Bal Sauve.

Conducting Research with Children and Adolescents

Design, Methods and Empirical Cases

Julie Tinson

 **Goodfellow Publishing**

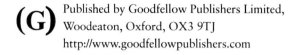 Published by Goodfellow Publishers Limited,
Woodeaton, Oxford, OX3 9TJ
http://www.goodfellowpublishers.com

British Library Cataloguing in Publication Data: a catalogue record
for this title is available from the British Library.

Library of Congress Catalog Card Number: on file.

ISBN: 978-1-906884-02-4

 Design and typesetting by P.K. McBride

Printed by Lightning Source, www.lightningsource.com

Contents

Acknowledgements

I am extremely grateful to the following willing contributors to the text:

S. B. Nimmo, Pete Nuttall (Chapter 9), Liz Forbat (Case 1), Ross Gordon (Case 2), Claire Ridsdale (Case 3) and Jennifer Thomson (Quantitative Analysis Section).

Thanks also to Clive Nancarrow as I have 'borrowed' from our work throughout the book.

To those who have been encouraging and have critically read (and re-read) versions of the chapters (who are not all listed here – but you know who you are!) – thank you.

And I am always indebted to Mum, Dad, Ade, Rebecca and Toby

1 Researching with Children: an Introduction

Objectives

- To introduce and contextualise the basis for the text

- To establish the terminology associated with children and the context in which it will be used

- To summarise the relevance of cognitive and social development

- To explore how and why researching with children is different to researching with adults

- To consider how to expand ideas on ways to research with children and to discuss how to develop aim(s) and objectives

Introduction

Ask the young. They know everything.

Joseph Joubert (1754-1824)

Joubert suggests that the young are knowledgeable and asking them what they know about a variety of different topics sounds reasonably straightforward. Yet the reality of researching with young people can be complex, not least because of what young people are prepared to divulge and the extent to which the young people engage with the research and the researcher. In addition there are a wide-ranging number of issues that need to be taken into consideration before the research can begin (e.g. ethics, research design and approach, engaging techniques and planning) and deliberation ought also to be given to the interpretation and dissemination of findings. The objective for this book is to provide an accessible text which will guide the (novice) researcher who seeks clarity and illustration through the entire process of researching with children. Whilst there have been a wide-ranging number of papers written about researching with children, these tend to focus on innovative research practices, ethical approaches or the nuances of ethics and interpretation. Not only are these articles diverse in what they focus on (see Box 1.1) but they represent studies conducted in a variety of different disciplines. This text will draw together the various contributions made by researchers who have conducted research with children and will endeavour to illustrate best practice across disciplines.

Food choice	Bullying
Hospitalization	Inter-personal violence
Exercise	Counselling provision
Space (and use of)	Materialism
Ridicule	Romance
Dislikes and disgust	Shame management
Health provision	Smoking and cessation
Advertising and brands	Extra-curricular involvement
Street children	Music use and consumption
Fashion	Self-esteem
Learning disabilities	Dyslexia friendly environments
Parents' involvement in education	Pester power
Hard to reach children and teenagers	Anti-social behaviour

Box1.1: Examples of research topics explored with young people

This book is designed to be a practical guide to researching with children whilst at the same time being underpinned with academic concepts. This text is primarily designed for final year undergraduate or MSc/MA students studying research methods courses, education modules or associated dissertation modules (although it could also be used by PhD students in the initial stages of their studies). The book is akin to a guidebook for those researching with children. It summarises seminal papers and salient issues (ethics, access, engagement, etc.) and provides actual examples of research projects (see Appendices 1, 2 and 3 for extended illustration of research practice) that have been conducted with children – how they were planned, how the research was designed, how consent was achieved, how the data was collated, the way in which the data was analysed and the 'equipment' used to facilitate the process.

There is a need for this book as there are an increasing number of students who choose to research with and write about children for a variety of courses and often their final-year dissertations. The research environment in relation to children and 'young people' is contentious and students are often unsure how to progress their ideas. However, children are an interesting and tempting group with which to conduct research. This book will guide novice researchers in terms of what they must do in relation to research planning and design and provides clear and concise guidelines as to how to approach the salient issues (ethics, access, engagement, etc.). For more experienced researchers, the book provides new and innovative approaches to facilitating research (specifically with adolescents – see Chapter 9) and will detail the way which greater insight can be generated with regard to topical child and adolescent related issues. This text will also facilitate the role of dissertation supervisors and project managers.

The complexities of researching with children and adolescents are to be explored. Research guidelines and professional codes of conduct are provided and illustration of how to follow these guidelines will be given. 'Equipment' to facilitate research with children will be explored and help on developing the 'topic' to be researched will be posited. Research design (consent, the role of experts, gatekeepers, teachers, ethics committees etc.) will be discussed. Interpretation of data will be examined and how to present the data will also be included. What to do once the research project is completed is also to be addressed. The book will cut through jargon and will be clear and concise in terms of what is appropriate when researching with children and how to achieve the greatest insight or understanding in relation to the chosen topic. This book, however, will not be appropriate for those researching highly sensitive issues in relation to children (e.g. mortality, abuse, etc.) where the highly experienced and well trained researchers in this area will follow their own very specific codes of practice in relation to these areas of vulnerability.

Although this text is designed to be easily accessible, the gravity of the principles of researching with children should mirror those observed (albeit in a more complex manner) across disciplines. As the practice of researching with children can vary in health, business, education, sociology and social work, researchers in different disciplines have the opportunity here to learn from one another (see for example: Richardson and McMullan, 2007). This text, whilst comprehensive, does not claim to be exhaustive on researching with children and further reading is both suggested and recommended throughout.

This chapter specifically will dispel any myths the reader has about researching with children and will ensure that the (novice) researcher seriously considers the implications of working with this unique group. It will also differentiate between children and adolescents and will address the key concepts relative to the child, including socialisation and development. It will also help the researcher when deciding on a research topic and/or exploring the nature of the research project to be undertaken. Having decided on or having considered the research topic to be explored, the way in which aims and objectives can be developed will be addressed. Finally preparing to research with children will be summarised.

'Children', 'adolescents' and 'young people'

The terms 'children', 'adolescents' and 'young people' are often used interchangeably and use of this terminology can sometimes simply denote that the individual(s) being discussed is less than 18 years of age. This can be confusing as the cognitive and social development of a 'child' will differ significantly depending on their age as well as their socio-cultural environment. Often researchers will justify the age of their sample by 'interpreting' age-related boundaries and attempting to reflect the abilities the age group are expected to display. Lind *et al.* (2003), for example, suggest that 'adolescence' has been broadly considered to extend from puberty to relative independence from parental control which could include the ages of approximately 10-18 years. Others would argue that at 10 years of age, comparatively with older adolescents, children do not possess the maturity or skills to process information and communicate in a more adult-like way. As such it would appear that defining the 'boundaries' of childhood or adolescence is somewhat problematic and calls for flexibility. Each group of young people then should be considered relative to their own social development, skills and abilities as detailed below (see the section below 'Cognitive and social development'). The gatekeeper(s) may be able to guide the researcher when research approaches are being planned and designed in this respect.

This text will consider researching with young people between the ages of 8-17 years. There is a difference researching with 8-year-olds and 17-year-olds and Chapter 3 illustrates the way in which a variety of methods can be employed to appeal to different age groups. In this text, young people have been categorised into three different groups; those aged 8-11 years for researchers interested in researching with children in the latter stages of primary school; those in early adolescence (12-14 years) and those in late adolescence (15-17). Harvey and Byrd (1998) indicate that early adolescence (12-14 years) is mostly about acquiring information and experience, while late adolescence (15-17 years) is characterised as being a period of identity development in which the information obtained earlier is used to build and consolidate a new identity. As such, the importance of the social context might change over the course of development and it appears to be appropriate to subdivide older children into these two age groups. This is considered as an 'ages and stages' approach.

However, it is accepted that child development models are not universal but socially and culturally specific (Woodhead, 1998). Social constructivism, that is, who we are and how we come to see ourselves is increasingly viewed as the ongoing and changing story we tell about our lives. It is a story that begins in the early childhood years and is actively constructed from the *'relational matrix'* of home, school, and community. Children 'construct stories of who they are in relation to others' (Korn, 1998: 223). As such, it is to be expected that children will have different experiences as a consequence of their role within the home, school and the community which may not be related to their age. Choosing to employ the research methods or techniques suggested here then should be done by taking into account the social development as well as the age of those you are researching with.

Cognitive and social development

These groups of young people (8-11 years, 12-14 years and 15-17 years) have been categorised for use in this text as the cognitive development stages of these age groups typically differ (with caveats). Piaget (1952) regarded the ages of 6 to 7 years as the 'age of reason'. It is said that at this age that children begin to take on others' viewpoints and engage in true communication. S/he can operate according to rules as well as compare what he or she hears, sees and knows. During middle and late childhood, it has been suggested that the child begins to co-ordinate two variables at the same time e.g. understand that a friend can be a boy and a child at the same time (Elkind, 1981). That is, 8 to 11-year-olds are typically in the 'analytical' phase of their cognitive development (Roedder John, 1999). Whilst 8-11 year olds are aware others may have a different view to them, they are unlikely to *simultaneously* consider other viewpoints at the same time as formulating their own opinions. Children of 8-11 years can also have difficulty using abstract concepts. That is, whilst an 8-year-old may not be able to readily describe the characteristics of someone they know (e.g. they are aggressive), they can describe the physical attributes of others (e.g. John is taller than James). Those over the age of 11 years are said to be in the 'reflective' stage of development. In this phase of early adolescence, young people are typically aware of the views of others and can take these into account when developing their own opinions or viewpoints (Elkind, 1981).

Piaget's theory (that children develop through the same sequence of stages before achieving rational mature thought) has been widely criticised. Wood (1998) summarises a number of the problems associated with Piaget's work including his small, unrepresentative sample, the way in which the importance of language was underestimated and the questions and tasks themselves that Piaget asked of the children which have been described as 'artificial' or 'unfamiliar'. Donaldson (1978) also argued that Piaget's theory neglected the cultural meanings of the materials used to test the children.

However, it is recognised that children's speed of mental processing increases with maturity. Halford (1992) accepts that children's speed of processing increases with age and also contends that children cannot process as much information simultaneously (as adults). Particular research methods then may be more appropriate when researching with children who have different cognitive abilities and these are likely to reflect, somewhat, the ages of the children.

In many respects those researching with children are interested in their socialisation or the social development of young people and how they form opinions, cope, learn and relearn attitudes and display particular types of behaviour. Within the fields of sociology, social psychology, psychology and consumer behaviour, there appears to be a consensus in the definition and meaning of socialisation as a term used to describe the change an individual experiences from the time they are attached and dependent upon their family environment (pre-social) to the time when they adopt more socially defined responsibilities and duties (adulthood). Socialisation is an inherently cultural process in which 'children, through insight, training and imitation, acquire the habits and values congruent with adaptation to their culture' (Baumrind, 1980: 640). Ward (1974) suggests socialisation research focuses on influences affecting individual development, both cognitive and social, and the processes by which individuals learn to participate effectively in the social environment. Socialisation (as well as cognition) is therefore as relevant for those researching with young people in health, sociology, social work, education and business. Given the interest in this specific period of development, the research approach adopted by the researcher needs to reflect both the cognitive (e.g. language skills) as well as the social development (e.g. cultural influences) of the children with whom the research is being conducted.

Children as a unique group

Although Chapter 2 summarises the ethical issues of researching with children (and the similarities and differences between ethical practices for differing groups of participants), it is useful here to highlight the differences between researching with children and adults. As 'educators, researchers and adults, we have much to learn about children and children's experiences from children' (Dockett and Perry, 2007: 48) and whilst historically adults have been used as proxies for children, the views of adults may not necessarily represent children's perceptions and experiences (see for example: Ben-Arieh and Ofir, 2002; Mishna et al., 2004; Irwin and Johnson, 2005; Cocks, 2006; Cook and Hess, 2007). It is now recognised that children as social actors are competent witnesses to speak for themselves and their experiences (James et al., 1998; Neill, 2005; Bray, 2007). This recognition is becoming increasingly widespread as their experiences take on a new importance. For example, over the last decade there has been an increased emphasis on the active involvement, participation and consultation of children and young people as users of the health service (Coad, 2007).

James et al. (1998) posit that there are two different ways of viewing children; that children are indistinguishable from adults or that children are similar to adults but possess different competencies. It is the latter of these two views that is generally supported, with adult researchers being asked to consider and question their own values throughout the research process to promote children's agency (Alderson, 2000; Edwards and Alldred, 1999) and to ensure children's studies consists of research with children as opposed to research on children (Mauthner, 1997).

Punch (2002), drawing on methodological issues, illustrates the way in which researching with children is different to how research would be conducted with a group of adults. It is important to note that children are typically marginalised in adult society and as such there is a power imbalance between the adult researcher and the child/ren. This is a contributing reason why there is such an emphasis on taking an ethical approach to researching with children (see Chapter 2). However, the power imbalance does not, for example, only affect consent to research with children but will also impact on the way in which the child engages (and is able to engage with) the research. Children are different to adults as their use of vocabulary is both limited and is used in a different way to that in which an adult would communicate. Children's understanding of words, their lack of life experience and their shorter attention span (Boyden and Ennew, 1997) also differentiate them from adults. As such, researchers must be careful not to impose their own perceptions on the children with whom they are researching and appropriate methods of research should be chosen to reflect the competencies of the children (see 'Social and cognitive development' above).

Children communicate differently to adults and as a researcher it is important to enhance validity and reliability with regards to the research data. That is, given children are different to adults, it is important that researchers can illustrate that they have effectively interpreted what the child/ren wanted to communicate. Morrow (1999) suggests creating favourable impressions with the children and Ennew (1994) recommends building rapport between the researcher and those children the research is being conducted with. Both of these approaches will ensure a 'shared understanding' of what has been communicated. Back translation (see Chapter 7) can also promote validity. Preventing boredom and sustaining interest is also important when researching with children (see Punch, 2002) and this too may ensure that the data is reliable as boredom often causes malresponse. Taking a reflexive and critical approach to researching with children will substantiate the research approach and facilitate the interpretation of the findings. It will also ensure that the children engaging with the research have a positive experience.

As children are clearly a unique group with whom to research, the topic (s) the researcher chooses (or is allocated) to explore with children should be given careful consideration. As the topic may influence the research approach the researcher has to reflect on the nature of the subject area and the way in which the child/ren may engage with the topic before preparing to research with the young people.

Deciding on a research topic

Deciding on an appropriate topic to research with children is essential if you are to develop a cohesive and comprehensive project. It may be that you have a broad area of research which needs to be narrowed or focused to ensure the project is manageable. It may be that you have a narrow but complex area of research that needs careful consideration and perhaps simplification. Conversely, a research topic may not have been considered at all, but as a researcher you are drawn to researching with children and are unable to decide on a specific area of study.

Often when advising students or researchers on an appropriate topic, it is easier to say what a topic should not be – for example, the area for consideration should not be too ambitious, it should not simply replicate other studies and it should not be overly complicated. However, researchers may find it easier to consider a more practical 'how to' list when developing an area for research:

◆   Do be clear about the relevance of your study. Think about not only what you want to find out but how it might be relevant to your discipline (in terms of theory building, informing policy, implications for curriculum development or business strategy).

◆   Do consider published work in the area you are considering researching. The majority, if not all, academic journal papers provide 'Implications for future research' towards the end of the articles. This will give you a number of options or ideas for your own research or may provide stimulus for your own creative ideas.

◆   Do be careful about the type of publication you refer to. Developing a 'hot topic' from a newspaper or magazine article may appear to be an interesting approach (e.g. 'hug a hoodie') but a topic developed from a substantial or more credible source will mean that researching libraries or texts to construct a literature review will be easier in the longer term.

◆   Do think outside your own discipline. Health researchers considering factors influencing healthy food consumption may benefit from looking at business or advertising-related journals. Those researching self-esteem in education might be well advised to think about how frameworks, theories or research conducted in psychology could be of use to them in developing a topic to research.

◆   Do make sure you are interested in the issue or topic you decide upon. Any half-hearted approach to research is likely to result in an unsuccessful outcome. If you have been attracted to researching with children as a result of being interested in a particular topic or issue and then, for whatever reason cannot follow through your idea, do not simply substitute your topic for another without clearly thinking through the consequences or implications. If you have to change your topic you must think of it as a 'new' idea and reconsider the ethical implications or the proposed methodological design.

◆   Do consider the nature of the subject or topic you wish to undertake. Are you considering one that may be sensitive? A sensitive topic may involve cultural differences, gender issues, issues of social power, the capacity of research to encroach on people's lives and/or the potential implications researching sensitive topics may have for the researcher. Whilst ethical issues will be explored here (see Chapter 2), further reading on sensitive issues can be considered outside this text (e.g. Sands *et al.*, 2007; Akiba and Miller, 2004). Think carefully before undertaking a research project that may be sensitive in nature. Do you think you are experienced enough to conduct the research? Have you fully researched issues that may emerge? Do you have a strategy for dealing with issues that may arise? Have you previously worked with children on a research project? Have you considered all the ethical consequences of researching with children in relation to your chosen or allocated topic? Have you sought expert advice and opinion?

♦ Do think about whether the children will wish to 'engage' with the topic. Do you wish to explore motivations, attitudes or behaviour? If so, is the topic one that children will be forthcoming about (e.g. shopping or celebrities) or one that they will perhaps not want to engage with (e.g. use of contraception or how sexually transmitted diseases are thought to be spread). Techniques to engage children and adolescents in research will be covered (see Chapter 4) but anticipating potential levels of engagement will allow for an appropriate degree of preparation and planning.

Importantly, the research practice proposed here does not necessarily reflect a more specialised approach that would need to be taken for very sensitive topics (e.g. verbal or physical abuse). Specialised guidelines are available (see for example, The Code of Good Practice) but specialist advice must be sought with regard to research of a very sensitive nature.

Having difficulty finding a topic?

There are a number of topics presented in this book (see Box 1.1 for examples). The case studies at the end of this text illustrate different research designs (each with their own ethical implications) and, where appropriate, suggest avenues for further research. Additional 'topics' may also be 'found' by reading the recommended texts or references supplied at the end of each chapter in this text. A research topic might not always come to you straight away. Sometimes it is an iterative process – and it may be that you read many articles or consider a number of topics before choosing one. Remember your research focus should be narrow and manageable. One research project will not produce everything you may want to know – but a well produced and meaningful set of findings (e.g. information relative to policy implementation or curriculum development) will be most useful for the children with whom you are researching.

Developing aims and objectives

It may be that as a researcher, a topic for researching with children has been allocated to you. In this case, deciding on the topic will not be an issue. However, understanding the nature of the topic and developing research aims and objectives ought to assist in appropriate planning and execution of a research project conducted with children.

What is the difference between an aim and an objective? The aim of a research study will clearly reflect the title of the project and the objectives will detail how the aim has to be achieved. For example, in Appendix 3, which considers the creation of dyslexia-friendly classrooms, the overall aim of the research is to evaluate the impact of the classroom environment on the children's ability to learn effectively. The objectives were (1) to explore the promotion of quality first teaching as an effective tool to raise the attainment of pupils with dyslexic tendencies, (2) to monitor the self-esteem of pupils with dyslexic tendencies throughout the duration of the study and (3) to consider the impact of the classroom environment on children who are not having to cope with dyslexic tendencies. In this way, the overall aim would be achieved if the enabling objectives were met. The aim(s) and objectives of a research study will be influenced by the researcher's philosophy (see Chapter 3). Whilst this text is designed to be a practical approach to researching with children, it is useful to reflect on how, as a researcher, your 'world view' will influence the way in which the project or study is designed, conducted and analysed.

Preparing to research with children

As a novice researcher it is sometimes easy to become over enthusiastic at the prospect of researching with children but going to the field too early (without adequate preparation) is a mistake. It may also be that the researcher is a nurse, teacher, social worker, parent or an aunt or uncle or a sibling and assumes, as they have good rapport with children in their family, that researching with children will require less preparation and will therefore be an easy option. This is not the case. The children that are familiar to the researcher in their capacity as a 'family member' are quite different to those children that may be researched with in a different environment. That is not to say that the ability to develop rapport with children is not important – it is – but it is also essential that ample time is given to ensuring that researching with children is conducted appropriately. Often researching with children has a limited time frame as the report, the dissertation or study the researcher has to prepare has a date by which it must be completed.

It is important at the outset of this text to highlight that researching with children is time-consuming as the preparation necessary to execute an ethical, engaging and detailed piece of research is not without potential setbacks. Equally, however, the process can be very rewarding.

This text will guide the researcher and will help to complete a rewarding, ethical and engaging piece of research. Each chapter summarises the salient issues that need to be considered and/or addressed when researching with children. Checklists are also provided for the researcher to ensure that the most important aspects of each chapter have been understood. Short case studies throughout the text illustrate specific aspects of researching with children and the three longer cases in the appendices, provide the researcher with an opportunity to consider different approaches to researching with children in varying age groups in their entirety. There is a glossary of terms (novice) researchers may not be familiar with and reflective questions at the end of each chapter to ensure the researcher has an understanding of the noteworthy issues that have been raised in relation to researching with children.

Summary

This chapter was designed to provide a brief context for the premise of the book. Initially the terms 'children', 'adolescents' and 'young people' were considered and their use generally (and more specifically in this text) were explored. The way in which this text is designed to reflect three categories of young people was also established although merely using age as a guide to cognitive and social development was raised as a problematic and caveats were suggested to ensure the abilities and social environment of the children being researched with are taken into account (as well as their age) when employing specific research methods. Socialisation and relevant cultural influences were also introduced. Deciding on and refining research topics to research with children were also addressed and developing aims and objectives were discussed with specific reference to Appendix 3. Finally the importance of preparing to research with young people (regardless of perceived experience) was emphasised and allocating ample time to ensure both ethical and engaging research with children was accentuated.

The following chapter focuses on employing an ethical approach to researching with children. The position of 'ethics' in this book signifies the importance of an ethical as well as an engaging piece of research with children. The topics explored within the next chapter (e.g. consent, assent, the Research Ethics Committee, gatekeepers' input, disclosure, etc.) can be time-consuming for the researcher. Having considered the procedure for obtaining access to children, the researcher will be better placed to assess the time it may take to complete their proposed study and the feasibility of this relative to the time frame for of their project. The following chapter will also illustrate the importance of the Data Protection Act, anonymity, avoiding covert research and managing the power imbalance in the relationship between the adult and the child/ren with whom they are researching.

Reflective questions

1 In what ways can the reality of researching with young people be considered complex?

2 Why does this text categorise young people into three separate categories?

3 What are the differences between the analytical and reflective stages of cognitive development?

4 Why has Piaget's theory of cognitive development been criticised?

5 In what ways can socialisation be considered as a cultural process?

6 List three ways in which researching with children is different to researching with adults.

7 What should you be aware of when generating ideas for a research project with children?

8 Give three reasons why it is important to prepare to research with children.

Checklist

☐ Do you know that each group of young people should be considered relative to their own cognitive and social development and who may be able to assist in this respect?

☐ Do you know how the speed of mental processing affects information processing and the implications this has for researching with children?

☐ Do you understand the differences between researching with children and adults?

☐ Do you understand why you should have a critical and reflexive approach to researching with children?

☐ Do you understand how to develop a focus for your own research project and how to develop the appropriate aim (s) and objectives?

☐ Have you considered the time implications of preparing to research with children?

References

Akiba, D. and Miller, F. (2004) 'The expression of cultural sensitivity in the presence of African Americans: an analysis of motives', *Small Group Research*, 35 (6), 623-642.

Alderson, P. (2000) 'Children as researchers: the effects of participation rights on research methodology' in P. Christensen and A. James (eds), *Research with Children: Perspectives and Practices*, London: Falmer Press, pp. 241-275.

Baumrind, D. (1980) 'New directions in socialization research', *American Psychologist*, 35 (7), 639-652.

Ben-Arieh, A. and Ofir, A. (2002) 'Time for (more) time-use studies: studying the daily activities of children', *Childhood*, 9 (2), 225-248.

Boyden, J. and Ennew, J. (1997) *Children in Focus: A Manual for Experiential Learning in Participatory Research with Children*, Stockholm: Radda Barnen.

Coad, J. (2007) 'Using art-based techniques in engaging children and young people in health care consultations and/or research', *Journal of Research in Nursing*, 12 (5), 487-497.

Cocks, A. (2006) 'The ethical maze, finding an inclusive path towards gaining children's agreement to research participation', *Childhood*, 13 (2), pp.247-266.

Cook, T. and Hess, E. (2007) 'What the camera sees and from whose perspectives: fun methodologies for engaging children in enlightening adults', *Childhood*, 14 (1), pp. 29-45.

Dockett, S. and Perry, B. (2007) 'Trusting children's accounts in research', *Journal of Early Childhood Research*, 5 (1), 47-63.

Donaldson, M. (1978) *Children's Minds*, Fontana/Collins.

Edwards, R. and Alldred, P. (1999) 'Children and young people's view of social research', *Childhood*, 6 (2), 261-281.

Elkind, D. (1981) *Children and Adolescents: Interpretive Essays on Jean Piaget*, 3rd edn, New York: Oxford University Press.

Ennew, J. (1994) *Street and Working Children: A Guide to Planning*, Developmental Manual 4. London: Save the Children.

Halford, G.S. (1992) *Children's Understandings: the Development of Mental Models*, Hillsdale, NJ: Lawrence Erlbaum.

Harvey, M. and Byrd, M. (1998) 'The relationship between perceptions of self-esteem, patterns of familial attachment, and family environment during early and late phases of adolescence', *International Journal of Adolescence and Youth*, 7 (2), 93-111.

Irwin, L.G. and Johnson, J. (2005) 'Interviewing young children: explicating our practices and dilemmas', *Qualitative Health Research*, 15 (6), 821-831.

James, A., Jenks, C. and Prout, A. (1998) *Theorizing Childhood*, Cambridge: Polity Press.

Korn, C. (1998) 'How young children make sense of their life stories', *Early Childhood Education Journal*, 25 (4), 223-228.

Lind, C., Anderson, B. and Oberle, K. (2003) 'Ethical issues in adolescent consent for research', *Nursing Ethics*, **10** (5), 504-511.

Mauthner, M. (1997) 'Methodological aspects of collecting data from children: lessons from three research projects', *Children and Society*, **11**, 16-28.

Mishna, F., Antle, B.J. and Regehr, C. (2004) 'Tapping the perspectives of children: emerging ethical issues in qualitative research', *Qualitative Social Work*, **3** (4), 449-468.

Morrow, V. (1999) 'We are people too. Children's and young people's perspectives on children's rights and decision making in England', *International Journal of Children's Rights*, **7**, 149-176.

Piaget, J. (1952) *The Language and Thought of the Child*, London: Routledge and Kegan Paul.

Punch, S. (2002) 'Research with children: the same or different from research with adults?', *Childhood*, **9** (3), 321-341.

Richardson, S. and McMullen, M. (2007) 'Research ethics in the UK: what can sociology learn from health?', *Sociology*, **41** (6), 1115-1132.

Roedder John, D. (1999) 'Consumer socialisation of children: a retrospective look at twenty-five years of research', *Journal of Consumer Research*, **26** (3), 183-213.

Sands, R.G., Bourjolly, J. and Roer-Strier, D. (2007) 'Crossing cultural barriers in research interviewing', *Qualitative Social Work*, **6** (3), 353-372.

Ward, S. (1974) 'Consumer socialization', *Journal of Consumer Research*, **1** (2), 1-17.

Wood, D. (1998) *How Children Think and Learn*, 2nd edn, Oxford: Blackwell.

Woodhead, M. (1998) *Children's Perspectives on their Working Lives: A Participatory Study in Bangladesh, Ethiopia, The Philippines, Guatemala, El Salvador and Nicaragua*, Stockholm: Radda Barnen.

2 Ethical Practice with Children And Adolescents: An Overview And Practical Application

Objectives

- To establish why it is imperative to employ an ethical approach when researching with children

- To identify the key characteristics of an ethical approach including informed consent, assent and dissent

- To consider best practice when employing an ethical approach and to identify the role of those assisting with the research

- To explore the policies and practices of an ethical approach when researching with children

- To summarise the role of the researcher in an ethical project with children.

Introduction

An ethical approach to research conducted with young people is essential given that 'children are particularly susceptible to intrusions of private space and behaviour by researchers' (Homan, 2001). An ethical approach to research design should not be considered retrospectively when the findings are being interpreted or when the study is being written up. The ethical implications of a study with children should be considered before any research is conducted and an ethical approach should be employed throughout the fieldwork and dissemination stages.

This chapter will explore what is meant by an ethical approach and will establish and discuss the key issues including consent, legal requirements, confidentiality, the role of the gatekeeper (those who control access to children) and the role of the researcher. The issues raised here should be carefully deliberated by the researcher whilst preparing for and designing a research project and should be re-examined throughout the duration of the study. An ethical approach to conducting research with young people is complex as 'it is important to recognise that childhood is diverse, with different children and their childhood experiences requiring unique approaches' (Young and Barrett, 2001). Not all young people will have the same lived experience and their understanding of what research is may be varied or non-existent. This chapter considers the ethical implications of researching with a variety of young people at different stages of their social development and the practical application of an ethical approach.

It is important to note at this early stage that research cultures across disciplines are not evenly developed (Munro *et al.*, 2005). It has been recognised by the Department of Health in *The Research Governance Framework for Health and Social Care* (2003) that in social care, for example, the arrangements for managing research and the associated ethical issues are not as consistent as those practised in the NHS. University research ethics committees have increasing authority (Scott *et al.*, 2006) although this typically applies to health related proposals. Consultation with respondents (young people) is often bypassed in educational research and it is frequently the case that consent is obtained not from the respondents (children) but those who are taking the decision on their behalf (teachers). As such, 'consent is assumed rather than informed' (Homan, 2001). In other subject areas (e.g. business) ethics committees in universities are still being formed and their role established with the majority of undergraduate and postgraduate dissertation research proposals not being subject to specific consideration by an ethics committee. Whilst guidelines are provided by the research industry bodies (e.g. the Market Research Society) the implementation of these procedures are not necessarily well practised (or indeed well known) amongst students and novices conducting work in this field. This chapter however does not seek to compare and contrast the differences between disciplines and their governance of research. Indeed as Soobrayan (2003: 107) suggests 'there is no single set of rules or practices that govern ethics, truth and politics of a research project'. Where appropriate, references will be made to subject groups but this chapter is specifically designed to illustrate best practice across disciplines and does not purport to be subject or discipline specific.

Ethical research with children in many respects is the same as ethical research conducted with adults (see '*Researching with children*', Chapter 1). It is important to gain respondent consent to research with adults, to ensure anonymity and confidentiality, to be sensitive to cultural issues and to be aware of how your research may impact on the respondents. Society, however, continues to see children as vulnerable, incompetent and in need of protection (Christensen, 1998) and this is where ethical research with children differs. This vulnerability could be developmental (and as such is equally applicable to groups who may have learning difficulties), social (e.g. lack of awareness of what should be disclosed), power related (e.g. children are typically expected to conform in a child–adult relationship) or comprehension of what is being expected of them. The role of the gatekeepers (see below) is to protect the children from embarrassment or distress. Ethical issues with regard to research with children, however, are insufficiently distinguished from issues in working with other vulnerable groups (Lindsay, 2000) and this needs further exploration.

As Morrow and Richards (1996) and Alderson and Morrow (2004) contend in everyday life adults typically do not respect children's views and opinions and this increases the challenge of developing research procedures that are both fair and respectful to children. Thomas and O'Kane (1998) argue that when children are involved in a participatory fashion in research, the overall rigour of the research is enhanced. As such it is important to address the ethical issues (as well as the research design approach) that are particularly relevant to researching with children to ensure their inclusion and input.

The following sections explore practical issues of consent and ethical practice when conducting research with children as Bray (2007: 448) contends: 'despite many papers discussing the issues of ethics in research with children (Alderson, 1995; Morrow and Richards, 1996; Thomas and O'Kane, 1998; Davis *et al.*. 2000; Cocks, 2006) there remains little practical guidance for researchers in the field conducting social research with children and young people'.

Informed Consent

The United Nations charter on the rights of the child (United Nations, 1989) is and has been a foundation for developing policies and making decisions about children (Harcourt and Conroy, 2005). Essentially children should be viewed as both capable and competent contributors to subjects that involve them. The rights of the child, however, increase the responsibilities of the researcher. Research that involves sharing of information or the transcription of ideas or thoughts children may have requires the consent or assent of the child in addition to the consent of any gatekeeper or parent/guardian. The view subscribed to here is the notion that an ethical approach to researching with children considers them able to contribute to research. Indeed, this approach should be adopted by researchers who wish to put the best interests of the child (and not their research) first. However, researching with children has a number of caveats and paramount in any study with children is obtaining consent.

(Legal) Requirements

Informed consent, as a consequence of the 1998 Data Protection Act, is now a legal requirement as well as a moral obligation (Scott *et al.*, 2006). Scenario 2.1 reinforces this requirement. When conducting research studies with children the minimum level of ethical requirement which must be met is that of informed assent by the child and/or informed consent of the parent/guardian. Of course there are opportunities to override these requirements and this may be of benefit to the researcher particularly as a more ethical approach to a study can lead to better quality data (Ferrell *et al.*, 1998). (See also 'Providing additional information' in Chapter 5.) '[T]he ethical principle of autonomy demands that consent should be informed and that elements of voluntariness, capacity and comprehension should be present for consent to be valid' (Lind *et al.*, 2003: 505). That is, individuals ought to understand the thing to which they are consenting and this is true of research being conducted in all disciplines and with regard to all research topics.

Scenario 2.1

Jonathan has just arrived at a hospital to conduct his research with children at an outpatient clinic. The bus he was travelling on broke down and he was late for his session. He realises, on pulling out his notes and consent forms that a number of children he has agreed to research with are 'missing'. Conversely there appear to be a number of 'new' outpatients. Jonathan is under pressure. The project has been delayed not least because of advice provided to him by the Research and Ethics Committee and he needs to submit his findings on time. Should he:

(a) Substitute a 'new' child for a 'missing' child to research with
(b) Re-arrange another session at the outpatient clinic
(c) Use the data he already has without completing the project
(d) None of the above.

Informed Assent or Informed Consent?

Informed consent is a person's autonomous authorization to participate in research (Beauchamp and Childress, 2001). There are a number of terms associated with obtaining consent from children and whilst these terms clearly mean different things they are often used interchangeably (Bray, 2007). *Informed assent* or *informed consent* are the most common terms and those most frequently referred to in the ethics literature. '*Informed assent*' is normally used where children are minors (under the age of 16). The elements of assent are described as information, comprehension and voluntariness (Belmont Report, 1979). Although informed assent and informed consent both involve asking the child if they want collaborate in the research process *informed assent* (typically for children 8 years and over) means the child is told about what will happen during the research process and agrees to the plan. It is generally agreed that children aged 7-12 years do have the cognitive capacity to judge information concerning their participation in research (Helseth and Slettebo, 2004) although it is recognized that some children and adolescents may have limited capacity and decision making abilities and, as such, assent and not consent would apply in this context (Lind *et al.*, 2003). Fixing an age at which assent can be given divides children into two groups (those with decision making ability and those without) and makes no allowance for those with developing autonomy (Strong, 1995).

As such, a developmental approach (see Rossi *et al.* 2003) which considers the capacity for consent as a continuum may be more appropriate (Miller and Nelson, 2006).[1]

If the researcher uses *informed consent* this will usually involve the participant (or their parent/guardian) signing a consent form which outlines the (research) process, any issues that may arise during the research, and what will happen to the research data when the project is complete. Arguably, where appropriate, children (under the age of 16) could also provide informed consent (in addition to that of their parents/guardian) and not just informed assent as 'a person of competent mind has the right to determine what is done to him/her and the right to determine what is not done' (Edwards *et al.*, 1998: 1825). This will depend, of course, on the topic or subject of research and the level of understanding of the child although Lind *et al.* (2003) note that responsibilities given to children who are aged 11+ when babysitting have been used to provide a contrast to adolescents' ability to consent to take part in research and have commented on the way in which the maturity of the children is assessed for these tasks. Koren *et al.* (1993) believe the issues of consent (given this comparison) are about power, control and poor communication as opposed to capacity for understanding.

It may well be the case that circumstances surrounding the research project (e.g. ill health, literacy, etc.) prevent parents (and children) from giving responsible and fully informed consent for participation in a study. In the field of health, for example, it has been suggested that consent may be granted because of lack of research background, insufficient knowledge about alternatives to experimental procedures and fear that withholding permission will result in denying the best possible care for their child (Lewis *et al.*, 1969). In other disciplines it may be the case that parents consent to their child's involvement in a research project so that the child does not feel 'left out' or is not open to questioning by their peers as to why they are not involved in the study.

The environment in which informed consent is given will also influence how and why consent is agreed. Pletsch and Stevens (2001) illustrate that where children are deemed to be in immediate danger (e.g. they have been diagnosed with cancer) their mothers have a sense of urgency (and unfamiliarity with the situation) and consent to research very quickly whereas in families where children have diabetes the trajectory of events is slower. If one of the principles of informed

---

1 The issue of competence of children and young people with specific reference to clinical decision making became focused not only on age but on maturity, understanding and intelligence as a consequence of the case of Gillick vs West Norfolk and Wisbech Area Health Authority (1985). The Gillick ruling only applies to interventions that are potentially of direct benefit to the health of the child and **not** 'non-therapeutic' medical research or social research.

consent is autonomy (the assumption being that individuals are the best judges of what is in their own best interest) the nature and environment in which these decisions are being made rather blur the boundaries of consent.

Bray (2007) also recognises that despite recognition of the issues surrounding research with children, innovative methods used to enhance the process of gaining consent are scant. Her own research design (an activity using a board with visual images) to convey the topics of assent, consent and dissent that children and young people seem to struggle to understand illustrates a practical response to the issues of developmental levels and literacy issues.

Informed Dissent

It is important also to remember that consent is not an event but a process (Alderson, 1998) and that even when, as a researcher, you have obtained consent this consent must be on-going and the child must be able to withdraw their consent at any time. Using the language 'assent' and 'consent' rather supposes the child/children want to participate in the research being proposed. Both words are accepting of what is being suggested. Using language that allows the young person to disengage will empower the children taking part in the research. *Informed dissent* is one such way that the children can be given the opportunity to opt out of a research study and although this may be frustrating for the researcher it can be empowering for the child.

Informed Dissent in Practice

An example of informed dissent in practice would be a child who has given informed assent to participate in a study on household responsibilities. The parents have provided informed consent for their child's involvement and the sample has been carefully chosen by the researcher to be representative – whether this is by age, gender or socio-economic group. The sample has been pre-organised before the study commences. Upon arriving to conduct the study with the children, how willing is the researcher to give a child or children the opportunity not to take part? If informed dissent is used appropriately the children should be offered the opportunity to withdraw from the research even at this late stage. As children often want to give the 'right' answer, ensuring that they fully comprehend that they do not need to take part in a research project can be difficulty.

They will not want to upset the researcher or will not want the researcher to dislike them and this is particularly true of younger children (8-11 years). Yet informed dissent is best practice across disciplines. Providing the children with the opportunity not to take part in the research could take many forms:

♦ It may be that a group of children are chosen to be involved in the study and are told that *only* if they want to participate should they go to the room where the research is taking place.

♦ It may be that children are told that it is acceptable to leave the room where the research is taking place without having to ask the researcher if it is okay to do so.

A useful approach for informed dissent during an interview has been discussed and employed by Helseth and Slettebo (2004). If children are familiar with football they can use yellow and red cards to express their feelings. As children often find it difficult to verbalise dissent, if they are asked about something they do not want to discuss (if they feel uncomfortable) they can give a warning by holding up a yellow card. If they do not want to discuss an issue or want to end their participation they can hold up the red card.

Passive consent or informed assent is not the right to choose between A and B but the right not to participate (de Meyrick, 2005). Children must understand that participation is completely voluntary and that they can withdraw from the study at any time.

Conveying the Meaning of Informed Dissent

It has been established that informed dissent as a concept can be difficult to convey. Often the location of the research study will influence the extent to which a child is prepared to withdraw from a study. If, for example, a student teacher is using ethnography to research children's behaviour (in relation to say stimuli for dramatic play) then the child may not understand that they are being observed for research purposes or because they are in class at school think that they have no other choice but to be observed. Similarly, children taking part in research conducted in hospitals may think that the research is part of their overall treatment programme. They may be unable to establish what tests or questions relate to the research and what tests or questions relate to their health care.

The notion of negotiating ongoing consent (Flewitt, 2005) may facilitate in balancing knowledge and power between the researcher and the participant and could help the child understand what is meant by informed dissent. Whilst 'provisional' consent may be agreed before the study commences:

> [O]ngoing consent cannot be assumed but is negotiated in situated contexts on a minute-by-minute basis.

(Simons and Usher, 2000)

Where the researcher considers the child to be uncomfortable (e.g. whilst being observed, answering questions, drawing pictures or taking part in role play – see Box 2.1) it is the responsibility of the researcher to be sensitive to this and the researcher must respect any subtle signs of dissent (Diekema, 2006).

Where the researcher is a novice and/or where the child or children are unfamiliar to the researcher, the researcher can look to parents, guardians or those in loco parentis as 'a pivot for gauging the children's ongoing consent' (Flewitt, 2005). Relieving the child of the situation does not necessarily mean removing the child. Removing the child may cause further embarrassment or discomfort and as such the researcher temporarily taking leave from the research study (if this situation should arise) is more appropriate.

Avoiding eye contact
Fidgeting nervously
Showing a tendency to move away
Legs are crossed defensively
Hiding their hands
Clenching their fists
A combination of these gestures usually indicates a child is uncomfortable.

S.B.Nimmo, Primary School Head Teacher, 33 years

Box 2.1: Body Language, signs that convey discomfort

It has been demonstrated that there is a poor understanding in children aged 5-12 years of stopping participation, with many believing that this would just be a temporary state (Abramovitch *et al..* 1991). To that end, it is particularly important to be observant for signs of discomfort in younger children.

Anonymity and Confidentiality

An aspect of consent is reassuring the research participant and their parent(s) or guardian(s) that the research contribution made by the participants will be anonymous. Scenario 2.2 illustrates a dilemma faced by a researcher in this context. No one else ought to be able to attribute the comments or concepts to one specific individual. This is usually addressed in the writing up stages by both using pseudonyms to protect the identity of the participants and by carefully considering (if the research is qualitative) that the quote used to illustrate the argument or theme in the research is sufficiently free of the participant's personal information. If the study with children has been conducted at a particular venue (e.g. drop-in centre, school, hospital) and disclosure of that venue would perhaps allow identification of the participant(s) the venue too can be given a pseudonym. It is important to note that the meaning and significance of information depends on what is already known by those receiving it (Richardson and McMullan, 2007: 1117). It is important that the context of the quotes used is appropriately noted so that identification of individuals is impossible. Publication of personal thanks for the respondents' involvement may well suffice without giving the venue or group name. In addition to this, the information given by the respondent should remain private and ought not to be passed on to anyone else without the permission of the respondent.

Scenario 2.2

Jennifer asked some adolescents she was researching with to conduct some of their own interviews. She provided them with a tape recorder, tapes and a stamped addressed envelope (SAE) in order that the tapes could be returned to her. In her haste, she did not realise until the following week that the pre-printed SAE was addressed to the department and not to her personally. This potentially meant that the tapes would arrive into the department and would be accessed by unauthorised personnel. Should she:

(a) Do nothing and hope the department secretary would send an e-mail round when the tapes finally arrived so that someone could claim them

(b) Call the adolescents immediately to ensure that if the tapes had not already been sent back that the researcher's name was to be written on the SAE and inform the department secretary that any tapes that came into the department that were not addressed to an individual were likely to be hers.

(c) Claim the packages must have been lost in the post and deny all knowledge of the tapes.

(d) Inform the research ethics committee immediately.

(e) None of the above

However confidentiality in research with children is occasionally an ambiguous and confusing notion. If a child raises concerns about being 'harmed' at home or at school, as a researcher, this raises both professional and moral obligations. Whilst there is no legal mandate in the UK for individual practitioners to report any suspicions of child abuse, Williamson *et al.* (2005) identify guidance provided by what was the Department for Education and Skills (Dfes, 2003) – now the Department for Children, Schools and Families (DCSF) – and the British Sociological Association (BSA, 2002) in relation to professionals and researchers and the issue of children raising concern about being harmed. Essentially, if a child confides or reveals alleged abuse, the child must be told sensitively that the professional or researcher has the responsibility to tell the appropriate agencies. This notion of confidentiality (and the ethical concerns regarding non-maleficence and beneficence which underlie the need to engage in a risk/benefit analysis and to minimise risks) is also discussed and supported by Mishna *et al.* (2004). Researchers should make provision for the potential disclosure of abuse in the *planning stages* of the proposed study *regardless* of the topic being discussed or researched. Specialist advice and expertise should be sought where relevant *before* the research is conducted.

Research Ethics Committees

A Research Ethics Committee (REC) is designed to both protect patients and the general public from unethical research and to improve healthcare and health (Alberti, 2000). In the UK, any research involving participants – of any age –

recruited as past or present National Health Service patients or users requires ethical *advice* from the appropriate NHS Research Ethics Committee (www. nres.npsa.nhs.uk/). It is a requirement that a 'positive opinion' of a Research Ethics Committee is obtained before any research may start – subject also to the 'approval' of the host organization (Balen *et al.*.2006). Ethics committees however are not, as outlined in the introduction, the preserve of health institutions and are increasingly being used across disciplines with varying rigour. It is important to note, however, that the researcher is still responsible for ethical practice with regard to their research project and this should not be abdicated to an ethics committee (Alderson and Morrow, 2004). Whilst in theory the role of the REC is invaluable, there are a number of issues associated with research proposals that are subject to the approval of a REC. It has been noted, for example, that the number of applications to local NHS RECs reduced in 2003-2004 by 40% (Bently and Enderby, 2005) and that 'clinical researchers have reported problems with the REC review in particular how it may impede, delay and sometimes distort research' (Richardson and McMullan, 2007). To that end, an early application to the REC is recommended with time built-in to the project to accommodate any necessary changes to proposals.

Data Protection Act 1998

When applying to a REC it will be imperative to illustrate in your proposal how you are going to meet the requirements of the Data Protection Act 1998 (DPA). As with the RECs, the DPA is not without its problems:

> Although the implementation of the 1998 Data Protection Act has materially improved the way in which sensitive information is both collected and stored in the research process, issues concerning access to personal data have nevertheless become increasingly prominent in the last 2 or 3 years. Difficulties may arise due to different interpretations of legislation at both intra and inter agency level.

(Munro et al. 2005: 1028)

For the purpose of researching with children, it is important for those consenting to the research (children and their parent/guardian) to be made aware of the following by the researcher:

♦   What is the researcher collecting the data for?

♦   To what institution is the researcher affiliated to?

♦   Who will have access to the data?

The researcher is responsible for keeping the data current, accurate. What is more, it should be kept for no longer than is necessary (e.g. the duration of the project). Security measures must be in place to guard against it being lost or damaged. The researcher must also prevent processing likely to cause damage or distress and this will include ensuring anonymity.

In this exert from Appendix 2 on 'Assessing the cumulative impact of alcohol marketing on youth drinking' the following observations were made about the balance between obtaining a usable sample, consent and issues of data protection.

The first challenge of the research was to obtain a sample frame that was large enough to achieve the required total sample size that would ensure any research findings would be statistically significant. This proved to be particularly problematic given the relatively large sample size required ($n=1760$) and also that we were dealing with children as our respondents. There are many issues that require to be addressed when attempting to conduct questionnaire surveys with children including data protection issues, dealing with consent from parents or guardians as well as respondents, accessing a sample frame through negotiation with various gatekeepers and also the resources in terms of time and costs of materials involved in carrying out a survey. For this project our initial intention was to obtain a sample frame from the local health board; however it transpired that due to data protection issues this would not be possible.

It followed that there were months of careful and at times delicate and difficult negotiations with gatekeepers of other potential databases of children aged 13-15 years that could provide a suitable sample frame. Finally after considerable negotiations (and at a not insignificant cost) the research team was able to obtain a sample frame through the local authority that enabled the team to invite participation in the research to school pupils aged 13 by direct mail. An information pack was sent out directly to the homes of each school pupil in second year at high school that attended a school within the particular local authority with parental and respondent consent forms being included, and an incentive of a gift token for each respondent was offered. However due to data protection issues there were strict limitations on the research team as to how the process was carried out and only once respondents agreed to take part in the research was data passed on to the researchers. Therefore it became clear during this process that the various data protection laws and issues surrounding accessing the data of children as respondents are complicated and it takes some time, effort and understanding to negotiate and differs by region.

Once the invitation packs had been sent out to the pupils in the local authority area the response rate was found to be considerably lower (12%) than expected (35%). It was therefore necessary to boost the sample by drawing respondents from neighbouring local authorities. This involved another round of negotiations due to logistical issues it was not possible to invite participation in the study by directly mail therefore invitation packs were distributed through schools.

Visual Data and Anonymity

Given the technological advances in recent years, the widespread use of visual recording equipment (including data collected on mobile phones) and the growing support for ethnographic studies, it is useful to explore the concept of anonymity in this context. Whilst in written accounts it is easy to provide the child with a pseudonym, images on film make the children easily recognisable. Visual methods of data collection present specific ethical issues, particularly where the child is filmed in their own home when this can 'render parents and practitioners vulnerable to criticism, anxiety and self-doubt' (Flewitt, 2005). Special ethical consideration must be given to studies employing this research approach with particular reference to consent and the agreed purpose for the use of this visual data. The researcher must ensure that the data is only used for its intended purpose and then either destroyed or additional consent requested for further use or display.

Denzin (1989: 83) suggests 'our primary obligation in research is to the participants and not the study being conducted'. Flewitt (2005) supports this view with specific reference to visual data and indicates that by giving control or greater ownership of the visual data to the participants some of the issues raised by this type of data collection can be alleviated. She suggests that by asking the children (and their parents) to view the data collected (and to collect their own visual data where appropriate) reinforces trust and co-operation. Of course there are opportunities to obscure the faces of participants through technological procedures. This, however, may be problematic if the study is concerned with facial expression and in this instance it would then be necessary to have the full consent of the participant to display the visual images. These issues would similarly apply to background images – particularly where the participants had been filmed in their home environment.

Covert Research

Whilst informed assent or informed consent must be obtained to meet the minimum ethical and legal requirements it can also be used as 'evidence' by the researcher of an ethical approach. Researchers, however, can manipulate 'consent' and this has been described as 'covert research' by Homan (2001). Covert research uses informed consent to bypass research responsibilities. That is, once a researcher has a signature on paper to agree to the child being involved in the research process the researcher (and not the participant) is protected from any risks or outcomes as a result of the study. Where the study perhaps raises issues for the respondent, the researcher is under no legal obligation to address or facilitate a resolution for the respondent. Once the research has been completed the researcher does not have to consider how the child is to express any concerns they have about the issues that have been raised by the study. Covert research is also akin to the 'Pontius Pilate Plight' described by Walters (1989: 958). A researcher can conform to the formal role procedures of researching with children but can wash his/her hands of the responsibility of what follows the research because they obtained assent/consent and, as such, were 'honest' and 'open' about what the research involved. The children (and their parent/guardian) had formally and freely accepted the opportunity to engage with the research. However, as covert research often involves the details of the study not being made explicit or hidden in the small print of the consent form, this 'honesty' or 'openness' may be questionable.

Covert Research in Practice

An example of covert research can be seen by considering a study conducted with children on food consumption. The research could purport to be about 'food choice' but may actually be designed to explore issues of obesity, self-esteem and compensatory consumption. Whilst the researcher would look at food choice (healthy food, processed food etc.) the research project may make the child think about underlying issues relative to food consumption that had previously not been considered or had lain dormant. The child may wish to discuss these issues outside the research project but if the researcher is using a covert research approach then they will not have thought past the completion of the research study. This covert approach to research illustrates that it is possible to meet the legal requirements of a research study which does not demonstrate concern or moral obligation to the child involved. Covert research has to be avoided to ensure vulnerable or powerless groups are both respected and appreciated for their contribution to our overall understanding of their social worlds and their interpretation of their everyday worlds.

Employing the approach used by Bondi *et al.* in Appendix 1 ensures that an ethical approach (and not a covert one) is taken to ensure the welfare of the children during and after the research study. The researcher who conducted these interviews was a counsellor with extensive clinical experience of working with children and young people, including referrals via statutory services. He was selected to conduct this component of the study because of this background, which ensured that he would be able to address the research questions at the same time as being mindful of the potential for these conversations to stir up difficult feelings or memories for the young people concerned.

Power and Moral Obligation

Whilst it is increasingly recognised that young people have the right to participate in research and to express their views and opinions, this in itself raises pertinent issues in relation to competence and power (Curt and Murtagh, 2007). Viewing power as inherent to research emphasises that research is a practice that is part of social life rather than an external contemplation of it (Christensen, 2004: 166). That is, the research cannot be viewed objectively as the study being conducted with young people is an element of the structure of their existence – simply put, the research is part of their life. The social norms, values and expectations of control that the children have will be reflected in the study and associated data. Issues such as social or cultural life that can be sensitive to the issue of power should be considered and addressed.

If a white European researcher is, for example, interviewing Asian children, will this dynamic cause issues with data collection and data analysis? If the researcher is male and interviews a female respondent this may necessitate additional research and understanding of the cultural issues (e.g. the female may not be able to speak freely to a male because of the social norms within her culture). Of course these issues manifest themselves in all types of research and between, as well as across, gender (see, for example: Sands *et al.*, 2007). Whilst informed dissent can facilitate in shifting the balance of power from the researcher to the child (in this cultural context) it is appropriate to further explore the concepts of power in relation to capability (age), control and representation within the context of an ethical approach to research design and fieldwork.

The age of the child in addition to their own life experiences will undoubtedly influence the extent to which, within the research/participant relationship, there is a perception of discrepancy in control. It is likely, for example, that children between the ages of 8-11years will feel less empowered as social norms tend to dictate that they ought to show some deference to adults. Children at these ages are still in the analytical stage of socialisation (Roedder John, 1999) and consequently, whilst they may appreciate others have different opinions to them they do not necessarily consider these alternative opinions simultaneously with their own. This inability may lead to younger children feeling 'out of their depth' or confused by what is being asked. This is supported by Antle *et al.* (2004) who suggest that despite attempts to equalise the power between the researcher and those affected by the research topic under consideration there remains an inherent power imbalance in which the researcher has a distinct 'advantage' in the relationship (ibid.). Interestingly, younger children are more forthcoming if they can choose a friend to join their conversations with them (Hill 2007) and this illustrates that younger children feel more powerful when they have an ally. Children should not be excluded from research because they are 'quiet'. This does not make their views less valid.

In order that the sample and data is representative, children with a variety of communication abilities ought to be included even where this involves more work on the part of the researcher. The moral obligation of the researcher is to ensure that the children in the research study not only understand what is being asked of them but, where possible, will allow the younger children (8-11 years) to have a friend with them to make them feel more comfortable during the research and with whom they can confer. This too will benefit children who have lesser communication ability.

For older children (adolescents), the power imbalance may be more evident, although this may be reversed in the participant/research relationship particularly where the young person is marginalised. In the social work arena, despite 'listening to children' being a legal requirement, dialogue with disaffected young people can be hard to achieve. McLeod (2007: 278) argues that 'much that appears unsuccessful in [research] interaction can be understood in power plays, with young people resisting the adult's agenda and trying to impose their own'. She supports Antle *et al.* (2004) and adds that there is always an imbalance of power when an adult conducts research with a child.

Withholding information, changing the subject or fabricating responses are all strategies displayed by adolescents dealing with powerlessness. This powerlessness may be addressed by giving the adolescents a greater opportunity to be involved in the research process. Adult generated categories as described by Grover (2007) can pose difficulties when researching with young people. Allowing the adolescents (in this case) the opportunity to generate their own questions regarding the topic for discussion (see Chapter 9) may improve interaction, engagement and the quality of the data. Strategies that have been adopted to provide maximum possible scope for young people to exercise direct and indirect control over the nature and course of interviews (Sanders and Munford, 2005) are further discussed in Chapters 3 and 4.

Important to note here is that regardless of how much agency researchers may wish to give to children (with regard to consent procedures, question design, etc.) there are layers of gatekeepers who exercise power over children throughout the research study (see section 'Role of gatekeepers' below). The researcher is not just trying to negotiate power between themselves and the young people involved in the study but between the gatekeeper, themselves and the children.

Control or power is evident between the interlocutors of the research process (e.g. researcher and participant, researcher and gatekeepers) but can also be visible within groups of children. In groups, power and hierarchy manifest themselves as a child–child as well as a child–adult phenomenon (Hill, 2007). Depending on the research approach adopted, power plays within groups can be more or less evident.

Power Play in Practice

If, for example, a focus group is being conducted with children aged 8-11 years and the groups are made up of mixed gender (and depending on the topic) the girls or boys within that group may be more likely to dominate the conversation. If the topic is about fashion the girls may think they have more to contribute and the boys may wish to disassociate from the topic or feel embarrassed and say little, if anything. This may work in reverse if the topic is considered perhaps more risqué. It may be that the research design has to reflect the potential group dynamics and an alternative approach (e.g. single-sex groups, paired interviews or one-to-one interviews) which may alleviate some of these concerns will have to be employed. The gatekeeper may also be able to advise of any particular power plays that they are aware of with and between groups and have observed in practice.

Role of Gatekeepers

Gatekeepers are parents, head teachers, teachers, social workers, members of ethics committees, ward sisters, managers of after-school clubs and others who are in charge of children in a social or community context (scout leaders, guiders, youth club organisers etc.). In the context of researching with children, the *gatekeeper(s)* means the person or persons, who control access to young people and who, in some cases, are present when the research is being conducted.

This list is not exhaustive and invariably a researcher will be dealing with more than one gatekeeper in any one research project. The gatekeeper not only has a role of power but also has a burden of a responsibility and gatekeepers are tasked with ensuring the best interests of the child are taken into account. Parents, and to a lesser extent, teachers are still the dominant reference points when negotiating access, reflecting their socially superior position in the hierarchy (Wyness, 2006: 195) and children can only be approached for their informed assent or consent once the gatekeepers have established the boundaries as well as approved or agreed the aims and objectives of the research study.

There may be a hierarchical chain of access. That is there may be a specific way in which access to children should be sought through the various gatekeepers. This will largely depend on the nature of the project and probably geographic region. For example, if you wish to conduct research in primary schools the hierarchical chain of gatekeepers would probably involve asking a variety of people (see Figure 2.1).

In secondary schools, the process may be similar but there may be additional gatekeepers (e.g. the head teachers in the chain of command will be followed by individuals who are heads of the year group). Each of these gatekeepers will need to be aware of the research aim(s) and objectives and be satisfied that the children's best interests will be met.

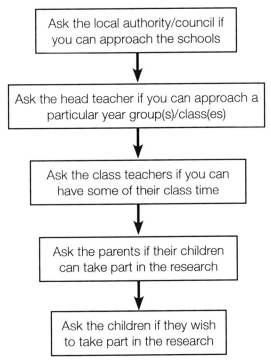

Figure 2.1: Possible Hierarchy for Primary School Gatekeepers

Gatekeepers and their Responsibilities

As with allowing the children informed dissent, the gatekeeper should also be allowed to withdraw their consent for the project if they believe the method or approach is inappropriate for children for whom they ultimately hold the burden of responsibility. This can be difficult, particularly where the gatekeeper is known personally to the researcher. It is essential, therefore to build in both formal and informal opportunities for participants to say no in a safe environment (Flewitt, 2005: 554) and to negotiate ongoing consent during the research process with the gatekeeper as well as the participants.

Role of Researcher

The role(s) of the researcher is fundamental to the overall ethical approach of the study. The researcher must not only identify the relevant ethics committees and procedures (where applicable) but must also develop a professional relationship with the gatekeeper(s) and take into account in the design of the research the advice of the *gatekeeper(s)* where appropriate and ensure both provisional and on-going assent or consent from the children taking part in the study. The complexity of the role(s) of the researcher in relation to conducting ethical research with children, disclosure and gender issues will be explored here.

Whilst a researcher may well be welcomed just because they are not a teacher (Morrow, 1999) – and this would apply equally in other disciplines – it is important for the researcher to explain their role to the young people they are going to research with. As children and young people will attribute some form of role to researchers rather than none (Edwards and Alldred, 1999: 276) it is both ethical and appropriate as a researcher to:

♦   Clearly state your background
♦   How you are proposing to conduct the research
♦   What your role is in the environment you are in.

For example, if research is being conducted in hospitals or GP surgeries it is important to disclose the level (or lack) of medical experience attributable to the researcher. Similarly in a school environment it is important for the children to understand the researcher is not a teacher. Whilst the setting will influence the data collection (see section 'Location of study', Chapter 5) this bias will be minimised by the researcher expressing clearly to the young people their role and research intentions.

Many of the discussions of fieldwork with young people have addressed the issue of the roles researchers assume (see, for example: Fine and Sandstrom, 1988; Mandell, 1988; Corsaro, 1997). These roles include supervisor, leader, friend, parent and 'least adult'. However, children's perceptions of the researchers' roles are less well documented (Nespor, 1998). In order to address the power imbalance the context of the research ought to be dynamic and processual. That is, researchers should recognise that interaction with the children with whom they research with does not necessarily circumscribe the social processes as the children experience them (Nespor: 375).

The concept of power in the young person/researcher relationship has already been explored in this chapter (see 'Power and moral obligation' above) but it is useful to remind researchers that playing the least adult role as described by Mandell (1991) may facilitate a more equitable relationship between the researcher and young person. Particularly when conducting research with young children (8-11 years) playing the least adult role (e.g. assuming the role of a learner, avoiding contact with other adults, ignoring requests to behave like an adult – such as resolving disputes between the children) may improve the credibility of the researcher. Although this makes the role of the researcher complex (it is important to maintain a positive relationship with the gatekeeper) the significance of developing a relationship with the young people that is different to the one they have with their social worker, teacher or medical consultant will help in overcoming the imbalance in power. It may be that the researcher, as well as managing a variety of roles during the research study, can feel vulnerable.

Notwithstanding the (sometimes bidirectional) power imbalance, feelings of vulnerability may also be a consequence of the gender of the researcher. Male researchers, for instance, may be concerned when researching with children (Horton, 2001) because of child protection issues and the unpredictability of children. There are ways in which some of these concerns can be assuaged. Location of research, adequate research planning and understanding of the key issues communicated by the gatekeeper(s) and a working knowledge of the behaviour the children may display during the research process may make the researcher more confident in their role. It is not unusual, for example, when researching young children for them to make physical contact with the researcher. This is not a problem in itself but knowing before the research takes place what strategies should be employed if this happens (such as moving position or engaging with the gatekeeper for advice if the contact is prolonged or the attention of the child cannot be diverted) is prudent. Moore (1992: 129) suggests that it is important to address the reality of ethics:

> If we are going to do work with children we are going to have to use the child within, yet at the same time retain our professional knowledge and judgement. We have to be comfortable with ourselves as we are.

As such, the researcher must be confident in their ethical approach to the research they conduct with children and this confidence may be enhanced by obtaining disclosure. Indeed this may be a requirement of having access to children and as such may have to be obtained before any research with young people takes place.

Disclosure

What is 'disclosure'? Disclosure (or Disclosure Scotland) is where an individual (or organisation) can apply to process police checks through the Criminal Records Bureau (CRB) in accordance with the Police Act 1997. The applicant can be checked against police records for convictions, cautions, reprimands and warnings and enhanced disclosure will provide detail on any records that are held about an individual by the Department for Children, Schools and Families, the Department of Health and any other relevant bodies. Being in receipt of disclosure as a researcher illustrates not only that the researcher has 'nothing to hide' but that they are professional in their approach towards researching with children. Obtaining disclosure may enhance not only the confidence of the researcher but the confidence of the *gatekeeper(s)* in relation to the ethical research design and approach. Disclosure may also be a requirement to gain access to the children with whom you wish to research and may be advised by a REC.

Completing the Ethical Research Process

It is important to remember to refer to the initial informed assent or consent on completion of the research project and the Data Protection Act (DPA) requirements as summarised earlier. The young person(s) with whom you have researched will have been promised confidentiality and anonymity (see above) but it is also typical to agree to destroy any information/data collected during the research process on completion of the study (see DPA above). It is imperative that this is done but also that it is done in such a way that any information (e.g. transcripts, photographs, drawings, and visual data) cannot be retrieved once the researcher has destroyed it. (See Chapter 8 for additional details on project completion.) The use of shredding machines is normal practice for destroying items and if this is not available to the researcher the information must still be destroyed using confidential waste procedures.

Summary

This chapter explored what is meant by an ethical approach to researching with children. Key issues including consent, legal requirements, confidentiality, the role of the gatekeeper and the role of the researcher were all explored in depth with the complexities of some of these issues identified. Additional themes such as culture, dissent, covert research and disclosure have also been discussed. Suggestions have been made as to how to ethically research with children and how best practice can be achieved. Case study examples have been used to illustrate the issues of obtaining consent and role of the researcher in relation to power and moral obligation. Whilst all the ethical issues raised here will reappear throughout the text (given the holistic ethical approach to researching with young people subscribed to here), this chapter should serve as a reference point for the foundation of a research project being designed to include the views, ideas and insights of children and adolescents at different stages of their social development.

Reflective Questions

1   What are the differences between researching with adults and children and between researching with children and other vulnerable groups?

2   Identify the differences between informed consent and informed assent.

3   Why is it difficult to convey the meaning of informed dissent?

4   What is the primary role of a Research Ethics Committee?

5   Name three important aspects of the Data Protection Act for the purpose of obtaining consent.

6   What is covert research and what could be the consequences of employing this approach?

7   How might adolescents deal with feelings of 'powerlessness'?

8   Taking into account ethical guidelines for your own discipline, who is/are likely to be the gatekeepers for your proposed research study?

9   What role could you adopt as a researcher and how would you communicate this to the young people with whom you are researching?

10 How and why would you obtain disclosure?

Checklist

☐   Do you understand why it is imperative to employ an ethical approach when researching with children?

☐   Do you know informed consent is a legal requirement?

☐   Do you understand the differences between informed consent and informed and would you know which to use in different scenarios?

☐   Do you understand how to encourage informed dissent and the signs to look for that convey discomfort?

☐   Do you know if the research you are proposing to conduct needs to pass through a Research Ethics Committee and what associated paperwork needs to be completed before the proposal is submitted?

☐   Do you know what information, as a researcher, you must provide to those you are researching with?

☐   Have you considered the ways in which the data you will collate will remain confidential and anonymous?

☐   Have you considered how power might influence your data collection and how the role of the gatekeeper might affect the research?

References

Abramovitch, R., Freedman, J., Thoden, K. and Nikolich, C. (1991) 'Children's capacity to consent to participation in psychological research: empirical findings', *Child Development*, **62**, 1100-1109.

Alberti, K.G.M.M. (2000) 'Multicentre Research Ethics Committees: has the cure been worse than the disease?', *British Medical Journal*, **320**, 1157-1158.

Alderson, P. and Morrow V. (2004) *Ethics, social research and consulting with children and young people*, Barkingside: Barnardo's.

Alderson, P. (1995) 'Will you help us with our research?', *Archives of Disease in Childhood*, **72** (6), 541-542.

Alderson, P. (1998) 'Informed consent: ideal or reality?', *Journal of Health Services Research Policy,* **3**, 124-126.

Antle, B.J., Regehr, C. and Mishna, F. (2004) 'Qualitative research ethics: thriving within tensions', in A.R. Roberts and K. Yeager (eds), *Handbook of Practice-Focused Research and Evaluation*, New York: Oxford University Press, pp. 126-136.

Balen, R., Blyth, E., Calabretto, H., Fraser, C., Horrocks, C. and Manby, M. (2006) 'Involving children in health and social research. "Human becomings" or "active beings"?', *Childhood*, **31** (1), 29-48.

Beauchamp, T.L. and Childress, J.F. (2001) *Principals of Biomedical Ethics*, New York: Oxford University Press.

Belmont Report (1979) http://www.hhs.gov/ohrp/humansubjects/guidance/belmont.htm (accessed Jan 2009)

Bently, C. and Enderby, P. (2005) 'Academic medicine: who is it for?', *British Medical Journal*, **330**, 61.

Bray, L. (2007) 'Developing an activity to aid informed assent when interviewing children and young people', *Journal of Nursing Research*, **12** (5), 447-457.

BSA (2002) Statement of ethical practice for the British Sociological Association. http://www.britsoc.co.uk/Library/Ethicsguidelines2002.doc (accessed May 2008).

Christensen, P.H. (1998) 'Difference and similarity: how children's competence is constructed in illness and its treatment', in I. Hutchby and J. Moran-Ellis (eds), *Children and Social Competence: Arenas of Action*, London: Falmer, pp. 187-201.

Christensen, P. H. (2004) 'Children's participation in ethnographic research: issues of power and representation', *Children and Society*, **18**, 165-176.

Cocks, A. (2006) 'The ethical maze, finding an inclusive path towards gaining children's agreement to research participation', *Childhood*, **13** (2), 247-266.

Corsaro, W. (1997) *The Sociology of Childhood*, Thousand Oaks, CA: Pine Forge Press.

Curt, M. and Murtagh, J. (2007) 'Participation of children and young people in research: competence, power and representation', *British Journal of Occupational Therapy*, **70** (2), 67-72.

Davis, J., Watson, N. and Cunningham-Burley, S. (2000) 'Learning the lives of disabled children: developing a reflexive approach', in P. Christensen and A. James (eds), *Research with Children*, London: Falmer Press, 201-224.

Data Protection Act (1998) http://www.hmso.gov.uk (accessed May 2008).

de Meyrick, J. (2005) 'Approval procedures and passive consent considerations in research among young people', *Health Education*, 105 (4), 249-258.

Denzin, N.K. (1989) *Interpretive Biography*, Newbury Park, CA: Sage

Dfes (Department for Education and Skills) (2003) http://www.dfes.gov.uk/publications/guidanceonthelaw/10_95/schools.htm#Confidentiality (accessed May 2008)

DoH (Department of Health) Research Governance Framework for Health and Social Care (2005)

Diekema, D. (2006) 'Conducting ethical research in paediatrics: a brief historical overview and review of pediatric regulations', *Journal of Pediatrics*, 149, 3-11.

Edwards, R. and Alldred, P. (1999) 'Children and young people's view of social research', *Childhood*, 6 (2), 261-281.

Edwards, S.J.L, Lilford, R.J., Thornton, J. and Hewison, J. (1998) 'Informed consent for clinical trials: in search of the "best" method', *Social Science and Medicine*, 47, 1825-1840.

Ferrell, M.D., Hartline, S.W. and McDaniel, O.C. (1998) 'Codes of ethics among corpora te research departments, marketing research firms, and data', *Journal of Business Ethics*, 17 (5), 503-516.

Fine, G.A. and Sandstrom, K.L. (1988) *Knowing Children: Participant Observation with Minors*, Newbury Park, CA: Sage.

Flewitt, R. (2005) 'Conducting research with young children: some ethical considerations', *Early Child Development and Care*, 175 (6), 553-565.

Gillick vs West Norfolk and Wisbech Area Health Authority (1985) All England Law Reports, AC 112.

Grover, S. (2007) 'Why won't they listen to us? On giving power and voice to children participating in social research', *Childhood*, 11 (1), 81-93.

Harcourt, D. and Conroy, H. (2005) 'Informed consent: ethics and processes when researching with young children', *Early Child Development and Care*, 175 (6), 567-577.

Helseth, S. and Slettebo, A. (2004) 'Research involving children: some ethical issues', *Nursing Ethics*, 11 (3), 298-308.

Hill, M. (2007) 'Children's voices on ways of having a voice: children's and young people's perspectives on methods used in research and consultation', *Childhood*, 13 (1), 69-89.

Homan, R. (2001) 'The principle of assumed consent: the ethics of gatekeeping', *Journal of Philosophy of Education*, 35 (3), 329-343.

Horton, J. (2001) 'Do you get some funny looks when you tell people what you do? Muddling through some angsts and ethics of (being a male) researching with children', *Short Communications*, 4 (2/1), 159-166.

Koren, G., Carmeli, D.B., Carmeli, Y.S. and Haslam, R. (1993) 'Maturity of children to consent to medical research: the babysitter test', *Journal of Medical Ethics*, **19**, 142-147.

Lewis, M., McCollum, A.T., Schwartz, A.H. and Grunt, J.A. (1969) 'Informed consent in pediatric research', *Children*, **16**, 143-148.

Lind, C., Anderson, B. and Oberle, K. (2003) 'Ethical issues in adolescent consent for research', *Nursing Ethics*, **10** (5), 504-511.

Lindsay, G. (2000) ' Researching children's perspectives: ethical issues', in A. Lewis and G. Lindsay (eds), *Researching Children's Perspectives*, Buckingham: Open University, 3_20.

Mandell, N. (1988) 'The least-adult role in studying children', *Journal of Contemporary Ethnography*, **16** (4), 433-467.

Mandell, N. (1991) 'The least adult role in studying children', in F.C. Waksler (ed.), *Studying the Social Worlds of Children*, London: Falmer Press, pp. 38-59.

McLeod, A. (2007) 'Whose agenda? Issues of power and relationship when listening to looked-after young people', *Child and Family Social Work*, **12**, 278-286.

Miller, V. and Nelson, R. (2006) 'A developmental approach to child assent for non-therapeutic research', *Journal of Pediatrics*, **149**, 25-30.

Mishna, F., Antle, B.J. and Regehr (2004) 'Tapping the perspectives of children: emerging ethical issues in qualitative research', *Qualitative Social Work*, **3** (4), 449-468.

Moore, J. (1992) *The ABC of Child Protection*, Aldershot: Arena.

Morrow, V. (1999) 'We are people too. Children's and young people's perspectives on children's rights and decision making in England', *International Journal of Children's Rights*, **7**, 149-176.

Morrow, V. and Richards, M. (1996) 'The ethics of social research with children: an overview', *Children and Society*, **10**, 90-105.

Munro, E.R., Holmes, L. and Ward, H. (2005) 'Researching vulnerable groups: ethical issues and the effective conduct of research in local authorities', *British Journal of Social Work*, **35**, 1023-1038.

Nespor, J. (1998) 'The meanings of research: kids as subjects and kids as inquirers', *Qualitative Inquiry*, **4** (3), 369-388.

Pletsch, P.K. and Stevens, P.E. (2001) 'Children in research: informed consent and critical factors affecting mothers', *Journal of Family Nursing*, **7** (1), 50-70.

Richardson, S. and McMullen, M. (2007) 'Research ethics in the UK: what can sociology learn from health?', *Sociology*, **41** (6), 1115-1132.

Roedder John, D. (1999) 'Consumer socialisation of children: a retrospective look at twenty-five years of research', *Journal of Consumer Research*, **26** (3), 183-213.

Rossi, W., Reynolds, W. and Nelson R. (2003) 'Child assent and parental permission in pediatric research', *Theoretical Medicine*, **24**, 131-148.

Sanders, J. and Munford, R. (2005) 'Activity and reflection', *Qualitative Social Work*, **4** (2), 197-209.

Sands, R.G., Bourjolly, J. and Roer-Strier, D. (2007) 'Crossing cultural barriers in research interviewing', *Qualitative Social Work*, **6** (3), 353-372.

Scott, J.K., Wishart, J.G. and Bowyer, D.J. (2006) 'Do current consent and confidentiality requirements impede or enhance research with children with learning disabilities?', *Disability and Society*, **21** (3), 273-287.

Simons, H. and Usher, R. (2000) *Situated Ethics in Educational Research*, London: Routledge Farmer.

Soobrayan, V. (2003) 'Ethics, truth and politics in constructivist qualitative research', *Westminster Studies in Education*, **26** (2), 107-123.

Strong, C. (1995) 'Respecting the health care decision making capacity of minors', *Bioethics Forum*, **11** (4), 7-12.

Thomas, N. and O'Kane, C. (1998) 'The ethics of participatory research with children', *Children and Society*, **12**, 336-348.

United Nations (1989) *UN Convention of the Rights of the Child*, Geneva: United Nations.

Walters, K.S. (1989) 'Limited paternalism and the Pontius Pilate Plight', *Journal of Business Ethics*, **8** (12), 955-962.

Williamson, E., Goodenough, T., Kent, J. and Ashcroft, R. (2003) 'Conducting research with children: the limits of confidentiality and child protection protocols', *Children and Society*, **19**, 397-409.

Wyness, M. (2006) *Childhood and Society: an Introduction to the Sociology of Childhood*, Basingstoke: Palgrave Macmillan.

Young, L. and Barrett, H. (2001) 'Ethics and participation: reflections on research with street children', *Short Communications*, **4** (2), 130-134.

Useful websites

Department for Children, Schools and Families: www.dcsf.gov.uk/

British Sociological Association: www.britsoc.co.uk/

Department of Health: www.dh.gov.uk/

3 Research Design for Researching with Children and Adolescents

Objectives

- To explore how a researcher's philosophy may influence how they conduct research

- To establish a variety of methods that can be employed when researching with young people taking into account their age and development

- To identify different ways in which the data can be recorded and suggestions to overcome issues that may arise as a consequence

- To summarise employing a mixed methods approach and the different models that can used to collate data.

Introduction

The previous chapter explored the ethical issues that must be considered and addressed before starting a research project. A comprehensive design that incorporates and employs a practical yet ethical approach is the type of research considered in this chapter to further illustrate best practice for researching with children. Before considering types of research, however, the researcher's philosophy and its possible influence on research approach will be explored. There is a wide variety of choice in relation to methodological design and the strengths and weaknesses of these approaches (qualitative and quantitative) will be summarised. The method section consists of two distinct phases, namely researching with younger children (8-11 years) and researching with older children (12-17 years). Researching with older children will be further subdivided into early adolescence (12-14 years) and late adolescence (15-17 years) where appropriate. The recording of the data and the implications of this (in an ethical research context) will also be explored.

Research Philosophy

The case for choosing any research method, whether qualitative or quantitative, is almost impossible to present in the abstract. It is important to provide an explanation of the researcher's assumptions about the nature of knowledge and the methods through which that knowledge can be attained. These assumptions, together with the nature of the phenomena to be investigated, need to be examined in the context of the wider and deeper ongoing debate surrounding the rival methodologies of social enquiry.

There are generally thought to be two main research paradigms, or 'consensus of thinking' (Kuhn, 1970) and agreement on the methodological rules to be followed (Hussey and Hussey, 1997). These are what Burrell and Morgan (1979) describe as the interpretivist (or phenomenological) and functionalist (or positivist) paradigms. Both these major paradigms have been given a variety of names including objectivist, scientific and traditionalist (to represent the positivist paradigm) and subjectivist and humanistic (to represent the interpretivist paradigm). Each set of assumptions along the objectivist/positivist–subjectivist/interpretivist continuum are intended to provide a rough typology for thinking about the numerous views that different social scientists and marketing and business researchers hold about human beings and their world.

It is accepted that both positivist and interpretivist paradigms are valid research philosophies and as such have had a bearing on research design and execution (Channon, 1982). Channon also notes that the influence of 'instrumental validity' and 'organisational validity' has tended to steer researchers towards the positivist paradigm. Barker *et al.* (2001) however, report a growing incidence of interpretivist-based research in applied research journals and illustrate the apparent dominance this model has had within the most recent discussions on paradigms. Whatever the 'accepted' methodology might be in any given discipline, the appropriateness of the one employed in any study must be derived from the nature of the social phenomena being explored and the researcher's own ontology, if it is to be a credible and transparent piece of research. In the context of research methodology, is the author's own assumptions about the nature of knowledge and the methods through which knowledge can be obtained (Morgan and Smircich, 1980) that are important. Johnson and Duberley (2000: 4) argue that there:

> [There] are no incontestable foundations from which we can begin a consideration of our knowledge – rather what we have are competing philosophical assumptions about knowledge that lead us to engage with management and organizations in particular ways.

The philosophies underpinning the competing paradigms therefore offer an 'intellectual authority' (Hughes, 1990). This foundation for the social research theories of knowledge can help to identify and understand the nature and origination of the perceptions and presuppositions or 'nature of reality' that the researcher brings to the study. This is supported by Guba and Lincoln (1994: 105) who argue that paradigms are:

> [T]he basic belief system or world view that guides the investigator, not only in choices of method but in ontologically and epistemologically fundamental ways.

Ontology describes the researcher's theory of existence, that is, his/her view on what really exists outside that which simply appears to exist (Bullock and Trombley, 1999). It is how a researcher defines the form and nature of reality and what may be known about it. It is therefore what the researcher considers to be 'acceptable knowledge' or 'truth' that is fundamental to the design and execution of a study and overall research approach and methodological choices (Bryman, 1992). In other words, the researcher's ontological position is a reflection of his or her view on 'reality' and what constitutes truth and the presuppositions that underpin this viewpoint.

Deetz (1996) explores the key characteristics displayed by positivistic researchers. Essentially, positivism presupposes there are law-like relations among objects and that problems addressed by this type of research approach include inefficiency and disorder. The narrative style for positivists is that of science. Those defending a positivistic approach suggest that 'the purpose of any science is to offer causal explanations of social, behavioural and physical phenomena' (Schwandt, 2000: 190). However, those defending the interpretivist paradigm argue that 'human sciences aim to understand human action' and, as such, an active perspective of consumers is not necessarily found in positivism. Treating respondents as independent, non-reflective objects 'ignores their ability to reflect on problem situations and act on these' (Robson, 1993: 51) in an independent way.

However, post-positivism moves away from the purely positivist contention that there is a reality out there that can be studied, captured and understood to a stance that supports a more interpretivist notion that reality can never be fully apprehended, only approximated (Guba, 1990). Although post-positivism relies on multiple methods to capture as much of reality as possible, it still places emphasis upon the discovery and verification of theories (Denzin and Lincoln, 2005).

Whilst there are other 'types' of researchers and a number of critical debates that are ongoing in relation to different approaches to research (see 'Reading List: Understanding Research Philosophy') it is important to remember that regardless of a researcher's philosophical 'stance', the type of research adopted by the researcher ought to reflect the research aim(s) and objectives of the *current* study. Methodology (research philosophy) is not always predictive (Silverman, 1997). That is, a researcher may have an objective or scientific view of the world but it does not mean that he/she should simply use a quantitative approach. Indeed, a significant amount of the work conducted (particularly with younger children) in the most recent past appears to be of a qualitative nature. This may be for a number of reasons outlined below:

♦ Research findings from quantitative research may have been inconclusive or contradictory (this may be because the children have not understood what is being asked of them or are disengaged with the research and could (purposely) complete the questionnaires incorrectly).

♦ Children engage with research to a greater extent when the method used for researching with children is less 'formal'.

♦ A greater depth of data can be collated when researching with children if the social worlds of the children are explored through their eyes (and not through predetermined factors or variables identified by the adult researcher).

♦ To understand children is to be 'child-like' and this is less likely to be achieved if research conducted with children is adult focused.

Despite this, quantitative research conducted with children in some cases (e.g. health research) *is* important for the purpose of generalising the findings of a study to the population of children as a whole (see 'Sampling', Chapter 5). If questionnaires, for example, are being used to establish attitudes and behaviours that children have towards types of medical treatment or intervention it is important to ensure that (a) the children understand what is being asked of them (the meaning of the statements or questions) and (b) that the questionnaire adequately or appropriately reflects the concerns of the children with regard to the topic being researched. The 'philosophical stance' of the researcher then is less important than having a *shared meaning* or understanding between the adult researcher and the young people or persons with whom the research is being conducted.

This notion of shared meaning is one that permeates the rest of this chapter. Regardless of the type of research approach adopted, the meaning of what is being asked in any given context must be understood by the researcher and those being researched – and the understanding should be the *same*.

Variety of Research Types and Approach

Once the 'world view' of the researcher has been reflected upon and the research aim(s) and objectives have been established, the type of research appropriate to meeting the aim(s) and objectives should become clearer. That is, if, as a researcher you wish to 'have a deeper understanding of children and their social and cultural lives' it is likely that you will use a qualitative approach. This means that you do not necessary wish to measure 'cause and effect' but that you want to use research questions (as opposed to research hypotheses) to generate a greater insight or understanding of behaviour. For example, it may be that you want to understand the social context and the role of family structure in relation to children and their behaviour. Whilst it is not impossible to use a questionnaire to achieve this objective, the research approach is likely to be one which lends itself not to 'looking for factors or variables which may influence behaviour' but one which 'seeks to understand the role of family structure relative to the behaviour of children'. Qualitative research in this context does not generally presuppose the influence of the family structure but the data collection will be used in order to understand the concept of family, the perception of roles and an interpretation of behavioural outcomes.

If, however, you wish to generalise your findings to children as a whole, a quantitative approach will probably meet the research objectives. Taking the same example of the influence of family type on behaviour, you could ask the gate-keeper/parent to identify the family type of the respondent (e.g. intact, step or single parent) and ask the children/parents to indicate the behavioural outcomes relative to a variety of scenarios (e.g. propensity to seek peer group affiliation, parental rule-making and breaking (autonomy and regulation) or 'misbehaviour' in relation to consumption such as shoplifting, anti-social behaviour). If you ask an appropriate number of children and their parents (see 'Sampling', Chapter 5) as a researcher you will be able to establish the extent to which family type influences behaviour.

Of course, questionnaires can be used to collate qualitative data through the use of open questions and content analysis may be used with qualitative transcripts to provide numerical data. Questionnaires can also be used in small samples where the research study has an expected outcome (see Appendix 3, which considers an appropriate learning environment for children with dyslexia). It is evident that there is the potential to capture data using a variety of approaches.

This is a simplistic view of qualitative and quantitative research but the examples given above are specifically to illustrate the most basic differences between the concepts of qualitative and quantitative research. As already identified, having a world view does not preclude a researcher from employing a particular research approach (Silverman, 1997). As each research method is discussed in the following sections, the complexities of the approaches will be identified and explored and suggested reading will be provided to facilitate a greater understanding of qualitative and quantitative research outside of this practical text.

Depending on the size and type of the sample (see 'Sampling', Chapter 5), it may also be possible to develop hypotheses. That is, as result of existing literature or pre-existing knowledge (or supposition), it may be possible to 'predict' the outcome of the research (e.g. children residing in intact or traditional families are less likely to seek peer group affiliation). The number and types of responses secured from the questionnaires will then allow the 'null' hypotheses to be proven (or not). In this way, the research findings may be able to provide 'cause and effect' variables that are generalisable across a population.

It is important that whichever the approach, it not only meets the aim(s) and objectives of the research study but that the approach is understood (and practised) by the children taking part so that the findings are 'meaningful'. Indeed engaging children in the research (e.g. asking them to help through piloting questions or asking them what they think is 'meant' by particular questions) may provide more robust and reliable findings when the data is collated on a wider scale.

Types of Research Method

It would be possible to cite many texts on research methods to explore different types of research methods available to you as a student or as a researcher. In your current or previous studies it is likely that you have at some point taken a research module or had some training in research methods or methodology. This chapter then does not simply seek to replicate what you would find elsewhere but will consider the advantages and disadvantages of research approaches in relation to researching specifically with children and will further develop this by considering the appropriateness of different methods for varying age groups. It is important to reiterate, that although researching with children needs special consideration, the methods employed by the researcher may not differ in principle to methods used for researching with other (vulnerable) groups. Modifications to research approaches for researching with children, however, will be discussed here where relevant. Qualitative research methods will be considered initially, followed by quantitative methods for younger and older children in turn and this chapter will conclude by exploring a mixed methods approach.

Researching with Younger Children

Research with younger children (typically 8-11 years) requires special consideration as they can (a) often provide data the researcher does not need (e.g. familial information which does not need to be divulged and can put the child or researcher in an awkward position); (b) often have a very short attention span; and (c) may be worried or anxious about being researched or can simply say what they think the researcher wants to hear. Consequently, there are particular types of methods that lend themselves to researching with children still in the 'analytical stage' of socialisation (Roedder John, 1999). Children of this age, although able to identify the views of others, do not do so simultaneously whilst establishing their own thoughts. As a result they may provide considerable insight for the researcher and have a different understanding of their social world than adolescents (children typically aged between 12-17 years).

Both qualitative and quantitative methods can be used to research with younger children and these types of methods will be considered here respectively and are summarised in Tables 3.1 and 3.2 at the end of the chapter.

Younger Children and Qualitative Research Methods

The types of qualitative research methods that can be useful for engaging a younger group of children are as follows: participant observer, paired friends or friendship pairs and creative groups. These research methods can be used individually or in combination (see 'Mixed methods' below) and the data can be further enhanced by conducting one-to-one interviews if or when the researcher considers that this would benefit the data being collated. Interestingly, Darbyshire *et al.* (2005) note their use of multiple methods increased the children's opportunity to have control over how they wanted to contribute and this may be a consideration for researchers planning their study. Whilst this list is not exhaustive, and other methods can be employed, these given here are likely to encourage younger children to become interested in the research topic particularly where engaging techniques are used (see Chapter 4).

Participant Observer

Although it is possible to use observation for any group or sample, the participant observer method can be a particularly useful way in which to build trust and rapport with younger children. Younger children can be shy and unsure of their responses to questions and will be the group of children most likely to want to give the 'right' answer to the researcher (see Cohen *et al.*, 2000; Dockett and Perry, 2007). By using the role of participant observer the confidence of the children will be enhanced if they know and feel comfortable with the researcher. There are issues regarding the role of participant observer but in the context of observation as a research method the following key issues must be considered:

♦ What is participant observer research?

♦ What are the possible roles of the researcher?

♦ And how will the data be recorded?

What is a Participant Observer?

Participant observer research is one strand of an 'ethnographic' approach to research design. Ethnography explores the 'lived order' of the respondents. This means that this particular research approach allows the researcher to understand the attitudes, behaviours and/or motivations of individuals (or groups of individuals) simply by watching and noting the way in which he/she/they interact and behave. Participant observer research as a method can be further explored outside this text (see for example: Kacen and Rozovski, 1998; Monahan and Zuckerman, 1999; Labaree, 2002) and as with any research approach there are proponents and those that urge deliberation and caution in using this method. Participant observer research is not particular to researching with children and has certainly been used elsewhere (see, for example, Schouten and McAlexander, 1995) but as a researcher conducting a study with children, you will never be able to be a child (although you can be child-like). As such you cannot simply observe as a 'member' of the group. If you use participant observer research to gain a deeper understanding of the behaviour of children, you will have a 'role'. You must understand that this 'role' will affect the way in which the children interact with you as a researcher and this must be taken into account when writing up the data.

What are the Possible Roles of the Researcher?

The following section considers the possible 'roles' of a participant observer. Discussions of fieldwork with young people have been preoccupied with the issue of researcher 'role' (see, for example, Fine and Sandstrom, 1988; Adler, 1996; Corsaro, 1996) but less attention has focused on the children's understanding of 'research'. However the cognitive capacity of minors has been underestimated as children as young as 6 years of age can demonstrate a basic understanding of the purpose of research (Broome et al., 2001). It is useful, then, to ensure that when as a researcher you adopt a 'role' that the children are aware of and understand it. The topic being considered here is, 'understanding how children learn to swim'. The initial 'role' considered here is that of a swimming instructor. The second role, namely that of a 'teacher-helper' will also be explored in the context of observing behaviour, collating data and recording field notes. The following examples are to explicitly illustrate the different roles a researcher may have when researching with children. It is possible to have overlapping roles (e.g. teacher-helper and teaching assistant) but for the purpose of demonstrating the adoption (or ascribing) of a role, the following examples show how the research data may be captured differently depending on the role adopted by or ascribed to the researcher.

If, as a part-time lifeguard or swimming instructor, you are interested in how children learn to swim (e.g. what their fears are, how these fears are overcome, how peer group influence affects the performance of those who cannot swim, how those who are strong swimmers are positioned within a group) then, with the permission of the children and their gatekeeper(s) you will be able to observe how the children learn to swim by taking part in their instruction. If this instruction lasts for say a 6-10 week period it may be possible to develop an understanding of the interaction and behaviour of the children as individuals and as a group and to make notes of how both interaction and individual behaviour changes over time. As a researcher you may also consider it necessary to interview some of the children to ensure your 'understanding' of the observed behaviour has a shared meaning, e.g. your perception and that of the child/ren is the same. Note also that if you do take part in the instruction, that the children are likely to consider you as a 'teacher' of sorts and this will influence the way in which they interact with you. Of course, over time and because they will probably enjoy learning this particular skill, they will begin to trust and build rapport with you. The field notes on their interaction with you, as well as with one another, may illustrate this change over time.

If in the context of swimming lessons you are not the instructor but a teacher-helper who assists the teacher with school trips your role will be different. Your participation will be less involved than that of instructor and the trust and rapport that the children will develop with you over time (and vice versa) may be less than that of an instructor as a result. You are also likely to be perceived or positioned as 'the teacher's friend' and this will most certainly affect the way in which the child/ren responds to you as a researcher. You may also know one or more of the children in the class personally. The role the children ascribe to you may be as a result of the relationship that child/ren has with the other children in their class. This is not to say that your observations will be any less valid but that you must use this context when analysing your data. If you are accompanying the children on a bus to get to the swimming pool or walking with children to a leisure centre or school where the swimming lessons are, you will be a unique position where you can observe the interaction and behaviour of the children before, during and after the swimming lessons and observe this behaviour over time. Your 'one-to-one' interviews may simply involve 'chatting' to different children on the bus on or the walk to develop a deeper understanding of their interaction or behaviour whereas the instructor would have to conduct any interviews outside the context of the research (e.g. not at the swimming pool). This is likely to be because of logistical reasons. The teacher will have a limited time to get to the swimming pool and back to school and the children will have a routine for getting changed and onto the bus or ready to walk back to school. The instructor, then, if they wish to interview the children, will probably have to go to the school or the home of the child/ren outside the context of the interaction and behaviour. This could have recall implications for the children (e.g. if the swimming lessons take place on a Monday and the child/ren are interviewed on a Thursday, they may not remember in detail what happened before, during or after the lesson) and could also have 'role' implications. That is, you would be an 'instructor' or 'teacher' at the swimming pool but what is your role at school? Again this may affect the way in which the children interact with you.

This example illustrates that as a participant observer it is possible to have a number of roles and that the note-taking, observation and possible interviews with the child/ren may be affected as a result. It also demonstrates that the children may ascribe a role to you (e.g. 'teacher') if they do not understand what your role is or what your research involves. It is, therefore, very important that when participant observation is being employed, the child/ren clearly understand the purpose of the research. This is not just for ethical reasons but so that the child/ren has a clear understanding of the topic and can frame their responses accordingly.

How will the Data be Recorded?

In the discipline of ethnography, of which participant observer is only one aspect, it is normal practise to write 'field notes'. These notes will not only record actual behaviour but can also provide a context to the interaction and behaviour of child/ren. For example a participant observer making a note that before the first swimming lesson 'Lucy told me her cat had to be put down and she was very sad about it' may provide a context for Lucy's behaviour during the first swimming lesson. That is, rather than simply recording 'Lucy had trouble concentrating and found the first swimming lesson difficult', the context for why the swimming lesson may have been more problematic than anticipated and why Lucy's progress is slower than others may be external to the research focus but equally as relevant. It also helps the researcher 'paint a picture' of the interaction and behaviour rather than merely recording what has happened and surmising why Lucy may not be progressing (e.g. 'Lucy had trouble concentrating, perhaps she is afraid of the water?'). If Lucy is later interviewed this can be explored as a possible reason for her lack of involvement and this, again, helps to create a shared meaning.

If interviews are conducted in addition to the participant observing, it may be that the interview will be voice recorded if the appropriate permission has been sought (see Chapter 2). This will help the researcher for a number of reasons namely: it is difficult to make eye contact with children if you are constantly trying to write down what they say, often it is difficult to contextualise the notes you have made if you have no record of the conversation (e.g. number of pauses in the dialogue, etc.) and the intonation of the voices of the researcher and the child/ren are available so that the researcher can be sure of their interpretation of the way in which the child/ren commented on a topic or issue.

Where appropriate, it may also be possible to visually record the observed behaviour. If, for example, your research considers food choice in the dinner hall at school, with permission of those involved, you may visually record pupils making their food choice so that you can play back their particular 'moment of choice' to them to facilitate discussion. However, there are times where the visual recording of observed behaviour should be considered inappropriate (e.g. issues of privacy and child protection issues). As such, in the above example of understanding how children learn to swim, visually recording these children would be inappropriate (not least because the children would be dressed in their swim wear) notwithstanding the unlikelihood of gatekeeper(s) consent. Be a considerate researcher and *not* a researcher who will seek to collect data at any cost.

Paired Friends or Friendship Pairs

Conducting research with younger children can seem daunting to them and, as already established in Chapter 2, allowing children to have a friend with them when the research is being conducted can reduce any power imbalance and can help to allay any anxiety. Researching with paired friends or friendship pairs can also provide a greater level of insight as younger children, in a safe environment, are likely to talk or discuss more readily. What is the difference between paired friends and friendship pairs? *Paired friends* will typically be children known to one another but will be part of a wider circle of friends (e.g. members of a friendship group). *Friendship pairs* are usually 'best friends' or children who know one another very well. If you are interviewing paired friends this may be because the interlocutors (e.g. social workers, teachers) have selected and paired the children for you. There are advantages and disadvantages to this sampling approach, however, in the context of research design, the difference between paired friends and friendship pairs can affect data collection and subsequent interpretation of results and this will be discussed here.

Deciding between Paired Friends and Friendship Groups

If you have a choice, considering the following in relation to your specific research topic may help you to decide which approach to take. Paired friends may be quieter or less communicative than friendship pairs because they are not as close as friendship pairs. They may however take any task or questions you set them more seriously because they consider the activity to be more 'work' than 'play' centred. However, friendship pairs know one another much better than paired friends and this may prevent socially desirable responses (e.g. it will be more difficult for the children in a friendship pair to say what they think the researcher wants to hear as typically the other child will 'correct' them). This is also true of 'sibling pairs' if there is an opportunity to interview brothers or sisters together. Paired friends may seek more guidance from the researcher rather from one another as they may be less trusting of their 'pair' as they do not know them as well as their other friend(s). Important to note here, is that younger children often argue but also more readily make friends again. If you are interviewing friendship pairs it is important to ascertain with the gatekeeper if there has been any 'fall outs' or animosities between the friendship pairs that the research will reignite.

Researching with either friendship pairs or paired friends can be akin to conducting an interview with two children as opposed to one. This means that you can give both children your attention (as opposed to trying to manage a larger group) and you will be more aware of when the conversation is slowing down. You can use a variety of techniques to involve the children whilst you are researching with them (see Chapter 4) but this method is recommended for novice researchers who have had little, if any, previous research experience with younger children as it (a) minimises the need to manage a larger number of children (b) allows the researcher to practise their techniques slowly and carefully to build up their experience and (c) most importantly provides a safe and comfortable environment in which the children can be heard.

How will the Data be Recorded?

If initial consent has been obtained from the gatekeeper(s) and the child/ren and on-going consent has been given by the child/ren, voice or visual recording of the friendship pairs or paired friends can be used. This will allow the researcher to fully engage with the children and not have to worry about writing down what the children say whilst trying to maintain a discussion. If voice recording is being used but not visual recording, body language and facial expressions can be observed and noted by the researcher where appropriate (to provide context for interpretation and analysis). Destroying this voice recording and any transcripts on completion of the project is both required by law and good practice (see Chapters 2 and 8).

Creative Groups

For more experienced researchers or those more experienced in dealing with children, creative groups as described by Melzer-Lena and Middelmann-Motz (1998) may allow data collection with a larger number of children over a shorter period of time. Creative groups can involve the children with whom you are researching in role play, drawing, collages or inventing stories. These projective techniques and ideas for engaging children during research will be covered in Chapter 4. Creative groups can have between 6-10 children although this number allows for subdivision (e.g. groups numbering 4, 3 and 3). If you choose this as a research method for researching with younger children, the following must be taken into account:

♦ Younger children have a short attention span. Make sure you have thought through how long it will take them to complete any activity. The younger the child, the shorter the time they will take to complete a task. Conversely, ensure you have allowed enough time to discuss the output/creations of the children after completion of the task (Darbyshire *et al.*, 2005).

♦ Younger children particularly (although not exclusively) need praise and appreciation to complete activities. Ensure that if the group is large (more than 4 children) that you have a second researcher or moderator to help explain the task and encourage the children throughout the activity. If this is not possible think about reducing the number of children in a group or the number of groups.

♦ Do not automatically expect that the children will know what to do. Use short sentences to explain what you would like them to do and check regularly to make sure they are happy and comfortable with the task in hand.

♦ In the interests of safety, if the children are (for example) making a collage, make sure they are well supervised and that all equipment (e.g. scissors) are being used appropriately and carefully.

As with all other methods used to research with children, ethical consideration in relation to consent and the area being researched needs to be addressed before the research can take place.

How will the Data be Recorded?

As with friendship pairs or paired friends the general approach to recording the data will either be voice or visual recording (with appropriate consent) or both. Recording the data from creative groups, however, can be problematic. Visual recording can only capture a small number of children up close or a large number at a distance. The interpretation of this data would be limited to either a small number of children or may provide very little detail. Voice recording also has limitations in this context as children tend to speak all at the same time or talk over one another and some of the data can be lost. If resources allow, using a number of voice recorders (and where applicable, visual recorders) can maximise the amount of 'conversational' data that can be captured. Using other researchers or moderators as observers to make notes during the research process may also add to the body of data and may help contextualise the 'findings' to a greater extent.

Younger Children and Quantitative Research

Whilst recent research (particularly with younger children) has featured a greater number of qualitative research approaches, quantitative research has also been used to generate an insight into understanding the behaviours, attitudes and motivations of young people. It is more unusual to use quantitative research approaches with *younger* children because levels of literacy mean the types of questions you can ask may be limited (e.g. questions that require 'yes', 'no' or 'not sure' answers may have to replace agree/disagree scales). Nevertheless, there is general agreement that survey research is feasible with children from the age of 7, albeit with carefully adapted questionnaires (Scott, 1997; Borgers *et al.*, 2000). Oppenheim (1996) argues, with adults in mind, that question wording or sentences should not exceed 20 words and this number should be considerably reduced, even halved, for younger children and it may therefore be difficult to convey exactly what you 'mean' in a statement. Although it has been suggested that some clear and helpful introductory text may prove to be an advantage even if it does result in a longer question overall (Borgers and Hox, 2000) remember that questionnaire completion is a limited activity and may not engage the children. Younger children have a short attention span and therefore any questionnaire has to be reasonably short (minimising the amount of data that can be collated) and should not have a wide number of options (e.g. should be limited to yes/no) (De Leeuw *et al.*, 2002). Bell (2007) also suggests that questions based in the 'here-and-now' are preferable to retrospective questions about children's behaviour as children do not have the same recall as adults. There is also a fine line between 'helping' younger children to complete a more complex question-naire and 'biasing' the findings.

Quantitative research, however, does have its advantages. It is possible to gen-eralise findings (although this will be dependent on the sampling approach) and it can provide enough volume of data to make a convincing case to facilitate strategic or policy related decisions. What is important is to make sure that the younger children know what is being asked of them. When designing a question-naire for children (see, for example, Appendix 3) the researcher should think about the ways in which the questionnaire can be both interesting and (where possible) fun. Computer-based questionnaires are often popular with young chil-dren as they can be very computer literate and given the features available to the researcher, a questionnaire has the potential to be very engaging.

Online or computer-based questionnaires can utilise colour, animation, presen-tation opportunities (e.g. one question per screen), noise (music, positive sounds, e.g. applause) and interaction (e.g. drop-down menus, click and drag, etc.). Computer-based questionnaires can also minimise non-response as the respond-ent will be unable to progress to the next question until the question posed on screen has been answered. To be able to design and manage an online ques-tionnaire, the researcher needs to be computer literate themselves and for the children (who must also be computer literate) to have access to a computer for the study. Depending on the time frame of the study, the researcher may want to have a paper-based contingency plan in place in case the technology fails. Use of software (e.g. SNAP) that can help the researcher design a questionnaire using a variety of interactive methods can be placed online and should also facilitate easier analysis. Inputting is automatic with this type of online questionnaire and data can be exported to commonly used Microsoft programs (e.g. Excel) to ex-pedite analysis.

Regardless of the method used to collect quantitative data, and as with all other research methods, it is important to encourage the children and praise them regularly for their contribution. Often on paper-based questionnaires, using '☺' or encouraging words ('nearly there, you are doing so well!') will not only moti-vate the child but will help them concentrate too.

The role of the gatekeeper(s) and experts is also important in ensuring that the children understand statements or questions asked on a survey. Tinson and Nan-carrow (2005) illustrate the significance of *preparing* quantitative research to be conducted with children. Their particular study focused on 10-12 year olds and provides guidance for designing a questionnaire for children that is useful to note here. They suggest inviting a variety of people pertinent to the research (experts, gatekeeper(s) and children) to consider the questionnaire that has been designed. Ask them if they think the wording is appropriate, if they understand what is being asked and establish how user-friendly the questionnaire is in terms of design (e.g. too long, disengaging, similar statements that are difficult to differentiate between, obvious omissions, irrelevant questions or questions that may cause embarrassment or upset). This is supported by Bell (2007) who advocates pretesting of questionnaires for children. As younger children may not be as vocal and/or as literate as older children, the role of the gatekeeper(s) in this scenario is of particular significance.

Older children may of course have the skills and abilities to become more involved in the research process and this will covered somewhat in the section that follows next but also in Chapter 9.

Older Children and Qualitative Research Methods

The types of qualitative research methods that can be useful for engaging with a *younger* group of children can be modified or adapted to research with older children (typically ages 12-17). For example, as participant observer you might opt to coach a teenage football team or offer to share a skill you have (e.g. first aid) to study the behaviour, attitudes or motives of adolescents in relation to a variety of topics. However, this method will not be covered again here as the same guidance would apply to researchers using participant observer with younger or older groups of children. The reason participant observer has been suggested as research method for *younger* children is that they may be less self-conscious when being observed. As adolescence is a time of 'storm and stress' with young people trying on different behaviours (see, for example, Montemayor, 1986) it may be more difficult to try to find a 'role' within that group. Adolescence is a period of autonomy and regulation (Csikszentmihalyi and Rochberg-Halton, 1981) and even as a participant observer you may be unwelcome amongst a group of teenagers trying to establish 'who they are'.

Of course there can be considerable differences in the experience and perception of adolescents who are 12 years old and adolescents who are nearly adult (17 years). Harvey and Byrd (1998) indicate that early adolescence (12-14 years) is mostly about acquiring information and experience, while late adolescence (15-17 years) is characterised as being a period of identity development in which the information obtained earlier is used to build and consolidate a new identity. As such, the importance of the social context might change over the course of development and it may be easier to subdivide older children into these two age groups. For example, early adolescents may be less comfortable being observed as regulation will be high and autonomy low and additional perceived constraints on their behaviour (e.g. 'being watched') could be resented. Conversely, late adolescents may be more comfortable being observed (as regulation will be lower and autonomy higher) as they may be more comfortable with who they 'are'. Deciding on participant observation as a method for researching with early or late adolescence will depend on the existing relationship you may have with the children (e.g. social worker, teacher), the topic being researched (e.g. engaging, sensitive, etc.) and how comfortable you would feel creating a role for yourself in a potentially isolating situation.

It may be that instead of using a participant observer method with adolescents another qualitative research approach would elicit the same rich type of data. For example, instead of using paired friends, friendship pairs or creative groups (suggested for researching with *younger* children) consider larger groups of friends or scene interviews. Scene interviews as described by Melzer-Lena and Middelmann-Motz (1998) are those that use scenario research to allow teenagers the opportunity to express and present themselves. This type of research will be covered in greater depth here as will the use of diary studies. As before, these research methods can be used individually or in combination and the data can be further enhanced by conducting one-to-one interviews if or when the researcher considers that this would benefit the data being collated.

Scene Interviews

Early adolescents, in particular, use adolescence to acquire information and experience. To this end, it has been observed that teenagers often find it easier to disassociate themselves from other 'types' of people or different 'types' of behaviour than identifying with them. Hogg and Banister (2001) for example, illustrate that 'refusal of tastes' may say as much about us individuals as what we choose to consume (or how we behave). That is 'what becomes clear is that "good taste" exists only through a thorough knowledge of what constitutes "bad taste" (ibid: 76) and this could be equally applicable in the context of health or learning behaviours. This may be because early adolescents do not have enough information or experience to feel comfortable enough to 'commit' to a particular type of behaviour. Using scene interviews or 'scenarios' in an interview situation may, therefore, allow the teenagers the opportunity to express their views and opinions without them overtly providing information about themselves or their attitudes or behaviour (and importantly may make them feel more comfortable).

Scenarios or 'scenes' (also known as vignettes) during interviews may involve role play. Vignettes have long been used to study attitudes, perceptions, beliefs and norms within social science (Finch, 1987). Vignettes are simulations of real events depicting hypothetical situations (Wilks, 2004). This type of approach to collating research is used across disciplines although it is less popular than, say, a semi-structured interview. This may be because it is easier to develop a semi-structured interview that focuses specifically on the research issue (e.g. how does having eczema affect your day-to-day life?) rather than using an abstract vignette and hope that the children the involved will see the relationship between the scenario and the research issue (and possibly themselves). There is no guarantee that the responses to a given vignette will in some way mirror actual behaviour of the respondent. However, as stated, using scenarios as a projective technique (see Chapter 4) may (a) elicit more information and (b) may be more engaging for the adolescent and (c) address social desirability issues (Hughes, 1998). It is, however, important to gauge the levels of literacy of the adolescents to ensure they understand the concepts being presented in the scenario. Ask the gatekeeper(s) or experts to give you their opinion of the vignette or illustration before it is distributed. Examples of scenarios used to help children think about school bullying are provided by Ahmed and Braithwaite (2004).

Whilst scenarios or vignettes have been used across disciplines they are not always used in researching with children e.g. it may be that as a researcher you can adapt a research approach used in a more adult way as the following example shows. Gill and Coad (2007) report their recent findings on nurses' understanding and knowledge of children and young people with eczema, having used vignettes supported by a questionnaire. Importantly, however, this research could have been adapted to research with children about their condition. One of the scenarios used is that of a fictitious child who had severe eczema and was suffering psychosocial effects as a result. Although the scenario was used in this reported research to examine practical aspects of nursing care and decision making, the scenario could equally have been used to explore the way in which eczema affected the day-to-day life of an adolescent and could afford the adolescent the opportunity to discuss their condition in a more objective way.

Scenarios or vignettes can be supported by other research methods (as here with questionnaires for the health research) but can also be enhanced by pictures, photographs or cartoons that illustrate the concepts described in the narrative. There are a number of reasons why researchers may wish to use pictures when interviewing adolescents. Firstly, children have different learning styles and these can typically be mapped using the Visual, Audio and Kinaesthetic (VAK) model (see Dunn *et al.*, 1984). VAK approaches to learning vary between children and some children respond better to seeing rather than hearing information. (The VAK model does not just apply to adolescents but to all learners – greater discussion on its use and applicability will be detailed in Chapter 4). However, it is important to note here that all learners can benefit from multisensory approaches and that using pictures, photographs or cartoons may enhance the research experience of the adolescent and enable all adolescents that you are researching with to understand the concepts being posed. Second, adolescents tend to be media literature and are constantly exposed to interactive material. As such using a multisensory approach to research design is likely to be more familiar and encouraging to them. Finally, the adolescent can choose to associate or disassociate themselves from the character(s) described in a scenario or depicted in a cartoon. This may improve the conversation between the researcher and the adolescent and more important, may make the adolescent feel more comfortable.

If you are going to choose a vignette that has a picture, photograph or cartoon associated with it this can influence the data collection. For example, if as a researcher you are exploring the subject of pregnancy with teenage girls and you use a photograph of a pregnant woman to stimulate discussion, the photograph itself provides a context. For example, if members of the group with whom you are exploring the issues are living in poverty and the photograph introduced is that of a white, affluent, middle-class woman, the discussion may be less about pregnancy and more about poverty. It is important to remember that as a researcher it is easy to impose your own views and more difficult to illicit the views, opinions, attitudes and motivations of others.

How will the Data be Recorded?

It is likely that as with other types of qualitative research, the interview will be audio and/or visually recorded (with the caveat of the researcher having obtained consent and ongoing consent). The only 'unique' aspect of recording this type of data is that using scenarios or vignettes in an interview situation can, methodologically, be done in two different ways. That is, the scenario can be issued before the interview and can be discussed when the interview takes place or can be given to the adolescent during the interview. If the scenario is issued before the interview, the adolescent may use this opportunity to think carefully about how they want to react to the narrative or illustration. They may show it to their friends, parents or family members to seek their views too. In this situation it is much more difficult to record the data as the impact of the narrative or illustration may be lost and/or the opinion of the adolescent with whom you are conducting the research may be difficult to ascertain because of the influence of others.

Alternatively if the scenario is presented during the interview, the researcher must allow the adolescent enough time to (a) read and digest the piece and (b) clarify any issues that might arise from the material that has been presented. Audio and/or visual recording of this process may also be insightful for the researcher and will also provide a context to the discussion that follows.

Diary Studies

Adolescents (12-17 years) will *typically* have greater levels of literacy than younger children (although it is acknowledged that this will largely depend on the sample and location of research) and as such giving them the opportunity to record their own behaviour can seem less intrusive than other methods of research (e.g. one-to-one interviews). The advantages of using a diary approach when researching with adolescents include:

- **Privacy** – Completing a diary for research purposes can be akin to keeping a private diary. As the researcher ought to ensure confidentiality (see Chapter 2) the adolescent should be reassured that the information they are providing will not be used for any purpose other than the research. The diary entries can be made by the adolescent in a (private) location of their choice and the ethical issues of a researcher being physically present in the private space of the adolescent is negated.

- **Timing** – When researching with adolescents, it is often more difficult to arrange times and days that they will be available to meet the researcher (although again this will depend on the sample and the location). Using the diary method means that the adolescent is free to choose the time of the day or week in which they complete the diary entry and they can also decide when they want to interact with the research project.

- **Ownership** – Depending on the design of the 'diary' (see below) the adolescent(s) will be able to personalise their diary entries. That is, if the adolescents want to draw, use illustrations or photographs to record their behaviour, opinions or motivations this is possible in a way that is not possible in say an interview situation. An 'interview' never can belong to them in the same way a diary can. A diary is also a productive document. Adolescents will themselves be able to see the development of the data and be more aware of themselves as 'producers of research'.

Of course there can be issues relating to the completion of diaries. Incomplete diaries or those with incorrect entries are difficult to analyse and detect. The adolescents need to be motivated enough to complete their daily entry and they need to know exactly what is going to happen to their data and how it is going to be used. The researcher needs to think carefully about the use of incentives and ways in which they can encourage the adolescents to complete the diaries. Completion of diaries may be facilitated by their design.

Design of the Diary (Recording of the Data)

There are two ways in which a diary can be presented to an adolescent for completion. It can be unstructured or semi-structured and depending on the research aim(s) and objectives of the research study being conducted, the researcher should choose carefully between these types of design. Given the new technology both available to young people and researchers it would also be possible to have a diary online that the adolescents could complete. This would also allow for 'prompts' to be employed (see Chapter 4).

Unstructured

An unstructured diary will be one that has no direction or instructions on it. Inevitably the researcher will have to choose the type and size of paper and the format in which the diary will be presented (one page of A4 paper or a booklet of A5 for example) and that may in itself be encouraging or discouraging to adolescents. Whilst any form of diary presentation is acceptable, note that the adolescents may complete their diaries in different ways with different volumes of data depending on the amount of space they have been given. Also note that giving adolescents more space to write does not necessarily equate with greater volume of data. An unstructured diary may be more appropriate when you are exploring behaviour, attitudes and motivations. For example, if the research is designed to capture the diet of children, a diary that asks children to record 'breakfast', 'lunch' and 'dinner' does not take into account their snacking behaviour or their varied eating patterns. However, offering the adolescents an opportunity to write at leisure about what they have eaten and when they have eaten (and with whom if applicable) may provide greater insight into food consumption than simply asking them to record their eating habits in a traditional (perhaps unrealistic) manner. In this example (food consumption) there will inevitably be aspects of misinformation, for example, the adolescent(s) may not record that they ate three bars of chocolate at lunch time but instead suggest that they had a salad or a healthier option. However, using a diary approach should reduce socially desirable responding because the adolescent(s) does not have to explain their choice (only record it) and so will not have to look for face-saving excuses (as they may do in an interview situation).

Semi-Structured

There are advantages to giving adolescents some direction in relation to diary completion (although the choice of this type of approach would depend on the research aim(s) and objectives). Trew *et al.* (1999: 56) illustrate the benefits of using time diaries to record adolescents' main (sporting) activities out of school hours during term-time as in their study it provided 'an independent basis for establishing the time devoted to sport by young people with differing levels of commitment to competitive sport'. The adolescents in this study were each asked to complete a diary comprised of one page per day, over a four-day period. They were asked to note when they got up, had their main meals and went to bed as well as noting the times they started and ended activities, where they were and who they were with. School days were divided into three parts with the weekend divided by meal times. This type of diary design could be applied to any piece of research if the researcher was seeking information on frequency or percentages of adolescents taking part in an activity and the possible influence of any referent (peer) influence. This approach affords less ownership for the adolescent but greater management (and numeric analysis) opportunities for the researcher.

It is important, however, to afford the adolescent the opportunity to record their own thoughts as well as those predetermined by the researcher. The reasons for this are twofold. First, it is essential that the adolescent considers their input to be valuable as this will motivate them to complete the diary and enhance their research experience and second, the adolescent may provide insight previously not considered by the researcher that may, in turn, make the researcher re-evaluate the research aim(s) or the data analysis. (see Appendix 4 for a structured diary example).

A semi-structured diary is more akin to a quantitative approach (particularly if the researcher was seeking information on frequency or percentages of adolescents' behaviour).

Quantitative Research with Adolescents

Quantitative research has a number of advantages. By its very nature it strives for generalisation which can lead to prediction, explanation, and understanding. Quantitative research typically involves the use of structured questions where the response options have been predetermined. Generally a large number of respondents complete these questions in a questionnaire format.

The sample size for a questionnaire or a survey is calculated by using formulas to determine how large a sample size will need to be from a given population in order to achieve findings with an acceptable degree of accuracy (see 'Sampling', Chapter 5). Generally, researchers seek sample sizes which yield findings with at least 95% confidence interval (which means that if you repeat the survey 100 times, you would get the same response on 95 occasions). Many surveys are designed to produce a smaller margin of error.

In what ways then, do questionnaires for adolescents differ from (or indeed are the same) as surveys for younger children? (See 'Younger children and quantitative research methods' above.) In many ways, the principles for questionnaire design are the same regardless of those you are researching with. It is important, for example, to make questionnaires engaging so that those being asked to complete them are motivated to do so. An online approach as described in the section on 'Younger children and quantitative research' can also be employed with some modifications. It is important, for example, not to appear to be patronising and the use of language for adolescent questionnaires should also be chosen carefully. For example, be wary of using the word 'cool' as often adults doing so is an anathema.

Often with older children it is important to provide more detail with regards to the research project. The more adolescents know about 'why' they are completing a questionnaire the more likely they are to complete it properly. Malresponse is likely to occur when the adolescents do not know the researcher or their motivations and/or do not fully understand what the information is for or how it is going to be used.

Quantitative research conducted with both early and late adolescents is often appropriate when researching issues that could cause embarrassment or discomfort when asked in an open forum. An example is Giordano *et al.*'s 2006 study on the meaning of adolescent romantic relationships for boys. It is important when using questionnaires with adolescents that they understand *exactly* what is being asked about. As a researcher you may have a definition of romance that does not correspond with that of an adolescent. Simple definitions that precede different sections within a questionnaire can be extremely useful in ensuring that the adolescents understand what the researcher means in relation to an idea or concept. Asking the adolescents what they mean by 'romance', for example, and using this in a questionnaire will produce a 'shared meaning'. This approach is likely to involved mixed methods (see 'Mixed Methods' below).

A way of making sure the questionnaire reflects the views and concerns of adolescents is to ask for their help. They can contribute to an understanding of their social world and as such they can help design questionnaires or pilot surveys (or both). A recent example of researching with adolescents to understand the significance of the 'high school prom' as a way of both expressing an identity and as a 'critical moment' can be seen in the example of exploring ritual behaviour.

The purpose of the study was twofold: to establish the way in which the high school prom is adopted or adapted as a ritual experience in a different country, and to ascertain the way in which the ritual artefacts, script, roles and audience are used by the adolescents to facilitate their 'coming of age' celebration.

The research employed a mixed method approach which involves qualitative and quantitative approaches within or across the stages of the research process to increase the validity of data. Initially 12 interviews were organized with young adults (18-20 years of age) who had already attended a high school prom. They were tasked to consider what happens before, during and after a prom (preparation, event and post evaluation) and to indicate the extent to which they felt it had been a significant event for them. Second, a mini group of three 17-year-old girls were invited to discuss how they would research this particular topic with their peers. A questionnaire was designed by the authors using the data generated by the discussion group (as well as the data from the interviews) and underpinned by the notion of the high school prom being a ritual experience. The questionnaire was then piloted by the members of the discussion group and changes to its wording were discussed and addressed.

Box 3.1: Exploring Ritual Behaviour

(Adapted from Tinson et al. forthcoming)

Curiosity about ritual behaviour is global and in recent years, rituals practised in the USA have been embraced more fully in the UK (e.g. Halloween) with the ensuing commercialisation and consumption behaviour associated with such practices increasingly apparent. However, the extent to which these rituals are being adapted as well as adopted is less well documented and needs further exploration.

Historically, the principal notion of the school prom has been to mark the transition of youths to adulthood. It is inspired by the debutante ball which was of particular significance for young women as it signalled that they were ready for marriage. However, few scholars have used the concept of ritual behaviour to explore it. Best (2000) notes that we have less systematic research on high school proms and the associated rituals and practices because they are typically dismissed as 'trivial'. She suggests research in this area would generate insight into transitional behaviour and argues that the high school prom has wrongly been positioned as 'marginal'. Whilst Escalas (1993: 709) described the debutante ball as an 'insignificant' ritual because 'the lack of lasting behavioural change and rejection of social implications causes [it] to lose significance for the participants', she too called for an examination of other rites of passage present in modern-day society (e.g. high school proms).

Ritual artefacts (signs and symbols), a ritual script, performance roles and an audience have been identified by Rook (1985) as essential to a ritual experience. Escalas (1993) observes that these four components are central to the debutante ball and they are in some respects equally relevant for the high school prom. The gown, the meal, the photographs and the audience (internal and external) contribute to the overall event. Ritual artefacts, in particular, when used in a ritual context can convey specific symbolic messages. Symbolic consumption is an important means by which these young consumers define themselves: they use goods as materials with which to create, foster and develop their identity (Elliot and Wattanasuwan, 1998) and do so as part of this ritual experience. Although some ritual occasions have declined in popularity (such as the debutante ball), new rituals have emerged to take their place (Rook, 1985: 255). The high school prom has not only risen in popularity but has transcended continents.

This research explored how, if at all, the high school prom has been adapted in the UK and if it can generate an insight into the transition from youth to adulthood. The research was an exploratory study conducted with both adolescents who currently attend a secondary school in central Scotland and young adults who have attended a high school prom in the UK in the last three years.

The questionnaire was then self-administered by the female friends from the discussion group to their peers to facilitate completion of the survey and to generate interest in the research topic. Questions about the survey could be asked of the females by their peers and because of their input and understanding with regard to the questions being asked, the respondents were able to complete the questionnaires more readily and with support where necessary. Using this research approach allowed the research topic to be addressed in a more holistic way as it not only allowed the adolescents an opportunity to add their own insights but it may also have provided a more complete knowledge of the research issue because of the creation of 'shared meaning' with and within the respondent group.

Teenagers from a high school in central Scotland who were going to attend their prom were asked to respond to the questionnaire. The majority of adolescents completing the questionnaires were either 16 or 17 although a few of the youngest pupils were 15. Appropriate ethical consideration was given to this study with permission for the research to be conducted sought and given from the head teacher and ongoing consent given by the adolescents involved in the project.

As can be seen from the example above, this approach allows the knowledge from the research to be jointly constructed. In this paradigm, the researchers are not solely looking for affirmation of their views but rather are seeking to explore with, and jointly construct answers to, the research question with the adolescents. It has been noted that work that employs this perspective has pointed to the importance of attending to the ways in which power relations find their expression in research relationships (Oakley, 1981; Thompson, 1998).

The potential for knowing more about a phenomenon through the use of different methods is often discussed under the rubric of 'triangulation' (Moran-Ellis *et al.*, 2006). For example, Miles and Huberman (1984: 234) discuss the concept of 'within-methods' triangulation, that is 'using different kinds of measurements which provide repeated verification'. Holliday (2002: 61) discusses how to 'validate a conclusion'. That is, using a variety of questions (open-ended, probes, projective techniques, the draw and write technique) to ensure consistency of response using a range of questioning approaches. However, triangulation can also be used across methods as well as within methods and the following section discusses employing a mixed methods approach.

Mixed Methods

Qualitative and quantitative methods can of course be used together. There are advocates of this approach (see, for example, Greene *et al..*, 2001; O'Cathain *et al.*, 2007; Denscombe, 2008; Wilkins and Woodgate, 2008) although as a researcher your research philosophy (see 'Reading list – Understanding Research

Philosophy') may guide or influence the use of a mixed methods approach (remember, however, that research philosophy should not dictate method). It is important to remember that the type of research adopted by the researcher ought to reflect the research aims and objectives of the *current* study.

Whilst the results of quantitative research can seem shallow and abstract, the results of qualitative research can raise questions of objectivity (Buchanan, 1992). As such, employing a mixed methods approach may seem to be a promising strategy. Johnson and Onwuegbuzie (2004: 17) describe a mixed method approach as 'the class of research where the researcher mixes or combines quantitative and qualitative research techniques, methods, approaches, concepts or language into a single study'. The majority of mixed method research designs can be developed from two major types of mixed methods research:

Mixed Model

Mixing qualitative and quantitative approaches *within* or *across* the stages of the research process

Appendix 1 illustrates a mixed model approach. Service users were interviewed (qualitative) to help develop a questionnaire, a questionnaire was distributed (quantitative) and then focus groups and paired interviews were conducted (qualitative) with young people with a view to complementing and extending the evidence gathered from the questionnaire survey.

Mixed Method

The inclusion of a quantitative phase *and* a qualitative phase in an overall research study.

The 'Exploring ritual behaviour' case study in Box 3.1 illustrates the inclusion of a qualitative phase followed by a quantitative phase. This is a common approach to employing mixed methods. Whilst qualitative research was used to generate a deeper understanding of the high school prom (and to develop items for a questionnaire) the second phase was to distribute and analyse the findings using SPSS (Statistical Package for the Social Sciences) to reach a broader target and to generate a more holistic view.

Whilst there are clearly advantages to employing a mixed methods approach there are often difficulties in integrating qualitative and quantitative research (Moran-Ellis *et al.*, 2006). Appendix 1 used questionnaires to gather young people's awareness of the Youth Counselling Service, their thoughts on the location of counselling provision, the extent of young people's worries and the sources of support to which young people expect to turn if they are experiencing difficulties. This was then followed by a qualitative phase. This approach would be supported by Buchanan (1992) as he outlines a number of issues with regard to using qualitative data to inform a quantitative approach. For example, it is sometimes difficult to reduce qualitative data into statements for a 'standardised' questionnaire. The rich, thick data does not necessarily lend itself to being reduced to one or two concepts. In addition, whilst a quantitative approach offers 'psychological comfort by having firm, immutable standards' (ibid: 133), the reality is that sometimes it is truer to acknowledge that respondents simply do not 'believe' one way or another.

There are variations within these types of mixed methods (see, for example, Erzberger and Prein, 1997; Fielding and Schreier, 2001; Moran-Ellis *et al..*, 2006) but the complexities of these variations, such as integration, can be researched outside of this text (see Coyle and Williams, 200; Kelle, 2001; Foss and Ellefsen, 2002; Coxon, 2005). Mixed method research has a long history because it has often been thought that a mixed approach will best help to answer research questions (Johnson and Onwuegbuzie 2004). However, it is important to carefully consider the concept of a mixed methods research approach outlined here.

The benefits of using a mixed method approach with children is principally because of the shared meaning it can help create. Words, pictures and narrative can be used to add meaning to numbers and vice versa and this may be particularly important for validating data collated with children. The research topic can be addressed in a more holistic way which may afford the children an opportunity to add their own insights. It may be that a mixed methods approach can provide stronger evidence for interpretation and a more complete knowledge because of the creation of shared meaning.

The mixed methods approach has a number of caveats however and researchers would be well advised to consider the following before embarking on a mixed methods approach:

♦   Timing – an individual researcher may find it difficult to organise, conduct and interpret data from a mixed methods approach

♦   Knowledge of a mixed methods approach (and the complexities of such an approach) has to be learnt by a researcher

♦   Conflicting results may pose difficulties for interpretation

♦   The researcher may be guided by their philosophical stance.

Method	Advantages of employing this approach	Things to look out for	Recording the data (common approaches)	Can be used in conjunction with
Participant observer	Builds trust and rapport Conducted over a longer period of time so helps develop a more holistic understanding Gives an insight into the social world of a child	The chosen role of the researcher and the ascribed role of the researcher	Field notes Visual recording	Interviews Photographs
Paired friends or friendship pairs	Reduces power imbalance Reduces anxiety Can encourage the children to discuss/communicate to a greater extent Can reduce socially desirable responding	Differences between the two types of sampling approaches	Audio and visual recording where consent has been obtained and on-going consent is given	Photographs Draw and write
Creative groups	Data collection possible with a larger group of children over a shorter period of time	Children have a short attention span Check regularly to make sure the children know what they are doing	Can be noisy and spread out over a wider area so make sure you either have more than one piece of recording equipment or an observer to make notes on your behalf	Role play Drawings Collages Inventing stories
Questionnaires	Able to record a larger number of views about a topic	Make sure children know what is being asked of them but do not bias results by 'helping' too much	Variety of software available (e.g. SPSS) but when using online questionnaires, some programs input the data automatically and this can typically be exported to other applications	Colour Animation (online) Noise (online) Interaction (online)

Table 3.1: Summary of Research Methods for Use with Younger Children (8-11 years). See Chapter 4 for detail on techniques.

Method	Advantages of employing this approach	Things to look out for	Recording the data (common approaches)	Can be used in conjunction with
Participant observer	Builds trust and rapport. Conducted over a longer period of time so helps develop a greater understanding of adolescents (individual and group) and their peer interaction (dependent on where observation takes place)	Younger adolescents (12-14 years) may be less inclined to accept an 'adult' into their social group. Think carefully about your role and the role you may be ascribed	Field notes. Visual recording	Interviews. Photographs
Scene interviews	Gives teenagers the opportunity to express their views and opinions without overtly providing information about themselves. Will probably be more engaging than a general discussion and could make the adolescents feel more comfortable	The ability of the adolescents to see the relevance of the 'scene' or vignette to their own lives despite the situation being hypothetical. When the vignette is issued – before or during interview	Audio and visual recording	Interviews
Diary studies	Overcomes issues of privacy (adolescents can choose where and when to complete the task) and can give the them a sense of ownership/production	Boredom. Lack of interaction. Role of incentives	Structured or unstructured diary	Interviews. Photographs. Drawings. Collage
Questionnaires	Ability to generalise about larger samples of adolescents	Mal response. Disinterest/incomplete questionnaires. Poor response rates	Variety of software available (e.g. SPSS). When using online questionnaires, some programs input data automatically and this can typically be exported to other applications	Colour. Animation (online). Noise (online). Interaction (online)

Table 3.2: Summary of Research Methods for Use with Older Children. See Chapter 4 for more detail on techniques.

Summary

This chapter has been wide-reaching and the types of research method discussed were varied, with the advice proffered for a variety of age groups. Methods suggested for younger children can also be adapted for research with older children and this chapter detailed the way in which this could be achieved. The research philosophy of the researcher was briefly addressed but further reading on this particular area is suggested (see Reading List – Understanding Research Philosophy). A Mixed Methods approach is advocated here as a means of creating a shared meaning with the children you are researching with. Appropriate ways of recording the data have also been posited and holding/storing this data will be explored in depth in Chapter 8. In summary it is important to think about choosing a research design and method that will address the aim(s) and objectives of the project you are currently working on as well as being engaging for the children you are researching with (helping to build rapport). Involve the children you are researching with to create a shared meaning, for example, what do children understand by 'bullying' or 'policy' or 'treatment'. Be aware of not imposing your own perceptions (Punch, 2002) or imposing inappropriate interpretations of what is being said or communicated.

The following chapter will provide details of techniques that can be used to engage the children with whom you are researching and Chapter 5 will specifically address how to plan the research once the choice of method(s) has been made.

Reflective Questions

1 How might a researcher's philosophy impact on their approach to a study undertaken with children?

2 Give two reasons as to why researching with younger children (8-11 years) needs special consideration.

3 Using multiple methods can enhance engagement but does it provide different or just more data?

4 When employing a participant observer approach why is deliberation and caution encouraged?

5 What is the difference between paired friends and friendship pairs?

6 What are the advantages of using quantitative research with younger children?

7 How might computer-based questionnaires engage the children you are researching with?

8 What issues might arise if a researcher employs a participant observer method with adolescents?

9   What is the difference between early and late adolescence?

10 How might the use of diaries give a sense of ownership to adolescents?

11 How can adolescents contribute to the research design and execution of a project?

12 What are the different types of mixed methods that can be employed? List three caveats of employing a mixed methods approach.

Checklist

☐   Do you understand what is meant by a research philosophy and have you considered your own ontology?

☐   Are you aware of the differences between methodology and method and if/how one influences the other?

☐   Are you able to identify the best method for your own research project taking into account the age, development and any other circumstances particular to the children to wish to research with?

☐   Have you carefully considered how you will record the research data you will collate?

☐   Have you considered what role you will adopt when researching with young people and why?

☐   Have you established the role new technology may play in your research approach and what contingency plans you may have to put in place as a consequence?

☐   Do you understand what is meant by a mixed methods approach and the different models that can be employed when using this type of research approach?

Reading list – Understanding Research Philosophy

Blaikie, N. (2007) *Approaches to Social Enquiry*, 2nd edn, Cambridge: Polity Press

Crotty, M. (1998) *The Foundations of Social Research*, London: Sage

Deetz, S. (1996) 'Describing differences in approaches to organizational science: rethinking Burrell and Morgan and their legacy', *Organization Science*, 7, 191-207.

Hughes, J. and Sharrock, W. (1997) *The Philosophy of Social Research*, 3rd edn, Harlow: Addison Wesley Longman.

Johnson, P. and Duberley, J. (2000) *Understanding Management Research. An*

Introduction to Epistemology, Thousand Oaks, CA: Sage Publications.

Sayer, A. (2000) *Realism and Social Science*. London: Sage.

Teddlie, C. and Tashakkori, A. (2003) 'Major issues and controversies in the use of mixed methods in the social and behavioral sciences', in A. Tashakkori and C. Teddlie (eds), *Handbook of Mixed Methods in Social and Behavioral Research*, Thousand Oaks, CA: Sage, pp. 3-50.

References

Adler, E. (1996) 'Attributional shaming instrument', in *Life at School Survey*, Canberra: Australian National University, pp. 12-13.

Ahmed, E. and Braithwaite, V. (2004) '"What, me ashamed?" Shame management and school bullying', *Journal of Research in Crime and Delinquency*, **41** (3), 269-294.

Barker, A., Nancarrow, C. and Spackman, N. (2001) 'Informed eclecticism: a research paradigm for the twenty-first century', *International Journal of Market Research*, **43** (1), 3-28.

Bell, A. (2007) 'Designing and testing questionnaires for children', *Journal of Research in Nursing*, **12** (5), 461-469.

Best, Amy L. (2000) *Prom Night: Youth, Schools and Popular Culture*, New York: Routledge/Farmer.

Borgers, N. and Hox, J. (2000) 'Reliability of responses in questionnaire research with children plus coding scheme: a technical report', 5th International Conference on Logic and Methodology, 3-6 October, Cologne, Germany.

Borgers, N., De Leeuw, E. and Hox, J. (2000) 'Children as respondents in survey research: cognitive development and response quality', *Bulletin de Methodologie Sociologique*, **66**, 60-75.

Broome, M.E., Richards, D.J. and Hall, J.M. (2001) 'Children in research: the experience of ill children and adolescents', *Journal of Family Nursing*, **7** (1), 32-49.

Bryman, A. (1992) *Research Methods and Organisational Studies*. London: Routledge.

Buchanan, D.R. (1992) 'An uneasy alliance: combining qualitative and quantitative research methods', *Health Education Behaviour*, **19** (1), 117-135.

Bullock, A. and Trombley, S. (1999) *The New Fontana Dictionary of Modern Thought*, 3rd edn, London: Harper-Collins Publishers.

Burrell, G. and Morgan, G. (1979) *Sociological Paradigms and Organisational Analysis*, London: Heinemann.

Channon, C. (1982) 'What do we know about how research works?', *Journal of the Market Research Society*, **24** (4), 305-315.

Coffield, F., Moseley, D., Hall, E., Ecclestone, K. (2004). *Learning Styles and Pedagogy in Post-16 Learning. A Systematic and Critical Review*, London: Learning and Skills Research Centre.

Cohen, L., Manion, L. and Morrison, K. (2000) *Research Methods in Education*, 5th edn, New York: Routledge.

Corsaro, W. (1996) 'Transitions in early childhood: the promise of comparative longitudinal ethnography', in R. Jessor, A. Colby and R. Shweder (eds), *Ethnography and Human Development*, Chicago: Chicago University Press, pp. 419-457.

Coxon, A. (2005) 'Integrating qualitative and quantitative data: what does the user need?', FQS (Forum: *Qualitative Social Research*) 6 (2) http://www.qualitative-research.net/fqs/fqs-eng.htm (accessed Jan 2009)

Coyle, J. and Williams, B. (2000) 'An Exploration of the Epistemological Intricacies of Using Qualitative Data to Develop a Quantitative Measure of User Views of Health Care', *Journal of Advanced Nursing*, 31 (5), pp.1235-1243

Csikszentmihalyi, Milhaly and Rochberg-Halton, Eugene (1981) *The Meaning of Things: Domestic Symbols and the Self*, Cambridge: Cambridge Uinversity Press.

Darbyshire, P., MacDougall, C. and Schiller, W. (2005) 'Multiple methods in qualitative research with children: more insight or just more?', *Qualitative Research*, 5 (4), 417-436.

De Leeuw, E., Borgers, N. and Strijbos-Smits, A. (2002) 'Children as respondents: developing, evaluating and testing questionnaires for children', invited paper at the International Conference on Questionnaire Development, Evaluation and Testing Methods, Charleston, South Carolina, November.

Deetz, S. (1996) 'Describing differences in approaches to organizational science: rethinking Burrell and Morgan and their legacy', *Organization Science*, 7, 191-207.

Denscombe, M. (2008) 'Communities of practice', *Journal of Mixed Methods Research*, 2 (3), 270-283.

Denzin, N.K. and Lincoln, Y.S (2005) 'The discipline and practice of qualitative research', in N.K. Denzin and Y.S. Lincoln (eds), *Handbook of Qualitative Research*, 3rd edn, Thousand Oaks, CA: Sage Publications, pp. 1-28.

Dockett, S. and Perry, B.(2007) 'Trusting children's accounts in research', *Journal of Early Childhood Research*, 5 (1), 47-63.

Dunn, R., Dunn, K. and Price, G.E. (1984), *Learning Style Inventory*, Lawrence, KS: Price Systems.

Elliot, Richard and Kritsadarat Wattanasuwan (1998) 'Brands as symbolic resources for the construction of identity', *International Journal of Advertising*, 17, 131-144.

Erzberger, C. and Prein, G. (1997) 'Triangulation: validity and empirically-based hypothesis construction', *Quality and Quantity*, 31 (2), 141-154.

Escalas, Jennifer Edson (1993) 'The consumption of insignificant rituals: a look at debutante balls', *Advances in Consumer Research*, 20, 709-716.

Fielding, N. and Schreier, M. (2001) 'Introduction: on the compatibility between qualitative and quantitative research methods', FQS (Forum: *Qualitative Social Research*) 2 (1), http://www.qualitative-research.net/fqs/fqs-eng.htm (accesssed June 2008)

Finch, J. (1987) 'The vignette technique in survey research', *Sociology*, **21**, 115-140.

Fine, G. and Sandstrom, K. (1988) *Knowing Children: Participant Observation with Minors*, Newbury Park, CA: Sage.

Foss C. and Ellefsen B. (2002) 'The value of combining qualitative and quantitative approaches in nursing research by means of method triangulation', *Journal of Advanced Nursing*, **40** (2) 242-248.

Gill, S. and Coad, J. (2007) 'An exploratory study into nurses' understanding and knowledge of children and young people with eczema', *Journal of Research in Nursing*, **12** (5), 567-583.

Giordano, P.C., Longmore, M.A. and Manning, W.D. (2006) 'Gender and the meanings of adolescent romantic relationships: a focus on boys', *American Sociological Review*, **71**, 260-287.

Greene, J., Benjamin, L. and Goodyear, L. (2001) 'The merits of mixing methods in evaluation', *Evaluation*, **7** (1), 25-44.

Guba, E.G. (1990) 'The alternative paradigm dialog', in E.G. Guba (ed.), *The Paradigm Dialog*, Newbury Park, CA: Sage Publications, pp. 17-30.

Guba, E. and Lincoln Y.S. (1994) 'Competing paradigms in qualitative research', in N.K. Denzin and Y.S. Lincoln (eds), *Handbook of Qualitative Research*, Newbury Park, CA: Sage Publications, pp. 105-117.

Harvey, M. and Byrd, M. (1998) 'The relationship between perceptions of self-esteem, patterns of familial attachment, and family environment during early and late phases of adolescence', *International Journal of Adolescence and Youth*, 7(2), 93-111.

Hogg, M.K. and Banister, E. (2001) 'Dislikes, distastes and the undesired self: conceptualising and exploring the role of the undesired end state in consumer experience', *Journal of Marketing Management*, **17**, 73-104.

Holliday, A. (2002) *Doing and Writing Qualitative Research*. London, Sage.

Hughes, J.A. (1990) *The Philosophy of Social Research*, 2nd edn, Harlow: Longman

Hughes, R. (1998) 'Considering the vignette technique and its application to a study of drug injection and HIV risk and safer behaviour', *Sociology of Health and Illness*, 20, pp.381.

Hussey, J. and Hussey, R. (1997) *Business Research. A Pactical Guide for Undergraduate and Postgraduate Students*, Basingstoke: Macmillan Press.

Johnson, P. and Duberley, J. (2000) *Understanding Management Research. An Introduction to Epistemology*, Thousand Oaks, CA: Sage Publications.

Johnson, R.B. and Onwuegbuzie, A.J. (2004) 'Mixed methods research: a research paradigm whose time has come', *Educational Researcher*, **33** (7), 14-26.

Kacen, L. and Rozovski, U. (1998) 'Assessing group processes', *Small Group Research*, **29** (2), 179-197.

Kelle, U. (2001) 'Sociological explanations between micro and macro and the integration of qualitative and quantitative methods', FQS (Forum: *Qualitative*

Social Research) 2 (1), http://www.qualitative-research.net/fqs/fqs-eng.htm (accessed Jan 2009)

Kuhn, T. (1970) *The Structure of Scientific Revolutions*, 2nd edn, Chicago: University of Chicago Press.

Labaree, R.V. (2002) 'The risk of "going observationalist": negotiating the hidden dilemmas of being an insider participant', *Qualitative Research*, 2 (1), 97-122.

Melzer-Lena, B. and Middelmann-Motz, A. V. (1998) 'Research among children', in C. McDonald, and P. Vangelder (eds), *The ESOMAR Handbook of Market and Opinion Research*, 4th edn, Amsterdam: ESOMAR, pp. 957-969.

Miles, M.B. and Huberman A. (1984) *Qualitative Data Analysis*, Thousand Oaks, CA: Sage.

Monahan, J.L. and Zuckerman, C.E. (1999) 'Intensifying the dominant response', *Communication Research*, 26 (11), 81-110.

Montemayor, R. (1986) 'Parents and adolescents in conflict: All families some of the time and some families most of the time', *Journal of Early Adolescence*, 3, 83-103.

Moran-Ellis, J., Alexander, V.D., Cronin, A., Dickson, M., Fielding, J., Sleney, J. and Thomas, H. (2006) 'Triangulation and integration: processes, claims and implications', *Qualitative Research*, 6 (1), 45-59.

Morgan, G. and Smircich, L. (1980) 'The case for qualitative research', *Academy of Management Review*, 5 (4), 491-500.

Oakley, A. (1981) 'Interviewing women: a contradiction in terms', in H. Roberts (ed.), *Doing Feminist Research*, London: Routledge, pp. 30-59.

O'Cathain, A., Murphy, E. and Nicholl, J. (2007) 'Integration and publications and indicators of "yield" from mixed method studies', *Journal of Mixed Methods Research*, 1, 147-163.

Oppenheim, A.N. (1996) *Questionnaire Design, Interviewing and Attitude Measurement*, London: Pinter.

Punch, S. (2002) 'Research with children: The same or different from research with adults?', *Childhood*, 9 (3), 321-341.

Robson, C. (1993) *Real World Research: a Resource for Social Scientists and Practitioners-Research*, Oxford: Blackwell.

Roedder John, D. (1999) 'Consumer socialisation of children: a retrospective look at twenty-five years of research', *Journal of Consumer Research*, 26 (3), 183-213.

Rook, Dennis W. (1985) 'The ritual dimension of consumer behavior', *Journal of Consumer Research*, 12, 251-264.

Schouten, J.H. and McAlexander, J.W. (1995) 'Subcultures of consumption: an ethnography of the new bikers', *Journal of Consumer Research*, 22 (1), 43-61.

Schwandt, T.A. (2000) 'Three epistemological stances for qualitative enquiry: Interpretivism, Hermeneutics and Social Constructionism' in N.K. Denzin and Y.S. Lincoln (eds), *Handbook of Qualitative Research*, 2nd edn, Thousand Oaks, CA: Sage Publications.

Scott, J. (1997) 'Children as respondents: methods for improving data quality', in L.E. Lyberg, P. Biemer, M. Collins, E. De Leeuw, C. Dippo, N. Schwarz and D. Treman (eds), *Survey Measurement and Process Quality*, New York: John Wiley and Sons.

Silverman, D. (1997) 'The logics of qualitative research', in G. Miller and R. Dingwall (eds), *Methods and Context in Qualitative Research*. London: Sage.

Thompson, S. (1998) 'Paying respondents and informants', *Social Research Update*, **14** (16), 03-06.

Tinson, J. and Nancarrow, C. (2005) 'The influence of children on purchases: The development of measures for gender role orientation and shopping savvy', *International Journal of Market Research*, **47**, 1, 5-27.

Tinson, J., Nuttall, P. And Thomson, J. (2008) 'Exploring adolescent symbolic consumption in the context of the high school prom', submitted for the European Marketing Academy Conference (EMAC), Nantes, France 2009

Trew, K., Scully, D., Kremer, J. and Ogle, S. (1999) 'Sport, leisure and perceived self-confidence among male and female adolescents', *European Physical Education Review*, **5** (1), 53-73.

Wilkins, K. and Woodgate, R. (2008) 'Designing a mixed methods study in pediatric oncology nursing research', *Journal of Pediatric Oncology Nursing*, **25** (1) 24-33.

Wilks, T. (2004) 'The use of vignettes in qualitative research into social work values', *Qualitative Social Work*, **3** (1), 78-87.

4 Keeping the Children and Adolescents Engaged

Objectives

- To establish different learning styles and how these may influence the way in which children engage with research

- To identify a variety of techniques that can be employed in different situations to engage the children with whom you are researching

- To explore the merits of using engaging techniques and to consider the age and development of the young people when employing these approaches

- To discuss the views of young people in relation to research methods and techniques

Introduction

The previous chapters considered designing and developing an ethical approach to researching with children. Having chosen the method that will be employed for the research project (e.g. creative groups), this chapter now suggests a variety of techniques that can be used to engage the young people you are researching with. This chapter contains examples of innovative methods of researching with children and also provides suggestions from 'experts' in different disciplines (as well as young people themselves) as to how best to research with children.

Preparing Tasks

Having gained access, obtained consent and chosen a research method(s) the researcher should carefully consider the best ways in which to keep the children they are research-ing with engaged during the project. As previously noted, younger children (ages 8-11) are likely to have a shorter attention span in comparison with their older counterparts (young people aged 11+ years) and as such it is important to engage younger and older children in different ways. It is often useful to consider more than one technique for younger children as they are likely to be less reflective and can complete any tasks that are set for them more quickly than older children. Older children (11+ years) are in the reflective stage of socialisation (Roedder John, 1999) and as such can take longer to reflect on or discuss material they are presented with or they have created. There is no absolute guide as to how long a task will last because this will depend on the nature of the topic (e.g. children may be more comfortable talking about celebrities than they will be about why smoking is bad for their health).

The timing of the task might also depend on the research method and sampling ap-proach (e.g. the size of the creative group and the group dynamics). This is because if the creative group is small and the group is made up of 'quiet' children the task will be completed in a shorter time. There are ways in which you can overcome these issues including piloting or practising the tasks with a smaller number of children before con-ducting the actual study. This has a number of benefits as the researcher is able to see what the children enjoy, how the tasks might need to be adapted and what the levels of comprehension are relative to what the children are being asked to consider. Addition-ally you can ask the gatekeeper to consider what you propose and ask their advice on how long they think the task will take.

Learning Styles

What type of tasks would be most appealing to the young people you are researching with? Dunn, Dunn and Price (1984) illustrate the preferences individuals have for vis-ual, auditory or kinaesthetic learning (known as the VAK model). These principles on the way in which children learn could also be useful for the way in which the researcher can engage with children during the research project.

If children are visual learners they like to read a piece of narrative or text or can interpret diagrams. Auditory learners like to listen and discuss concepts. Kinaesthetic learners prefer to find out by 'doing': they like moving, manipulating, touching. It is likely that whilst children may have a preference for a particular type of VAK approach, a mixture of these approaches will be most beneficial to maintain interest amongst individuals or groups. Just as teachers have to acknowledge and address preferred styles of learning, the researcher has to understand these different approaches to communicating (and im-portantly, to being understood). For this reason, a range of research approaches may be most beneficial for the children you are researching with. A variety of activities within a session can accommodate different learning styles as well as being more engaging and preventing boredom. Engaging the children you are researching with is equally important when employing either qualitative or quantitative methods. In the following section, the techniques used to engage the children with qualitative research with will be explored first, followed by a summary of the ways in which quantitative techniques can be made more appealing.

Engaging Research Techniques

There are a variety of techniques that can be employed to engage young people when using qualitative and quantitative methods. When employing qualitative methods, these include asking the children to take photographs, employing the draw and write technique, role play, the creation of collages and the keeping of diaries. These will be explored here with examples of the way in which these techniques have been previously used with children. An indication of the best way in which these techniques can be employed (and the potential pitfalls of these approaches) will also be considered.

Many of the research approaches suggested in this section are 'visual methodologies', the use of which has faced criticism in the past (Silverman, 1993). It is claimed that the interpretation of images is subjective and riddled with ambiguity. This is true of visual methodologies used for adults as well as children. However, the ambiguity or subjectivity is presumably most questionable when the researcher tries to interpret the image(s) without the input of the person who, for example, took the picture or made the drawing. It is essential that when a researcher employs an innovative technique that they obtain the creator's opinion of what has been 'made'. The interpretation of a photograph or a picture without any discussion or input from the person(s) who created the image can rightly be subject to criticism. Whilst it is possible to identify recurrent themes in photographs or pictures, it is difficult to understand why these themes may be produced time and again without a more in-depth discussion with the creator. It is essential then that the innovative techniques described here are not used in isolation but are used as part of more traditional forms of research (e.g. interviews, creative groups, friendship pairs). Analysing this type of data is discussed in Chapter 7.

Photographs

Asking children to take photographs before, during or after the research can be both fun and engaging. Using photographs in research has been a long-established technique in many disciplines including anthropology, psychology and education. Although there has been little formal research on photographic methods used in health care and social care settings, there are now an increasing number of examples that can be drawn on (Coad, 2007). Photographs are said to be a powerful if underused and undervalued tool (Prosser, 1998), although more recent studies have considered adolescents' reactions to images in women's sport, health and fitness magazines (Hurworth *et al.*, 2005) and to elicit views about what it means to be young in Birmingham, UK (Coad and Needham, 2005). A practical example of how photographs can be used is illustrated in Scenario 4.1.

Scenario 4.1

George wanted to know more about what adolescents (children aged 12-17 years) valued in their lives and was interested in how this may be affected by the family type (intact, blended/step parent or single parent family) in which the adolescent was being raised. He was also interested in how these values might change over time and how they could be affected by the life events or 'transitions' the adolescents might experience (e.g. death of a family member or friend, illness, exams, relationships etc.). To facilitate the research George decided to ask the adolescents to photograph six things that were most important to them (and this could be literally anything) to facilitate the research process. The adolescents were given disposable cameras and the photographs were developed by George. The photographs were then brought to the interview by George so that the adolescents could discuss the photographs they had taken. This was done at the beginning of the interview. George interviewed these same adolescents six months to a year later and the adolescents were asked to take another six photographs (to see if things that the adolescents valued had changed over time). The original and new photos were compared and contrasted at the beginning of the second interview and the first set of photos provided a benchmark of what was originally of most importance to the adolescent when the research began.

The timing of the photography may influence the types of pictures that are taken. If the photographs are taken before the research, the children will have already considered the topic you wish to discuss and it may help in building rapport between the researcher and the young person(s). If the pictures are taken during the research, the items photographed may be more spontaneous than those 'chosen' before the research. An example of this would be if during the research, you asked children to take pictures of things that made the hospital seem more like home. As such the 'data' and discussion regarding the photos taken during the research could vary from that of a discussion about photos taken before the research commences. This will also be true of photos taken after the event as these photos could be more reflective or could illustrate a different understanding or insight about the research topic as the young person will have had the opportunity to reflect on the issue(s) to a greater extent.

Depending on the timing of the photographs being taken (before, during or after the research), the type of equipment (camera) used may differ. If the photos are taken before the research takes place, 'throw away' cameras can be used by the children and developed by the researcher. This is an inexpensive way in which to engage the children and the researcher. The child, in this scenario, does not have to be unduly concerned about damaging expensive equipment. Using disposable cameras however does require some planning as the camera film will need to be developed before the interview takes place. There are some disadvantages to this method too as the young person will not be able to see the picture they have taken before it is developed. If the pictures are of poor quality, the researcher and child/ren are unlikely to be able to remedy this before the research commences and this may be disappointing for the child/ren. However the use of photographs as a visual prompt and benchmark can outweigh any potential disadvantages.

If, however, the photos are taken during the research, disposable cameras will not necessarily be appropriate particularly when the researcher wishes to discuss with the child/ren what they have taken pictures of and why. Photographs taken during research projects will probably have to be taken on a digital camera. Note that this can be expensive to resource and the equipment should be insured in case of accidents. Older children often have a mobile phone which may have a camera facility and they may be happy to use their phones for research purposes. This is beneficial for a number of reasons. They have control over the data and the cost to the researcher is negligible. Do not, however, rely on the adolescents all having mobile phones and/or that they will be prepared to use them. If this is the approach you wish to use, this must be planned and agreed to before the research takes place. As a researcher it is your job to ensure that none of the children you are researching with feel isolated or 'left out' so only ask the children to take photographs if they are *all* able to do so (this might involve teaming up young people who have/do not have a camera on their phone but the 'ownership' of the photograph is likely to favour the person who actually owns the camera).

Disposable cameras can be used for photos taken after the research has been completed but the researcher must think carefully about why they would want the young people they are researching with to do this (e.g. are the pictures to be shared on a website, or displayed on a notice board) and what the advantages of this would be (e.g. to allow the children to share their thoughts with one another as opposed to the researcher or to remind the children that they have been producers of the research).

Cook and Hess (2007) illustrate that the use of photographs can be easy, fun and engaging for the children with whom you are researching because children often find taking pictures easier than writing. Using photographs could also be more inclusive. Lewis and Lindsay (2000) indicate that children experiencing learning difficulties and those who find it difficult to develop abstract concepts when using direct interview techniques could overcome these difficulties if photographs were used. It is important to remember that children and young people might differ from adults in their use of cameras and understanding of photographs (see, for example, Smith and Barker, 2004) and that their skill in taking pictures may differ by both experience and cognitive development.

Finally, as with any technique that can be used to engage children with the research, consider carefully the level of instruction that is given to the young people when they are given the camera. The more instruction the researcher gives about what to take pictures of, the less likely the children are to take pictures they want to take and are more likely to take pictures they think they should take. To that end, there is loss of 'shared meaning'. Little guidance in the way of what should be photographed and more of an emphasis on the general theme of the research should give the children enough to work on without biasing the photographs that are taken.

Draw and Write Technique

Projective techniques such as the draw and write technique have been advocated by a variety of researchers (see, for example, Harris, 1963; Buck, 1981; Engel, 1995) as children's ability to retrieve information that is encoded about their experiences may be more readily accessed by stimulating their perception senses than by semantic stimulus (Driessnack, 2006). 'Projective techniques involve the use of vague, ambiguous, unstructured stimulus objects or situations in which the subject "projects" his or her personality, attitudes, opinions and self-concept to give the situation some structure' (Donoghue, 2000: 47). Drawing is often referred to as the universal language of childhood (Rubin, 1984) which reflects feelings and information concerning psychological status and interpersonal style of the child (Malchiodi, 1998). Projective techniques were developed in the discipline of psychology and are based on the principle that, in this context, children will be able to interpret and respond in their own way to stimulus (using their ego defence mechanism) to express their inner feelings. Children can use drawings to express emotion (Councill, 1993) or poorly understood feelings in an attempt to bring them to order and clarity (Bentley, 1989). A drawing can be a window to cognitive and developmental maturity, coping styles and personality (Councill, 1999). What the children produce cannot be taken at face value but should be discussed with them to develop an understanding of it.

As with different learning styles, children can have a preference for the way in which they express their ideas and opinions. When employing the draw and write technique it may be that the child/ren are reluctant to draw as they might think they cannot draw very well and may be uncomfortable about their drawing technique or style. This will probably be true of older children as opposed to younger children as the latter regularly take part in 'art' related activities. Ensuring that the children are reassured about their drawing abilities and encouraging those less able to 'draw' to employ signs or symbols that convey the same meaning as a 'drawing' may help overcome the issues of 'being able to draw'. The draw and write technique can also be adapted and using a structure for the draw and write technique may help younger children, in particular, focus on the research task in hand. Banister and Booth (2005), for example, discuss their use of an 'animated tree' to illustrate a particular 'theme' (e.g. disgust). The children in Banister and Booth's research were provided with 'leaves' and were encouraged to write on the leaves to express their ideas on the given theme. In this way, the words on the leaves on the 'tree of disgust' were then discussed and the concept developed. There are also specific types of write and draw techniques. The Kinetic Family Drawing (KFD) projective technique has become more popular with children in healthcare settings over the past 30 years (see, for example, Instone, 2000). Rollins (2005) found that by employing this technique, action (kinetic) drawings were more informative than those with akinetic instruction.

Backett-Milburn and McKie (1999) posit that the draw and write technique is increasingly becoming popular when researching with children in health education research and, although Horstman et al. (2008) agree, they suggest that much of the published work has centred on healthy children. Future work in this area may enhance our understanding of children's hopes and fears in this context.

Driessnack (2006) introduces the concept of the 'draw and tell' technique in her study where she explores young children's fear experiences. It has been recognised that stories can be poignantly depicted and narrated by children with drawings (Malchiodi, 1998) although Driessnack (2006) suggests that previous work in this area has focused on the researcher's as opposed to the children's interpretation of what has been created (see, for example, Koppitz, 1968, 1984; Ryan-Wenger, 1998). Driessnack's study (2006) focuses on 9 and 10-year-old respondents (although the draw and tell approach could be adapted and used for older children too). Driessnack (2006: 1418) indicates that 'the opportunity to draw is familiar, typically perceived as fun and non-threatening, and [is] unlike most school based testing'. The children in her study were offered different size paper and a variety of drawing materials (e.g. pencils, pens, markers) to give a sense of power and control to the children from the outset of the study. The study was analysed by not only asking the children to discuss their pictures but by using linguistic and thematic analysis (see Chapter 7 on analysis and interpretation). The key benefit of using the draw and tell approach is that the children more readily engage with the research compared with children who are expected simply to 'tell' as opposed to 'draw and tell'. These findings support the work on the draw and write technique conducted by Backett-Milburn and McKie (1999) whose findings indicate that children can more readily communicate their thoughts in a drawing than in any conversational language. Similarly, Gabhainn and Kelleher (2002) describe their study conducted with 7-8-year-old children on healthy eating. A questionnaire was distributed amongst the year groups followed by a drawing task completed in the classroom with the drawings analysed using a theme-based approach.

Understanding of Drawings

Guillemin's (2004) study centres on using the draw and write technique to research illness with adults. However a number of her suggestions in relation to engaging and discussing drawings are relevant for researching with the children and their drawings. These are as follows: In what context (e.g. environment) has the drawing been made? What was the response of the drawer to the image? What is the relationship between the drawer and its subject? What is being shown? How is it arranged? Is the image in colour? If so, how has the colour been used? If a grey pencil has been chosen, is this so the drawing can be rubbed out and there is less 'commitment' to the picture by the child/ren (Driessnack, 2006) and if the image is contradictory to data collected at interview or survey stage (if there has been an interview or survey) why might this be the case?

The drawing in Figure 4.1 are taken from a research project that considered the meaning of music to adolescents (Nuttall, 2006). One adolescent (Male, 16) was able to convey how he felt about music by describing his drawing as follows:

> [Y]ou can't freeze frame it [music]…you can't look at it and say this is what is happening…it's fleeting cos it's always moving, it's always changing. If you stop it or pause it it dies. It's better than everything else and uncontrollable because no-one can say what music you can't play."

Figure 4.1

In this way, the data was richer and more insightful that those obtained by writing (or even discussion) alone.

Figure 4.2 considered the same topic but was drawn by a girl in the early stage of adolescence. It can be seen from her drawing that music, for her, represented money, brands and celebrity. In this way the use of the draw and write technique allowed a discussion on the meaning of music based on what the adolescents believed music 'meant' as opposed to what the researcher thought music meant to adolescents.

It is possible to ask the children you are researching with, over time, to draw a series of pictures (as was the case for the research outlined above). The same individual will demonstrate constant structure and form although the content

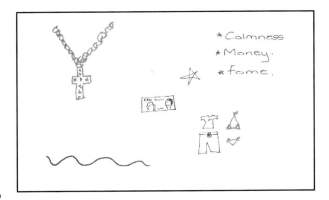

Figure 4.2

may vary. Such techniques are supported (see, for example, Welsh and Instone, 2000) as they allow children to freely express their perceptions and experience. These drawings will be unbiased by right or wrong answers, cultural influences or the expectations of the researcher. The draw and write technique may be most appropriate when *exploring* topics (see Table 4.1). If there are specific issues that need to be addressed, it may be that by employing role play more explicit areas can be considered.

Role Play

Role play can be considered in two different ways. First, role play can actually involve the child/ren you are researching with adopting a different role and acting out this role – usually with other children. Second, children can role play by 'putting themselves in the "minds" of others' without having to *act* as if they were someone else. The first type of role play is illustrated by Scenario 4.2.

The example of role play in Figure 4.3 demonstrates that whilst it may be more difficult to ask older children to 'act' (because they may feel embarrassed or uncomfortable) if there are roles they would like to adopt, using this type of approach may provide rich data as part of a wider data set. Although this case focused on music, the technique could be adapted and employed in a variety of disciplines. In a health care environment, for example, the child/ren could adopt the role of the consultant or the nurse or their parent(s) to illustrate how they think they may behave in a particular situation. In an educational context, the child/ren could adopt the role of a head teacher, class teacher, parent helper or visitor to the school to explore attitudes and motivations. In a business environment the child/ren could adopt the role of an advertiser, a supermarket manager, a parent(s) or a farmer to consider the interrelationships in a business context. Finally in a social context, the adolescent child/ren could adopt the role of a pregnant teenager, the parent(s), the boyfriend and members of the friendship group to investigate issues that might arise as a consequence of this type of situation occurring.

Scenario 4.2

Having friends or being part of a friendship or peer group is a significant social achievement for adolescents and an indicator of social competence (Berndt, 1990). Whilst it has been acknowledged that child peer influence varies with age, gender and product situations, previous findings do not consider adolescent peer influence in relation to the family structure and type. Ben wanted to explore how peer group influences consumption of music during adolescence and how this consumption is moderated by family type and gender. His study was not only to identify music consumption amongst teenagers but to contextualise this in relation to how they consumed and used music (publicly or privately), how often they listened to music and in what way. Additionally familial influence and peer influence were explored to ascertain the extent to which music consumption was situational and if music use and consumption varied for teenagers raised in a variety of family structures (intact, blended and single parent).

The initial stage of this research was to be largely exploratory, establishing current views and opinions on music consumption. Mini groups evolved as a natural choice for observation, allowing a wider range of information, insight and ideas than responses secured privately (Malhotra and Birks, 2003). Four pairs of friends (mixed gender) were invited to take part in the research and were subsequently divided into two mini groups. The children were aged between 13 and 14 years. To aid the discussion on choice, use and consumption of music, the teenagers were given a task to pre-prepare for the group (see Figure 4.3).

The mini groups were designed to simulate a group of friends listening to music together. Consent and on-going consent was obtained for this research (see Chapter 2). The research took place at the university and the groups were set up in one room with the researchers being on-hand in another. The mini groups were video-taped and tape recorded and the adolescents were given a task to facilitate the group dynamics (as per the letter in Figure 4.3). This task involved them having to bring three CDs with them (electing to play three tracks) and choosing two features from a (music) magazine given to them before the mini-group to talk about with the other group members. They each had a 'set' and were encouraged to be DJs, inviting comments from the rest of the group about their choice of music. This approach is particularly supported by Efken (2002) who suggests that simulating creativity within a group of adolescents encourages them to contribute more than they would without props.

Despite the expected use of posturing, the mini group was useful in (a) observing how adolescents discuss (language), use and choose music and how they want to express this and (b) establishing referent group influence. The observations also revealed certain aspects as regards the everyday use and consumption of music by respondents, which helped to formulate and guide the development of questions for the interviews that followed this exploratory stage of research.

Hi there

'Choice of Music': What's it all about?

Thank you for agreeing to take part in our research project, which looks at the way in which you listen to and enjoy music. We really hope you have fun doing this and we can't wait to see what you come up with for your 'radio programme'.

Why do we need your help?

We would like to understand a little more about the music you enjoy and why you like it. We are hoping that by asking you to select some of the music you like and discussing your choice with your friends we will learn more about what music means to you. What we learn will help us to sort out the kind of questions we might ask other people your age about the music they are into and why.

What are you going to be doing on Thursday afternoon?

Have you ever wanted to be a DJ? Well now is your chance. OK, so it's not Radio 1 or Ibiza but what we would like you to do is create a short radio show of your own. Select three tracks of music on CD that you really like, anything you like, but try and select three different singers or bands, and bring them along.

We would like you to imagine you are a radio DJ and have a slot on the radio to play your three tracks and talk about two articles that you have read in the magazine we have given you (you can keep this – so write all over it if you want!). Choose anything from the magazine that interests you and make some comments on the radio about it. You could repeat what's in the article or feature or talk around it – it's up to you.

Your Radio show could go something like this...

1. Introduce and play record one, then talk about the first magazine feature, then introduce and play record 2...
2. After record 2, talk about your second magazine feature and then introduce and play your final record...
3. At the end of the last record, invite your listeners (mates!) to 'call in' with comments and views about your choice of records and features and have a 5-10 minute phone-in.

That's it – you can be as chatty as you like, or keep it brief, you're the DJ! Enjoy!

What we will we be doing?

Well we are not going to get in the way – it's your show. However, what we would like to do is video-tape all the shows if that's OK. We will be around at the start just to help you get kicked off then it's over to you.

So what do you need to bring?

Yourself!

3 CDs to play three tracks from your radio slot

2 features to talk about from the magazine you've been given for your radio slot

A BIG thank you for doing this.

Figure 4.3: Letter sent to respondents

These potential role plays are not an exhaustive list but can be adapted or developed to meet the specific needs or objectives of the proposed research study.

The second notion of role play is that of asking the children to 'put themselves in the minds of others' (projecting) without them actually having to act out a specific part. The children may be familiar with this type of approach as the Social and Emotional Aspects of Learning (SEAL), which is used by both primary and secondary schools offers a framework for promoting the social and emotional aspects of learning: self-awareness, managing feelings, motivation and social skills. The materials provided by SEAL include a wide range of additional resources (See: Department of Children, Schools and Families) and, as one aspect of the resource, offer the opportunity for children to 'role play'. Considering the material that is already available, may help the researcher when designing their own methods of data collection.

Collages

Another way in which data can be collated is by asking the children you are researching with to make a collage. This is made up from assembling and gluing (or sticking) a variety of materials onto a piece of paper or canvas. The materials can be, for example, newspaper clippings, pictures or words from magazines, photographs and/or pieces of coloured ribbon or material. The size and shape of the collage is normally determined by the size of the paper or canvas and this too will affect the amount of material that can be assembled. Collages using cutting and pasting exercises have been discussed by a variety of researchers (see, for example, Banister and Hogg, 2001) but not all researchers use the cut and paste concept to develop collages. Instead, children can be asked to draw items by hand (Banister and Booth, 2005) and then these can be made into a collage although the analysis of this may be more akin to that of the draw and write technique (see Chapter 7). Scenario 4.3 illustrates a practical example of using collages when researching with children.

It can be seen from Scenario 4.3 that the use of collages can be helpful in engaging children with a research project. Whilst this scenario illustrates the topic of food choice, the method is equally useful when exploring other issues (e.g. depiction of women in advertising, materials associated with drug use and abuse, anti-social behaviour and the implications and/or outcomes or the portrayal of illness and resilience). Collages can also be useful as a basis for developing a questionnaire (see 'Mixed methods', Chapter 3) particularly when asking teenagers to become their own designers as well as producers of research (see Chapter 9).

Scenario 4.3

Anna wanted to know what types of food younger children (ages 8-11 years) ate at school and the variety of food these children consumed at home. She was interested in the attitudes and behaviours children display in relation to food and decided to use qualitative research to explore these concepts in greater depth. Anna decided to use creative groups and had 4 groups of 3 children to research with (6 boys and 6 girls). Two groups were conducted simultaneously in the same room. She divided the groups by gender so that the girls and boys worked separately. This was because her previous experience of trying to mix this age group by gender had resulted in the children naturally migrating to other groups as the girls wanted to work only with girls and the boys were keen to see what the other boys were doing. This approach is supported by Mauthner (1997: 23) who suggests that single sex groups can be more successful than mixed ones where boys who often talk more, more loudly and determine the conversation topics tend to overshadow girls. The children were asked to choose from a wide selection of magazines and to cut and paste images of food onto two collages – one collage that was labelled 'Food Eaten at Home' and the other labelled 'Food Eaten at School'. (Safety issues in relation to using scissors were carefully thought through before the research took place.) The children could write words on the collages if they wanted to and could write the names of food if they could not find pictures of it in the magazines. The collages, when they were finished, were pinned up in the room where the research was taking place and both groups (e.g. the two groups of three girls or the two groups of three boys) all looked at all the collages and discussed the differences between food choice, the variety of food, shopping for food and people who influence food consumption. In this way the children were fully engaged with the research as they were thinking about what was being asked of them, were able to reflect on this and actively seek images as well as contribute to a discussion on food and food choices.

Diaries

The design of diaries (e.g. unstructured or semi-structured) has been discussed in **Chapter 3** and the layout of the diary will undoubtedly affect the extent to which the children become engaged with the research project. It may be, for example, that by simply making the diary in an A5 'booklet' ('handbag' size) that those children you are researching with will feel more predisposed to completing them. It may be that you want to prompt the children when they are completing diaries, particularly if it is over a longer period of time. Postcard or e-mail reminders are useful for a number of reasons as they can let the child/ren know that as a researcher you are still engaged with the project. If the child/ren think you are disinterested or are simply expecting them 'to get on with it' they will be less inclined to engage. Second, the postcards or e-mails give the researcher an opportunity to suggest topics or themes the children might want to consider when completing their diaries. For example, if the child has been asked to complete the diary about their sporting activity, the postcard or e-mail might ask the child to consider anything that may have impeded their sporting activity (e.g. weather, injury, opportunities to engage in other activities) that particular day and include it in the diary entry. The postcard or e-mail may simply be a reminder. As with most research projects, the child/ren will invariably have other activities they can engage with (e.g. social networking, sport, etc.) and as such the research project may not be their priority.

It may be that for older children using an online diary may be more user-friendly. Given the electronic impact on research techniques, asking adolescents to complete an online version of an unstructured or structured diary may be more engaging. Instead of sending e-mails or postcards to remind the children to complete a diary entry, a 'pop-up' could appear when the child/ren signed in online. This would involve all the children in the study having access to an online facility and some technological know-how on the part of the child and researcher. There have been ethical issues with employing new technology to engage children with research (Nairn, 2006) but these have principally been in relation to commercial products.

Young people could also make an audio diary or a video diary (although the video diary has ethical implications – not least that all the children appearing in a video diary would need to consent/assent and would need to have parental consent - see Chapter 2). The equipment needed for this may be outside the realms of experience and resource for a novice researcher.

There is, however, a fine line between engaging the children and invading their private space. It is ill-advised, for example, to take the teenagers' mobile numbers and text them with research requests. This is likely to irritate as opposed to engage them and even if they initially consent to this type of contact it can become frustrating for the child/ren and have a negative impact on their research experience.

Miscellaneous Techniques

Not all methods used by researchers when researching with children fall into neat categories. Researchers often adapt techniques to meet the aim(s) and objectives of the current research study and more experienced researchers will know what has worked well in previous research studies and will incorporate this into their research design. Employing a hybrid of methods may seem appealing to a novice researcher as they may perceive that a mixture of techniques will be more engaging for the children they are researching with. Here is a note of caution for the novice researcher. Using one approach and using it well may be more engaging than using a variety or hybrid of methods which may seem more chaotic

Technique	Reason for use	Things to look out for	Age/Development considerations
Photographs	Fun Engaging Under-used Can show changes over time (temporal)	When the photograph is taken can influence discussion Can be expensive if camera not disposable Level of instruction (be careful not to bias the images that might be captured)	More inclusive – children with learning difficulties can engage with this technique more readily than with others
Draw and write	Universal language of childhood Reflects feelings and emotions Exploratory	Need to reassure children who think they are unable to draw Paper size and colours chosen by the child may be significant	Drawing can be a window to cognitive development, maturity, coping styles and personality
Role play/ scenarios	Enjoyable Opportunity to be 'someone else' Can be enquiry-specific	Can the children make the link between the scenario and themselves Engagement of all children taking part	Role play may be more difficult for young adolescents as they may feel uncomfortable – projection (scenarios) may be more useful in this instance
Collages	Exploratory Can be used as part of a mixed methods approach	Look for direction and ownership within the creative groups and for the engagement of all children	Given the 'sticking and pasting' nature of collages probably (but not exclusively) more appropriate for younger children
Diaries	Promotes privacy Child can choose time to engage with research Can give a sense of ownership and production	Boredom – particularly with unstructured diaries Disengagement – if the researcher seems disinterested	Data may well depend on levels of literacy – can adapt for younger children by asking them if they want to draw pictures and words rather than sentences
New technologies	Potential very engaging Familiarity to children	Can be exclusionary – make sure all children taking part have access to necessary equipment. Ethical issues may arise if using video diaries or recording equipment	Probably more relevant/appropriate for older children (12–17 years)

Table 4.1: Summary of Research Techniques

(particularly if they are badly managed) (for further reading see Darbyshire *et al.* 2005). Importantly, whatever technique(s) is employed, the data still has to be analysed (see Chapter 7). To that end, when choosing an approach to engage the children you are researching with, think carefully about how the data will be interpreted and more specifically how it will facilitate meeting the research aim(s) and objectives.

Alternative techniques for researching with children were employed in Appendix 1 (the Youth Counselling Service case study). For example, when asking the adolescents to consider their 'hopes and fears', they were issued with two Post-it notes. On one of these the adolescents were asked to identify one thing (or more) they would hope to gain from seeing a counsellor and one thing (or more) they would be frightened about if seeing a counsellor. These anonymous Post-its (and what was written on them) were placed on a piece of flip chart paper and were discussed relative to the positives and the negatives.

Other approaches outlined in Appendix 1 involved asking the children to design a poster for the counselling service that they thought would appeal to other people in the school. These posters were then shown to all the members of the group and a discussion on why the service could be 'marketed' in this way, followed.

Listing what young people worry about and asking them to prioritise which they think is most significant was also used as a way to engage children. Whilst there was no right or wrong answer to which was the most significant worry, the adolescents were engaged by the researcher as they were able to discuss the topics in a way which would appeal to them (as opposed to simply saying 'discuss these ideas').

Sanders and Munford (2005), in a separate study, drawing on their background in social work practice research, advocate the use of eco-maps and social network maps to provide a starting point from which to generate data. These approaches involve the young people identifying who they regularly come into contact with and then coding these relationships according to the nature and quality of their relational experience. This approach, building on Hartman's (1995) eco-map and Tracy's (1990) social network map, provided Sanders and Munford (2005) with a rich understanding of the complex and sometimes delicate nature of young people's relational landscapes.

Whilst most of the 'miscellaneous' techniques described here apply to Appendix 1, they all can easy be adapted to engage the children you are researching with. Using Post-its to facilitate a discussion on a variety of social topics, for example, bullying or discrimination, or health related topics such as implications of illness or resilience/coping with illness, could be beneficial in the data collection process. Asking children to prioritise what is most important to them on any given topic and why (in groups) can also help engage them. Employing social network maps may allow you to understand the context of the data to a greater extent.

Remember, whatever technique(s) you employ, ensure you have allocated enough time for each task and think carefully about the way in which the data you are collating will help you meet your research aim(s) and objectives.

Quantitative Research

Ensuring that quantitative research is engaging can be difficult compared to a qualitative research (which may be why employing a mixed methods approach may be more appealing to children and researchers – although this may depend on the researcher's philosophy). It has already been established (see Chapter 3) that when designing quantitative research there are a number of ways in which the presentation of, and the approach to conducting surveys, for example, can be enhanced. Using an online questionnaire can afford the researcher the opportunity to explore and employ a wide range of visual and engaging techniques. The use of colours, pictures, animation, click-and-drag and asking one or two questions per screen can be instrumental in securing a positive response. It is, of course, not always practicable to use a computer-based approach and a paper survey may be less technologically challenging for the researcher.

When using a paper-based quantitative approach, it may be more appealing if different colours of paper are used (and this may also be useful for analysis purposes – see Chapter 7). Children, regardless of age, can be influenced by colour (although it is important to remember that colour is deep rooted in culture and that if you are researching a group of children for whom colour may be important, take this into account). For example, red in China is considered to be lucky and white is representative of death. Of course it is important to make sure that whatever colour paper you choose, the words on the page are still readable. Test this *before* having all the copies you need printed.

When conducting quantitative research, children still need to be praised and the design of the questionnaire is extremely important in ensuring that children are engaged during the research study.

It may of course be that the questionnaire is self administered. That is, the researcher asks the children the questions from the questionnaire and completes the questionnaire for them. This has a number of advantages. The questionnaire completion is more akin to a structured interview and as the researcher is on hand to immediately respond to any queries, the response rate may increase. The researcher can also use prompts more effectively in this situation.

In Appendix 2 (Assessing the Cumulative Impact of Alcohol Marketing on Youth Drinking) a team of professional market researchers was briefed and administered the questionnaire in the home of the respondents (with parental/guardian consent and presence). Show cards were used for much of the interviewer-administered questionnaire so that the young people could point to the answers instead of talking out loud about alcohol consumption practices.

There are disadvantages to using a self-administered method too. One of the benefits of a questionnaire based approach can be anonymity and the resulting lack of socially desirable responses. However, by using a self-administered approach, the children may feel compelled to respond in a way they would not if they were left to complete the questionnaire themselves (this would be particularly relevant in Appendix 2 as outlined above and as such the show cards were designed to minimise this). Also given the volume of responses for a quantitative piece of research, adequate reflection time for the additional 'visuals' used during the administering of the questionnaire may not be given to the children. To minimise this, in Appendix 2, plenty of time was allowed for the administering of the questionnaire. The questionnaire was also placed in a sealed envelope when the interviewer had completed it to reassure the adolescents of confidentiality and anonymity.

Young People Give their View

Although Chapter 9 specifically details how to involve children as researchers, it would appear to be useful to include a section here on what children think would be engaging in terms of a research approach. Having asked children and adolescents after a variety of research projects what they enjoyed most and also having asked them if they were going to conduct research on a specific topic how they would do it, the following quotes are illustrative of their thinking:

On using projective techniques:

It would be easier if you just asked us [what you wanted to know].

(Female, 13 years)

On how to sample:

I mean you probably could have been more conversational with people you knew because then you would know you were on the same basic level in that sort of way.

(Male, 15 years)

On which research approach to choose:

Diaries would be good as a way [of researching] as it would be fun to record your journey from ideas [about what to wear to a formal dance] to final decision. However, people may not want to give up their time or would not want to tell the truth. Having a casual chat and asking if you can record what is said would be good as it may be more relaxed.

(Female, 17 years)

You could set up a Bebo page – type comments and blogs, upload pictures, have polls about what decision a person could make and have four answers available so they could see the outcome of their decision.

(Male, 15 years)

On employing an interview approach:

Just ask people generally where they normally hang out.

(Male, 14 years)

Younger children are particularly interested in how they are going to be 're-warded' for their involvement with the research project. This is not normally financial and can be tied to reward systems already in place in the school (e.g. house points). Often they are happy when they have something they can 'take away' with them to show others (e.g. parents/guardians, siblings or friends).

Summary

This chapter sought to explore how best to engage young people with research practices. Types and numbers of tasks that can be employed have been discussed and the usefulness of understanding learning styles has been explored. Different engaging techniques such as photographs, draw and write, role play and collages have been considered and the limits and the merits of using these approaches have been examined. Case studies have illustrated how techniques can be used and have demonstrated the subsequent advantages of employing engaging methods to collate data. Techniques to encourage young people to engage with quantitative methods have also been summarised and young people have suggested the best ways in which they can be researched with. The role of new technology in research has also been briefly considered.

The following chapter will address the issue of appropriate forward planning for researching with children whilst Chapter 6 explores what may happen when the researcher finally begins to conduct the fieldwork.

Reflective Questions

1   How long might a task related to a research project take and why?

2   How can an understanding of learning facilitate our chosen research approach?

3   List three advantages of using photographs in research and three potential drawbacks.

4   Why might the draw and write technique enhance our understanding of complex topics?

5   How can a researcher give 'ownership' to a child using the draw and write technique?

6   Describe the different types of role play that can be used when researching with children and suggest an alternative source of additional material for this purpose.

7   Suggest ways in which the researcher can build rapport with children who are completing diaries.

8   How can social network maps provide a context to or generate insight into the lives of young people?

Checklist

☐   Do you understand how and why different learning styles may influence the way in which children engage with the research?

☐   Do you understand why visual methodologies have faced criticism in the past and how to address these criticisms?

☐   Are you aware of how using photography during research can enhance both the engagement of the children you are researching with and the richness of the data?

☐   Are you able to identify the best techniques for your own research project taking into account the age, development and any other circumstances particular to the children to wish to research with?

☐   Do you understand the ways in which drawing allows children to express themselves?

☐   Have you considered what equipment/material you will need if you want to use the techniques suggested in this chapter?

☐   Have you considered the alternative techniques that can be employed to engage the children you are researching with and how they can complement the method (s) you have chosen to use?

☐   Do you understand why it is difficult to ensure quantitative methods are engaging and how these issues may be overcome?

References

Backett-Milburn, K. and McKie, L. (1999) 'A critical appraisal of the draw and write technique', *Health Education Research: Theory and Practice*, 14, 387-389.

Banister, E. and Booth, G. (2005) 'Exploring innovative methodologies for child-centric consumer research', *Qualitative Market Research*, 8 (2), 157-175.

Banister, E. and Hogg, M.K. (2001) 'Mapping the negative self: from "so not me"...to "just not me"', *Advances in Consumer Research*, 28, 242-248.

Bentley, T. (1989) 'Talking pictures', *Nursing Times*, 85 (31), 58-59.

Berndt, T. J. (1990), 'Distinctive features and effects of early adolescent friendships', *Advances in Adolescent Development*, Vol.2: From childhood to adolescence.

Buck, J. (1981) *The House-Tree-Person Technique*, Los Angeles: Western Psychological Services.

Coad, J. (2007) 'Using art-based techniques in engaging children and young people in health care consultations and/or research', *Journal of Research in Nursing*, **12** (5), 487-497.

Coad, J. and Needham, J. (2005) 'Snapshot: an exploratory survey of young people's perceptions of health and healthy living using a photographic record', *Heart of Birmingham*, tPCT Report, obtain from Dr Jane Coad, University of the West of England

Cook, T. and Hess, E. (2007) 'What the camera sees and from whose perspectives: Fun methodologies for engaging children in enlightening adults', *Childhood*, **14** (1), 29-45.

Councill, T. (1993) 'Art therapy with pediatric cancer patients: Helping normal children cope with abnormal circumstances', *Art Therapy, Journal of the American Art Therapy Association*, **10** (2), 78-87.

Councill, T. (1999) 'Art therapy with pediatric cancer patients', in C. Malchiodi (ed.), *Medical Art Therapy with Children*, London and Philadelphia: Jessica Kingsley, pp. 75-93.

Darbyshire, P., MacDougall, C. and Schiller, W. (2005) 'Multiple methods in qualitative research with children: more insight or just more?', *Qualitative Research*, **5** (4), 417-436.

Donoghue, S. (2000) 'Projective techniques in consumer research', *Journal of Family Ecology and Consumer Sciences*, **28**, 47-53.

Driessnack, M. (2006) 'Draw and tell conversations with children about fear', *Qualitative Health Research*, **16**, 1414-1435.

Dunn, R., Dunn, K. and Price, G.E. (1984), *Learning Style Inventory*, Lawrence, KS: Price Systems.

Efken, C. (2002) 'Keeping the focus in teen focus groups', *Advertising and Marketing to Children*, 3, 4.

Engel, S. (1995) *The Stories Children Tell: Making Sense of the Narratives of Childhood*, New York: W.H. Freeman.

Gabhainn, S.N. and Kelleher, C. (2002) 'The sensitivity of the draw and write technique', *Health Education*, **102** (2), 68-75.

Guillemin, M. (2004) 'Understanding illness: using drawings as a research method', *Qualitative Health Research*, **14** (2), 272-289.

Harris, D. (1963) *Children's Drawings as Measures of Intellectual Maturity*, New York: Harcourt, Brace and World.

Hartman, A. (1995) 'Diagrammatic assessment of family relationship', *Families in Society: The Journal of Contemporary Human Services*, **76** (3), 111-122.

Horstman, M., Aldiss, S. and Gibson, F. (2008) 'Methodological issues when using the draw and write technique with children aged 6 to 12 years', *Qualitative Health Research*, **18** (7), 1001-1011.

Hurworth, R., Clark, E., Martin, J. and Thomsen, S. *et al.* (2005) 'The use of photo-interviewing: three examples from health evaluation and research', *Evaluation Journal of Australasia*, 4 (1/2), 52-62.

Instone, S. (2000) 'Perceptions of children with HIV infection when not told for so long: Implications for diagnosis disclosure', *Journal of Pediatric Health Care*, 14, 235-243.

Koppitz, E.M. (1968) *Psychological Evaluation of Children's Human Figure Drawings*, New York: Grune and Stratton.

Koppitz, E.M. (1984) *Psychological Evaluation of Children's Human Figure Drawings by Middle School Pupils*, Orlando, FL: Grune and Stratton.

Lewis, A. and Lindsay, G.E. (2000) *Researching Children's Perspectives*, Buckingham: Open University Press.

Malchiodi, C. (1998) *Understanding children's drawing*. New York.Guilford

Malhotra, N.K. and Birks, D.F. (2003) *Marketing Research: An Applied Approach*, 2nd European edn. Harlow: Prentice Hall.

Mauthner, M. (1997) 'Methodological aspects of collecting data from children: lessons from three research projects', *Children and Society*, 11, 16-28.

Nairn, A. (2006) 'Commercialisation of childhood? The ethics of research with primary school children', *International Journal of Market Research*, 48 (2), 113-114.

Nuttall, P. (2006) 'Exploring the consumption and use of popular music as a means of expressing an adolescent's identity during the socialisation process', unpublished PhD thesis, University of the West of England, Bristol.

Prosser, J. (1998) *Image Based Research*, London: Falmer Press.

Roedder John, D. (1999) 'Consumer socialisation of children: a retrospective look at twenty-five years of research', *Journal of Consumer Research*, 26 (3), 183-213.

Rollins, J.A. (2005) 'Tell me about it: drawing as a communication tool for children with cancer', *Journal of Pediatric Oncology Nursing*, 22 (4), 203-221.

Rubin, J. (1984) *Child Art Therapy: Understanding and Helping Children Grow Through Art*, 2nd edn, New York: Van Nostrand Reinhold.

Ryan-Wenger, N.A. (1998) 'Children's drawings: an invaluable source of information for nurses', *Journal of Pediatric Health Care*, 12 (3), 109-110.

Sanders, J. and Munford, R. (2005) 'Activity and reflection: research and change with diverse groups of young people', *Qualitative Social Work*, 4 (2), 197-209.

Silverman, D. (1993) *Interpreting Qualitative Data*, London: Sage

Smith, F. and Barker, J. (2004) 'Contested spaces: children's experiences of our school care in England, Wales', *Childhood*, 7 (3), 315-333.

Tracy, E. (1990) 'Identifying social support resources of at-risk families', *Social Work*, 35 (3), 252-258.

Welsh, J. and Instone, S. (2000) 'Use of drawings by children in the pediatric office', in S. Dixon and M. Stein (eds), *Encounters with Children: Pediatric Behavior and Development*, St Louis: Mosby, pp. 571-589.

5 Planning the Fieldwork for Research with Children and Adolescents

Objectives

- To explore the concepts of disclosure, access and consent in the context of research planning

- To suggest the design of a consent form and determine the amount of additional information that it may be necessary to provide to the gatekeeper(s) or young person taking part in the research

- To identify how to sample for a research study with young people and where best to conduct the research with children

- To consider how and why it is necessary to have a contingency plan

- To explore the role of incentives.

Introduction

The previous chapters discussed the importance of an ethical approach to researching with children and illustrated a variety of methods and techniques that could be adopted and adapted for children and adolescents. The aims and objectives of the research project needs to be fully understood and addressed before the planning phase can begin. If you are reading this chapter, you will already have thought about the nature of your topic (e.g. sensitive, engaging, etc.), the age group of the children you will be researching with and the most appropriate research method to use. This chapter is designed to ensure that your proposed study is successful in its execution. Without adequate planning, researching with children is ill-fated. As many, if not all, projects have a time frame, a clear plan with a time line will be an effective aid to the successful completion of your project.

Preparing to Research

Timing is imperative to ensure that the research you are conducting with children ha a positive outcome. Any plan (but particularly a plan that involves researching wit young people) ought to consider what needs to be achieved but a contingency plan (se 'Contingencies' below) should also be considered in case of circumstances outside th researcher's control. Do not focus on what could go wrong but do retain a sense of flex ibility in your overall approach. The checklist at the end of this chapter outlines wha you need to include in your plan of research and the key people who will be involve in the plan you should prepare. Each aspect of this checklist is discussed in depth i this chapter and all of these items should be considered before your research proje is conducted. Figure 5.1 summarises what needs to be considered when preparing t research with young people.

Disclosure and Access

Chapter 2 outlined the need for an ethical approach to researching with children an the first item on a plan that involves researching with children is securing access t young people. Do not underestimate how long this process will take. Researching wit children is very rewarding but it is essential that access, consent and disclosure are i place before any research commences. 'Access' to children varies across discipline Chapter 2 discusses best practice across disciplines but it is important to note her that depending on the type of project you are proposing (e.g. health, education, bus

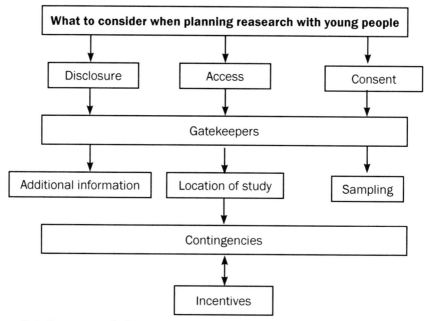

Figure 5.1: Summary of what to consider when preparing research with young people

ness, etc.) securing access will differ between disciplines. For example, health-related proposals will invariably be screened by a Research Ethics Committee (see Chapter 2) before the study is allowed to progress. This means that you must build this 'advice' process into your time frame and/or plan (see Chapter 2 for references and discipline-specific advice). If you are researching in other disciplines, your proposal may not have to be screened by a committee but this does not mean you do not have to secure access, gain consent or provide disclosure. Usually access, consent and disclosure are interlinked although access and disclosure will be agreed before consent can be sought.

Gaining access can be the most difficult aspect of your research. If you are trying to gain access to schoolchildren, once the local authority or council has agreed that you can approach a school(s), access is normally sought by approaching the head teacher (see Chapter 2, Figure 2.1). Some researchers know teachers in a local primary or secondary school (through social networking or because they are related in some way) and in some situations these teachers may approach the head teacher on your behalf. It is important to remember that invariably there is more than one gatekeeper and that there are different types of gatekeepers (which will normally be related to the organisational employment structure).

Even if you know the teacher you are approaching, be professional and ensure that you provide adequate information regarding the research you wish to conduct. Do not assume that the teacher will think your research topic is appropriate just because you are familiar to them. It is useful to know how the research may benefit the children before approaching the school. The SEAL material (discussed in Chapter 4) may be a useful starting point to gain an understanding of the type of work that is covered at primary and secondary schools.

Once you have permission to approach the school (see Chapter 2, Figure 2.1), to agree access with a head teacher and/or a class teacher you will need to provide the following: the research topic, aim(s) and objectives, the age group(s) of the children you wish to research with, the number of children you wish to research with, the type of research you are proposing (e.g. computer-based), the length of time you think the research will take place, the timing of the research (e.g. day of the week, time of the academic year), the benefit to the children you will be researching with, proposals for gaining consent and proof of researcher disclosure (see Chapter 2).

This list is not exhaustive and depending on your research proposal you may have to provide additional information. However, this list does provide a useful starting point and will ensure that you have fully considered the study you are proposing and that you fully understand the implications of what you are asking permission to do.

If you wish to interview children in a different environment (e.g. at home, at a local youth/community centre or at an after-school club) you will still need to provide the above information and you will need to clearly identify who has the responsibility for the children when you want to research with them. Once you have gained access to the children, you must seek consent from the gatekeeper(s) and the children themselves before continuing with the research. For example, the head teacher may permit access to the children but the class teacher and parents should also give their consent for the research to take place. There are practical difficulties associated with relying on gatekeepers. Researchers need to be aware that project requirements can impose considerable additional work on staff and organisational structure and resource issues can cause difficulties (Munro *et al.*, 2005).

Consent

The importance of consent is detailed in Chapter 2 and malpractice in relation to consent has also been discussed. When you seek consent to research with children you should be open and honest about what you intend to discuss with the children and you should clearly indicate what the data will be used for and who will have access to it. For an example of a consent form see Figure 5.1. Any consent form should detail where the research will take place, what will be expected of the young person during the research process and details of any additional information that will be made available. The person or persons involved in the research should be identified and their details provided. Confidentiality should be assured, on-going consent established and how the data will be stored and destroyed at the end of the project should also be included.

It is *essential* that if you use this approach, that the consent forms are signed and returned by the parents before the study begins. You can only sample from and research with the children who have permission from their parents.

There is another way in which you can obtain consent to research with children although this approach is not as robust or as rigorous as using consent forms. This approach is known as 'passive parental consent' where the school/youth group leader/after-school club manager will send letters home to the parents to explain what the researcher is proposing to do and will give the parent (s) the opportunity to ask for their children not be involved in the research project (Gans and Brindid, 1995). This approach ensures that the parents are aware of the programme of research and where ongoing consent is employed by the researcher (see Chapter 2) this method can still be considered as an acceptable approach. There is however a number of limitations to this approach and these must be considered before you obtain a particular 'type' of consent.

Whilst 'passive parental consent' may seem an easier option, the parents may not see, for example, the letter from the school (particularly if it is sent home and ends up in the bottom of a school bag) and may be unaware that the research is taking place. This approach also shifts the responsibility from the researcher to

Name of young person: _____

This is to confirm that those signing the form agree to the above young person being interviewed about [*insert research topic*]. The interview will take place at [*insert time and location*] and a task will be given to the interviewee to complete before the interview [*And/or indicate what will be expected of the young person during the interview. Include any details about additional information regarding the study if this is on a website or if a hard copy of additional material is available*]. Members of the research team who would then have access to the material include [*name*], [*name*] and [*name*].

We do/do not (delete as appropriate) give our consent to the named young person taking part in the above research.

We understand that:

1. This project is completely confidential and anything said during interview will not be passed on to anyone outside the research team.

2. The research can be stopped at any point and anything recorded will be given to the interviewee so it can be destroyed if necessary.

3. The interviewer may make notes on the interview, although these will be kept securely and only the research team will have access to them.

4. The tape-recording (if made) will be kept securely and will only be accessed by the research team. It will be destroyed securely at the end of the study.

5. At all times, the researchers will endeavour to treat what is said in this project with due respect to privacy and to conduct themselves in a proper and professional manner.

6. The researchers will ensure anonymity of the participants if this research is published in any form.

Name and signature of young person: _____

Name and signature of parent or guardian: _____

Contact telephone no. in case of emergency: _____

Date: _____

A COPY OF THIS LETTER WILL BE GIVEN TO YOU FOR YOUR OWN REFERENCE

[Details of the research team should be provided – tel nos/email addresses, affiliations]

Figure 5.2 : Consent form

the school or organisation helping the researcher to obtain consent. The onus is also on the parent(s) and not the researcher to ensure the child/ren can take part in the research. Confusingly, 'opt out consent' is also used interchangeably with 'passive parental consent'. In the context of Appendix 1, 'opting out' would mean that the children do not have to take part in research. *Best practice* would be employing the use of *consent forms*, despite them probably being more time-consuming and perhaps narrowing the sample frame (see 'Sampling', below).

Obtaining consent may of course be influenced by the gatekeeper (e.g. social worker, teacher) who can advise you on the best approach in relation to your chosen topic. The gatekeeper(s) may have a preference for the type of consent you obtain and may have experience in this area. Listening to the advice of those allowing access to the children should also be taken into account and may influence the type of 'consent' approach taken by the (novice) researcher. Where possible use the *best practice* approach.

Gatekeepers

The gatekeepers or interlocutors and their role have already been discussed (see Chapter 2). They are the person (or people) who control access to young people and who, in some cases, are present when the research is being conducted. First and foremost then is ensuring that the gatekeeper is fully aware of the aim(s) and objectives of the research project and how you are planning to research with the children. The gatekeeper may be able to provide advice on aspects of your research (e.g. any projective techniques you are proposing to use – see Chapter 4) and will be more familiar with the language used by the group you wish to research with (so may, for example, be able to consider the appropriateness of language used in a questionnaire). The gatekeeper will also be familiar with risk assessment – that is taking all reasonable steps to ensure that hazards to children, both indoors and outdoors, are kept to a minimum. They will have expected you to have considered if any of the research you plan to do with the children (e.g. using scissors) has been carefully thought through.

The gatekeeper will have the responsibility for ensuring the care of the child/ren with whom you wish to research. Their utmost concern is not necessarily the success of your research project but the welfare of their charges. It is important that you understand that the research you are proposing is only a (minor) part of the day-to-day activities the gatekeeper will share with the children. Where (one of) the gatekeepers is either a teacher or a social worker, for example, the researcher will have to be aware that the teacher(s) or social worker(s) will have their own role to maintain outside the research project the researcher wants to conduct. As such, the gatekeepers may expect certain behaviours of the children in relation to adults and vice versa and this can raise issues in terms of research approach and quality of data.

If, for example, a research project is being conducted with young children (aged 8-11 years) in school the researcher may want to appear to be 'child-like' in their role (see 'Role of the researcher', Chapter 2). This may involve asking to be called by their first name or sitting with the children at their desks. For some gatekeepers this may be problematic as retaining discipline in the classroom may rest on the balance of power between the teachers and children and the teacher may see this type of behaviour as potentially undermining the social structure of the class. Whilst innovative methods (see Chapter 4) have been proposed to engage and involve young people in issues that concern them (Weller, 2006) the gatekeeper (in this case the teacher) has to be comfortable with the approach.

The relationship with the gatekeeper is an important one to develop not least because the gatekeeper may be present (or on-hand) when the research is being conducted. This could be because of the environment in which the research is taking place (hospital, school, drop-in centre) and/or because the gatekeeper may be able to facilitate with the research and/or gauge the children's ongoing consent (Flewitt, 2005). The role of the gatekeeper(s) could also be to advise the researcher regarding additional information the participants or their parent/ guardian may need before the research is conducted (see 'Providing additional information' below). The gatekeeper could also be instrumental in facilitating the relationship between the researcher and the young people. The experience of the gatekeeper (length of employment or previous experience of working with researchers) may influence their confidence or perception of the researcher. Researchers need to demonstrate to the agencies with which they work that they will respect the rights of the service users (Ward, 2004). That is, as well as ensuring the well-being of the children, it is important to be sure that those indirectly participating with the research (e.g. the gatekeepers) will be recognised as playing a significant role in the process.

In some instances researchers within childhood studies have been able to persuade adult gatekeepers such as teachers and social workers that children can be treated as research collaborators and this is probably as a result of the relationship the researchers have developed with the gatekeepers as well as those relationships developed with young people. One effect or by-product of this might be that children are perceived by child professionals to be more competent (Wyness, 2006: 231) and the gatekeepers may feel more confident about the role of the researcher as a consequence.

When considering the gatekeeper and their role the researcher should take the following into account. It may be that access has been awarded by the overall gatekeeper (e.g. head teacher, ward sister, etc.) but that the gatekeeper in charge of the children or young person(s) you wish to research with (e.g. class teacher, nurse) is not known to you or familiar with the research study you wish to conduct. It is imperative that you try to develop a good rapport with the gatekeeper in charge of the children you wish to research with and not assume that because you have been given permission to research with these young people that all gatekeepers will be interested in or understand the concept(s) you are trying to explore. To this end, it is always useful to address how the research may be of benefit to the gatekeeper in charge of the children as well as how the research may benefit the overall gatekeeper. An example of this would be trying to ensure the research in some way reflected the curriculum for that particular year group (useful for the gatekeeper in charge of the children) as well as considering the benefits to the school (e.g. collaboration between schools and university, data that may help improve service provision, etc.).

Location of Study

The location of any research conducted with children must be part of a careful planning process. The location of some research studies may be predetermined by the nature of the research (e.g. clinical trials are likely to be conducted in a hospital environment) and the location of the research can sometimes add to the confusion about what constitutes the research and what part of any discussion or treatment specifically relates to health care (Broome *et al.*, 2001). However, it is often the researcher who has to consider the most appropriate location for the study to take place.

> **It is good practice not to conduct one-to-one or face-to-face interviews with children in a closed room on your own.**

This is for the safety and well-being of all involved. Where the environment allows, it is important that for the safety of everyone in the research that the researcher and participant are able to be observed by others albeit at a reasonable distance. Paired research (where two interviewers are interviewing different individuals in the same but large enough room to minimise noise effects) may overcome issues of having to conduct one-to-one interviews in an enclosed area. However, paramount in any decision made about the location of a research study with children is the comfort of the child participant. The researcher must balance the potential quality of the research data with respect for the young person involved in the study.

The location of a research study with young people may also be influenced by the chosen research method. For example, ethnographic work is grounded in a commitment to first-hand experience and exploration of a particular social or cultural setting. To conduct an ethnographic piece of research with children would involve exploring the social setting in which they grow and develop and arguably could involve interviewing or observing young people in their bedrooms at home whilst they talk with their friends or listen to music, etc. The research aim would be to understand more about the <u>social worlds of children</u>. However, this may appear to be intrusive to the young people (and their parents/guardians) and the data collected as a result may be incomplete or biased as the children are unused to having their 'space' researched. They may 'play up' to a camera or may simply feel uncomfortable. It is important to think of alternative locations to research the social or cultural settings of young people. It may be useful, for example, to ask children to photograph the items in their bedroom that are most important to them and ask them to discuss and give a context to the photographs. Whilst this may not provide as much insight as the researcher would like, the young person retains control over the research data and can maintain an appropriate level of privacy between themselves and the researcher.

The location may also be chosen to try and remove children from an environment that may bias their responses. Darbyshire *et al.* (2005), for example, conducted focus groups with children in an art/activities area adjacent to their classroom. The children seemed to accept that, because of this environment, the research was not 'school work' and the location helped create a more informal atmosphere where animated and interactive discussion could take place.

There has been in recent years, some debate about whether conducting research in school is appropriate (David *et al.*, 2001) and this has raised particular concerns when the focus of the research is not necessarily for 'educational' purposes. The debate is twofold. First, research should not take place in school as it diverts the attention of children from bone fide education. Second, the data collected at school will be influenced by the school setting so that the young people will just see it as another piece of school work (see, for example, Denscombe and Aubrook, 1992; Pole *et al.*, 1999). There are ways in which in which these issues can be addressed (see 'Role of gatekeepers' and 'Role of researcher', Chapter 2) although it is acknowledged that collecting data from young people during the school day or at school per se has limitations. The school setting will undoubtedly have an influence on the child and their responses (to varying degrees) although interestingly, parents have also been identified as 'agents of surveillance' (Danby and Farrell, 2002) suggesting data collected in the home environment will also have its own limitations. The nature of the topic and any additional information given to the participants will also influence the type of data collected. If the young person is given an adequate level of information regarding the study (and they feel comfortable with the topic and the location) they are likely to engage with the research and the researcher to a greater extent and provide useful insights into their behaviour.

Providing Additional Information

How much additional information do young people (and their parents) need about the proposed research study to be conducted? Chapter 2 has already discussed the malpractice of 'covert research' (see Homan, 2001) and the need to be open and honest about the nature, aim(s) and objectives of the research topic. There is, however, a difference between being informed and being overwhelmed by additional material. The level of additional information provided to young people (and their parents) will largely depend on the nature of the research topic, the expectations of the participants (and their guardians) and any expert advice provided to the researcher (by the gatekeepers or ethics committees).

If the topic is complex in nature (e.g. health related) the researcher has to be aware of the concept of 'credence'. This is when the participant and their parents/guardians cannot fully comprehend what is being tested or the way in which it is being researched but are comfortable to delegate the responsibility to those with the credibility or authority. This does not remove the onus from the health researcher in conveying information in a simple, comprehensive format but overloading the participant (and their parent/guardian) with complex detail regarding procedures or outcomes is unnecessary.

The obligation is to disclose all relevant information to respondent or participant and not to hide crucial stipulations in small print. If the topic is less complex in nature (e.g. business related) the researcher may want to provide details of the study to both the parent/guardians and to the child. Additionally, researchers can discuss methodological approaches with children and their parent/guardian if they feel this is appropriate. This can, however, raise questions rather than providing answers as children and their parent/guardian may not be familiar with research methods and their merits/disadvantages.

The overriding principle in relation to additional information ought to be common sense. David *et al.* (2001) had not initially planned to provide information leaflets about their project but decided they would serve as an introduction to the gatekeepers and the children. Three leaflets were designed (two specifically with children in mind) although the format of the leaflets was similar. These authors expressed concern about the level of information influencing the data (in a similar way to introducing visual stimuli that are 'predetermined' – see Chapter 4) and as such, too much information may impact on what the children say and how they behave.

Darbyshire *et al.* (2005) discuss giving schools, parents and children 'child-friendly' information sheets and clear explanations of what they wanted to talk to the children about. Where possible one side of A4 paper ought to be enough to clearly detail the nature and aims of the study, the duration of the research, the likely output and what will happen to the data when the project is complete. If additional information on the detail of the research approach is required, advised (see 'Role of gatekeepers' in Chapter 2) or requested by the participants (or their parent/guardian) this can be produced by the researcher and provided to the gatekeepers, participants or their parent/guardian. As knowledge is power, it may be that by providing additional information, a balance of power through the sharing of this knowledge will be maintained. As with other suggestions that refer to empowerment, asking the parent (or gatekeeper) or the young person to read the final report or asking the children if they want their responses included in the text can provide those engaged in the study with both a level of additional information and can enhance the illustrative content of the study.

Sampling

When planning to research with young people it is normally expected that you will know how many children you would like to research with. Indeed, when you approach gatekeeper(s) to request access or complete a proposal for an ethics committee to consider, one of the first questions you will have to answer is about the size of the sample.

Teddlie and Yu (2007) highlight the differences between purposive and probability sampling. The first type of sampling approach is used for qualitative research and the latter used for quantitative research. Purposive sampling allows the researcher to select cases he/she can learn most from and therefore those chosen for research are done so on their 'typicality' – that is how typical they are relative to the research issue or problem. As the respondents are specially selected the sample sizes are normally small (less than 30). The focus of the research is on the depth of understanding and the sample is chosen using expert judgement. The sampling frame is informal and the data is not generalisable. It is likely that if you are researching with children you will use a purposive approach to sampling. Quota or convenience sampling are also popular methods of sampling for qualitative research.

In terms of planning, sampling is important as it will give you an indication of how much time you need to collect data (although it is important to have a flexible approach). The saturation principle should be employed when collecting qualitative data. That is, if you plan to conduct 12 interviews but after the tenth interview there is no new information, it is not necessary to conduct the last two. If, however, after 12 interviews new data is still emerging then you must keep interviewing until there are no new insights (where practicably possible). When researching with children, the sample size should always be over-estimated. That is if you think you need to research with 12 children, ask to research with 16. This is to allow for informed dissent as children will not always want to engage with the research/researcher and it is less problematic with regard to data collection if there is a greater sample to draw on. Also some children are quiet by nature and whilst it is important to include their ideas to ensure rich qualitative data you might need to increase the number of children you research with. Further to this children can be absent and/or called away (e.g. through illness, music lessons, etc.) on the day or time of the research so that even though you have consent it is just not possible to research with that particular child. The gatekeeper may think it is more important for the child to be doing something else (this is particularly true when conducting research in schools) and as such the child may be busy elsewhere. It is important to ensure you have enough returned consent forms to conduct the research as planned.

It is important to remember that if children want to take part in the research and consent has been given by the children and their parents if they are not chosen (sampled) to take part then they may feel let down or disappointed. Whilst as a researcher you will want to over-recruit to ensure you have a large enough sample, there is also the possibility of having too many children to research with and some will inevitably be unhappy at being excluded. There is then, a balance between ensuring you have enough children to research with and managing their expectations in terms of taking part.

Of course this view of sampling presupposes that there will be no problem gaining an appropriate sample. Stalker *et al.* (2004) and Scott *et al.* (2006) detail the difficulties of gaining access to the research population particularly in health care situation (where the possible number of children who can be researched with can be small). In the latter study, the gatekeepers were described as facilitators with regard to the sampling and this serves to reinforce that developing a positive relationship with the gatekeeper(s) can be beneficial for a number of reasons, not least access. (For additional information on qualitative sampling see: Luborsky and Rubinstein; 1995; Thompson 1999; Green, 2001 and Collins *et al.*, 2007.)

If the research is quantitative, the sampling will be scientific. As a researcher you will use probability sampling although it is unlikely that the sample will be 'random' (particularly if you seek and gain access to a particular school or organisation). Scientific sampling seeks generalisability and as such the sample should be representative (typically numbering more than 50) of the young people you are researching. Using this type of sample ought to provide the researcher with breadth of information and the selection of the sample is often based on mathematical formulas. Again the sampling frame will typically be larger than the sample as mal or non-response is common although there are ways in which this can be minimised (see Chapter 3).

The sampling frame will also be dependent on what you wish to 'test' or 'find out'. Say, for example, you want to find out the difference between males and females and their attitudes towards snacking behaviour. If you ask 30 girls and 30 boys you will be able to conduct a meaningful test on this simple data set. If, however, you wish to conduct more complex analysis by considering, for example, gender, snacking behaviour, socio-economic group and level of literacy, the number of respondents would need to be much higher as you would need to have data that reflected at least 30 boys, 30 girls, 30 children from each socio-economic group and 30 children from each literacy group.

As a researcher using quantitative research you will focus on numeric data (see 'Research Philosophy', Chapter 3) but it is possible to generate narrative data through the use of open questions. (For additional information on quantitative and mixed methods sampling see: Gilbert, 2006; Teddlie and Yu, 2007; Collins *et al.*, 2007 and O'Cathain *et al.*; 2007.)

Contingencies

What is a contingency and when should it be employed? A contingency is a flexible approach to researching with children and can be employed when there are factors outside the researcher's control that impact on their research plan. A contingency is not something that is put in place when a research project has not been properly planned. A contingency can be employed for location of study, providing additional information and sampling (see for example Scenario 5.1). A contingency can *never* be employed for access, consent or disclosure. If access to children or young people is not recommended or approved, if consent is not given from the parents or gatekeepers and ongoing consent is not given by the children and the role of the researcher is not disclosed the research *cannot* take place. However, there are situations in which the research has been well planned but where external influences change the organisation of the research approach. Sarah's experience as described in Scenario 5.1, is one such example.

Scenario 5.1

Sarah's experience of conducting qualitative research in schools has been varied. In one particular school she researched with children about their food consumption habits and more specifically what they took to school in their lunch boxes. The research was to be conducted in the school dining hall to allow the children the opportunity to contribute to the study in a safe, reasonably quiet, environment. Upon arriving at the school, Sarah was told the windows were being replaced in the dining hall and that the research would need to be conducted outside the head teacher's office. Initially this seemed a good idea as there was space to lay out the pre-prepared lunchboxes and tables and chairs to sit at with the children. However, the area outside the head teacher's office soon became very noisy. The window fitters passed the area regularly and shouted encouragement to the children and Sarah herself. A child had been dropped off at school and had shut her fingers in the car door and understandably was upset and crying loudly at the sink outside the head teacher's office. Whilst Sarah tried to explain to one child she was researching with her particular area of interest, a child, dressed in a PE kit, arrived from seemingly nowhere and was sick all over the floor beside the lunchboxes. Sarah was trying to remain calm. The child she was researching with had, of course, seen it all before and was oblivious to the noise and melee. The child continued the conversation about food consumption and, grateful for the opportunity to research with this child, Sarah felt obliged to do the same.

Of course a contingency will influence the data that is collated. This is particularly true when using the same research method to compare and contrast data. If research data is more readily collated in one school and a contingency has to be employed in another, this must be taken into account when interpreting and writing up the data. Where possible, if a contingency has to be employed in relation to location of research, the sample size can be increased (this is relevant for Scenario 5.1). As the saturation principle is central to qualitative research, by increasing the sample size, any anomalies that might have occurred as a result of the contingency can be identified and/or overcome.

If the research is quantitative and the problem is lack of completed questionnaires again a contingency may need to be employed. See, for example, David's research issue in Scenario 5.2.

Scenario 5.2

David had used a mixed methods approach to conduct research on a forthcoming sporting event. He had conducted qualitative research with adolescents to establish reasons for attendance and who/what would influence attendance, preparation for the event and possible post-event evaluation. With agreement from the school, the young people with whom he conducted the initial qualitative research agreed to distribute the questionnaires for him before the event took place. David understood the benefits of this approach to be that the adolescents would be able to support their peers if there were any queries and the questionnaires would be completed in a more informal environment. However, with only a week before the event, less than 40 questionnaires had been completed. David contacted the head teacher who allowed him to speak to all the high school students at assembly so that he could provide additional information about the research study and was able to distribute questionnaires in the last ten minutes of assembly time. The pupils responded to David's appeal and more than 100 additional questionnaires were completed after assembly.

Again, because the first 40 questionnaires were distributed using a different methodological approach, the analysis and interpretation of the results would need to reflect this. However, Scenario 5.2 illustrates that it is possible to use contingency planning to ensure researchers are still able to collect the necessary data.

Appendix 1 illustrates that it may be necessary to implement a contingency plan. Although 200 questionnaires were left for young people to pick up, complete and return at the community centre with regard to the Youth Counselling Service, this yielded no returns at all. It was necessary to approach an organisation working with young people at the centre to ask for their assistance.

When factors outside the researcher's control impact on the proposed research plan, it is still possible to address the issues and have a positive (and ethical) outcome. If your research plan is not being met, use the following set of questions to see if it is possible to employ a contingency plan.

1. Can the sample size be increased to accommodate any anomalies that might arise because of a contingency plan?

2. What is the timeframe for collecting the data?

3. Can this be increased?

4. If so, what might the implications be?

5. Can the gatekeepers facilitate an increase in data through helping communication between the young person(s) and the researcher?

6. If you are employing one research method, could you employ a mixed methods approach to increase the type and amount of data?

7. Is there additional information that can be provided to the children (in an innovative way) that could encourage them to engage with the research?

Importantly, employing a contingency plan should be considered at an earlier rather than a later stage. If you have a research plan with a time line, it should become self-evident that your research objectives may not (even will not) be met. Regularly reviewing your research plan should afford you the opportunity to identify when a contingency needs to be employed.

The Role of Incentives

The use of incentives may appear to be an ethical as opposed to a methodological or planning issue as incentives can be considered as a 'bribe'. David *et al.* (2001) posit that an expectation appears to be emerging generally that young people will be compensated for their time and trouble (including payment as an incentive to participate). This is particularly true of children/adolescents who are experienced in the field of research (e.g. have previously been involved in a research study). A number of methodological (as well as ethical) issues arise as a consequence of this view, not least that young people may be being exploited for their insights without realising the value of their contribution or that children who would not otherwise engage in a research study may feel obligated or unduly pressured to take part.

Further to this, if the young people do receive payment for their input they may feel obliged to 'say' what they think the researcher wants to hear. It also raises issues for the (novice) researcher who may not have the funds to conduct their research in this environment. In a business context, it is commonplace to reward children for their involvement in projects but the insight generated by the participants tends to have a commercial benefit (e.g. the study may involve researching new product development and may ask children to taste test different foods or comment on packaging). In the social sciences discipline and in an academic business management context, data is typically gathered to further an understanding of children for policy development and/or to contribute to knowledge in this area. As such, unless the young people are being 'employed' as researchers or to 'tailor' or review reports (see Chapter 9) incentives or rewards should be kept to a minimum and they should only be distributed once the research project has been completed. It is also useful to be aware of any healthy eating policies/food related issues when considering which incentives to reward the young people with.

Ideas for rewarding primary school children are suggested in the Box 5.2 and may be agreed with the gatekeeper. A more innovative 'reward' can also involve allowing the children to sit at a 'golden table' during school lunch (which is decorated and is at some point visited by the head teacher). The gatekeeper(s) may be able to advise the researcher regarding appropriate incentives but a book token for the class or an educational PC game are 'neutral' rewards. It is also worthwhile to remember that effective dissemination (see Chapter 8) on completion of the study is often considered rewarding by the research participants.

Box 5.2: Top Five Rewards for Primary School Children

(Primary school children; surveyed Midlothian, Scotland, March 2008)
Being rewarded with a 'star' or sticker
Being able to take something home to show their parents
Being read to
Being allowed to use the sports equipment in the gym
Being allowed access to the computers

Remember the plan that you develop for your research project should be holistic. The plan should include a time line and ought to be reviewed regularly to ensure that the project is going to plan. In this way, the likelihood of a positive and successful outcome is increased.

The following chapter is designed to help the researcher think about what might happen during research. Novice researchers particularly can be surprised at what happens when faced with even a small group of children and the following chapter has been designed to 'dilute' the element of surprise.

Summary

This chapter sought to clearly explain exactly what the researcher needs to consider before researching with children. Planning is fundamental to a successful project outcome and a well-planned project is much more rewarding and always provides better quality data. The first step in the planning process is to secure access and this may be facilitated by obtaining disclosure (see Chapter 2). In order to secure access you will have to have thought carefully about your research and what you propose to do if you get the opportunity to research with children. This will include what you will do to obtain consent. Remember, there is normally more than one gatekeeper and whilst access can be permitted by one, it is important that the researcher engages with all the gatekeepers. An example of a consent form has been provided and it is best practice to ensure that a form such as this is adapted by the researcher and completed by those taking part (and/or those giving permission) before the research commences. The researcher has also been encouraged to think about the location of the research and an ethical approach to researching with children (see Chapter 2) ought to help the researcher make decisions about where the research should take place. The extent to which additional information should be provided has been discussed with the number of respondents necessary for qualitative and quantitative approaches raised and addressed. The researcher may also find it useful to consider the sampling approaches employed by the researchers and authors of the case studies provided at the end of this text. Of course not all research goes to plan and to that end the role of contingencies has featured in this chapter. Examples of when a contingency may be necessary have been provided and although these situations are not exhaustive they are illustrative of the need to be flexible in your approach to researching with young people. Finally the use of incentives has been addressed and the expectations and implications of using them explored.

Reflective Questions

1 What should you never underestimate in relation to access?

2 What is 'passive parental consent' and in what circumstances can it be used?

3 Why is it important to develop a good relationship with the gatekeeper(s)?

4 How might you choose the location for your research with children?

5 What caveats should you be aware of when researching with children in school?

6 How might you propose to choose a sample for your research project?

7 What is a contingency and when might you employ a contingency plan?

8 Discuss the role of incentives in the context of researching with children.

Research Plan Checklist

- ☐ Have you obtained disclosure (see Chapter 2)?

- ☐ Have you obtained access by providing the appropriate information required about your proposed research study (see below)?

- ☐ Have you decided on an approach for obtaining consent and do you understand the implications of your choice?

- ☐ Have you prepared adequate information for the gatekeeper(s) (NB the gatekeeper(s) may not be the same person who permits access)?

- ☐ Have you considered the location of the proposed research and the implications and limitations of this location?

- ☐ Are there ways in which you could provide additional information to facilitate data collection?

- ☐ Have you considered the potential power imbalances that may come into play during the research process? Have you a strategy for dealing with this?

- ☐ Have you thought about how you may deal with sensitive issues that might arise (see Chapter 2)?

- ☐ If you intend to use a particular type of engaging technique (see Chapter 4), do you have all the equipment/visual aids you will need?

- ☐ What contingencies do you have in place should the research project not go to plan?

- ☐ How will you monitor and review your plan?

- ☐ Have you considered the use (and implications) of using incentives?

References

Broome, M.E., Richards, D.J. and Hall, J.M. (2001) 'Children in research: the experience of ill children and adolescents', *Journal of Family Nursing*, 7 (1), 32-49.

Collins, K.M.T., Onwuegbuzie, A.J. and Jiao, Q.G. (2007) 'A mixed methods investigation of mixed methods sampling designs in social and health science research', *Journal of Mixed Methods Research*, 1, 267-294.

David, M., Edwards, R. and Alldred, P. (2001) 'Children and school-based research: "informed consent" or "educated consent"?', *British Educational Research Journal*, 27 (3), 347-365.

Danby, S. and Farrell, A. (2002) 'Accounting for young children's competence in educational research: new perspectives on research ethics', *Australian Educational Researcher*, 31 (3), 35-50.

Darbyshire, P., MacDougall, C. and Schiller, W. (2005) 'Multiple methods in qualitative research with children: more insight or just more?', *Qualitative Research*, 5 (4), 417-436.

Denscombe, M. and Aubrook, L. (1992) 'It's just another piece of schoolwork: the ethics of questionnaire research on pupils in school', *British Educational Research Journal*, **18**, 113-131.

Gans, J. and Brindid, C.D. (1995) 'Choice of research setting in understanding adolescent health problems', *Journal of Adolescent Health*, **17**, 306-313.

Gilbert, T. (2006) 'Mixed methods and mixed methodologies: the practical, the technical and the political', *Journal of Research in Nursing*, **11**, 205-217.

Green, E.C. (2001) 'Can qualitative research produce reliable quantitative findings', *Field Methods*, **13**, 3-19.

Flewitt, R. (2005) 'Conducting research with young children: some ethical considerations', *Early Child Development and Care*, **175** (6), 553-565.

Homan, R. (2001) 'The principle of assumed consent: the ethics of gatekeeping', *Journal of Philosophy of Education*, **35** (3), 329-343.

Luborsky, M.R. and Rubinstein, R.L. (1995) 'Sampling in qualitative research: rationale, issues and methods', *Research on Aging*, **17**, 89-113.

Munro, E.R., Holmes, L. and Ward, H. (2005) 'Researching vulnerable groups: ethical issues and the effective conduct of research in local authorities', *British Journal of Social Work*, **35**, 1023-1038.

O'Cathain, A., Murphy, E. and Nicholl, J. (2007) 'Integration and publications as indicators of "yield" from mixed method studies', *Journal of Mixed Methods Research*, **1**, 147-163.

Pole, C., Mizen, P. And Bolton, A. (1999) 'Realising children's agency in research: partners and participants?', *International Journal of Social Research Methodology: Theory and Practice*, **2**, 39-54.

Stalker, K., Carpenter, J., Connors, C. and Phillips, R. (2004) 'Ethical issues in social research; difficulties encountered gaining access to children in hospital for research', *Child: Care, Health and Development*, **30**, 377-383.

Scott, J.K., Wishart, J.G. and Bowyer, D.J. (2006) 'Do current consent and confidentiality requirements impede or enhance research with children with learning disabilities', *Disability and Society*, **21** (3), 273-287.

Teddlie, C. and Yu, F. (2007) 'Mixed methods sampling: a typology with examples', *Journal of Mixed Methods Research*, **1**, 77-100.

Thompson, C. (1999) 'Qualitative research into nurse decision making: factors for consideration in theoretical sampling', *Qualitative Health Research*, **9**, 815-828.

Ward, H. (2004) 'Managing social policy research', in S. Becker and A. Radley (eds),

Understanding Research for Social Policy and Practice: Themes, Methods and Approaches, Bristol: Policy Press.

Weller, S. (2006) 'Situating (young) teenagers in geographies of children and youth', *Children's Geographies*, **4** (1), 97-108.

Wyness, M. (2006) *Childhood and Society: an Introduction to the Sociology of Childhood*, Basingstoke: Palgrave Macmillan.

6 In the Field: Preparing for What may Happen During Research

Objectives

- To illustrate how to listen effectively to the children with whom you are researching

- To establish what the children may want to know about the researcher

- To explore ways in which to overcome issues that might arise during research such as children talking too much or not speaking at all

- To discuss the role of the gatekeepers during research with children

- To consider practical matters associated with collating data.

Introduction

The previous chapters describe exactly what needs to be done before a research study with children can be conducted and addresses issues such as an ethical approach to research, research design and engaging the children you are researching with. The chapters that follow this one consider the best approach to analysing, presenting and disseminating the data that has been collated during the research study. This chapter, however, is designed to ensure that the researcher is prepared for what may happen *during* the research study.

It may be that you have planned your study ethically and have incorporated a variety of techniques to engage the children you are researching with. The planning chapter, Chapter 5, detailed the need for contingency planning and the research design chapter, Chapter 3, posits a variety of methods for different age groups and encourages careful thought in both planning and executing any proposed research study with children. Yet novice researchers in particular may be surprised at what can happen when conducting research with children and this chapter is specifically designed to dilute that element of 'surprise'.

Regardless of how well a research study has been planned if, as a researcher, you are unfamiliar with children, there are a number of issues that may arise during the research that can cause confusion or cause for concern. The quality of the interview, for example, may not 'conform to expectations' (Irwin and Johnson, 2005) and the brevity of some responses may cause the researcher to question the quality of the data. Additionally, a commonly asked question by a (novice) researcher conducting studies with children is, 'what did they mean when they said that?' and this can be exacerbated if the child/ren does not or seems unable to elaborate on what he/she has said. Simply not understanding the response is commonplace when researching with children. This following section then will provide useful 'probes' and ideas to ensure the researcher is able to identify during the research process what the child is trying to express and how to develop or provide a context to the answers that are being given. This chapter will also explore the following: listening to what children say; children who like to talk and those who do not; children who want to become gatekeepers; gatekeepers who want to become researchers; gatekeepers, power and advice; setting parameters; and boundaries and technology and equipment.

Understanding what Children Say

> ### Scenario 6.1
>
> Joanna was interviewing Daniel, an 8 year old boy, about what food he brought to school in his lunchbox as the focus of her research was about peer group influence on what food children ate at school. The research considered 'swapping' of lunch items, shopping for lunch items and what the children's friends thought about the food choices the children made. Daniel had chosen a picture of fairy cakes from a pile of food items cut out of magazines by the researcher to help discuss food choice and volunteered that his Mum made fairy cakes. 'That's lovely', said Joanna. 'I really like fairy cakes', said Daniel. Joanna asked if Daniel brought the fairy cakes his Mum made into school in his lunch box. He nodded vigorously. Joanna asked Daniel if his friends brought fairy cakes to school too. He shook his head. 'If they don't have fairy cakes in their lunch boxes,' Joanna said, 'what do they have?'. 'Fish', replied Daniel emphatically. 'Fish?', repeated Joanna, somewhat surprised, 'Like tuna fish?' she said, just to make sure. 'I love tuna', smiled Daniel and went back to looking through the pictures of food items. Joanna was more than a little confused.

Having obtained consent and on-going consent and having designed the research in such a way that the children will be engaged, it may seem that the actual 're-search' is the easy part. Yet faced with even a small group of children who you may not have met before can be quite daunting and listening to what they have to say as well as managing the time you have with them effectively can be difficult. Darbyshire *et al.* (2005), for example, illustrate that it is possible to miss the opportunity to ensure enough time is created to discuss all the data produced by the children and thus facilitate greater discussion about the context of their everyday lives. Listening to what children say is only one part of the research study. Understanding what it is they are trying to tell you can be more problematic. Scenario 6.1 illustrates that it is commonplace to misinterpret what is being said.

The research described in Scenario 6.1 was conducted with a younger group of children (aged 8-11 years) and it is likely that the youngest children in this age group will become easily distracted. Gibson's (2007) discussion of 'fatigue' during research with younger children is useful in this context. That is, the researcher has exhausted the child's interest in this aspect of the overall topic. Given the number of food items Daniel was given to look through it is likely he had seen at least one image of a fish. He probably was not listening to Joanna's follow-up question about the fairy cakes and had already moved on to thinking about other food choices he made (at home or at school). Joanna could assume a number of interpretations from what Daniel said. First, that all Daniel's 8-year-old friends brought fish to school in their lunchboxes instead of sweet or treat items and second, that Daniel liked tuna fish (possibly on his sandwiches in his lunchbox). It is of course unlikely that Daniel's 8-year-old friends bring fish to school in their lunchboxes.

It is essential as a researcher that you keep a sense of perspective and reality when researching with children and ask the same question in a number of ways at different times during the study (e.g. in a friendship interview or creative group) to ensure you understand what is being expressed. Some children, depending on age and development, are unable to deal with the complexities of open-ended questions and it may be that the use of closed questions can put less weight on the child's verbal ability (Wilson and Powell, 2001). In the scenario above, Joanna waited until the end of the discussion with Daniel and then summed up what she thought he had communicated during the interview. When she said 'And all your friends just have fish in their lunch boxes', he laughed and said 'No, but I like fish – and chips'.

There are then a number of 'learnings' from Scenario 6.1 that can be effective for using in other research projects. For example, ensure that there is enough time to cover all the topics needed in order to meet the research aim(s) and objectives. In the research design (e.g. creative group guide) make sure you ask the same question in a different way more than once. Regularly 'sum up' what the children tell you and ask them if that is 'correct' or 'right' – do not assume that you fully understand what is being expressed. There is, however, a fine line here as if the children become bored with the topic or want the research to come to an end they may agree with you so they can 'escape'. Try to be sensitive to their level of interest and do not seek a 'finite' answer. There are ideas, notions and concepts that children have that you will never understand and you have a limited time to consider the topic in question.

Offer the child/ren different contexts in which the activity or topic you are discussing can happen – do not assume what is 'normal' for them because of your own experiences (e.g. you might assume that the child sits with the rest of his/her family and eats an evening meal and your questions may reflect or reinforce this view). Allow the child the opportunity to express what is 'normal' for them. Give the child the opportunity at the end of the research to add or clarify any points they feel are important – do not 'rush' them or assume they are 'finished' telling you their views. Follow up with back translation where possible as this too will allow the children to clarify what was expressed and how it was interpreted by the researcher.

Listening and understanding to what children say in relation to a research topic will rarely be conducted in isolation. Indeed, effectively conducting the research you have planned will involve managing a variety of people with different responsibilities, priorities and personalities (Balen *et al.*, 2006; Wanat, 2008). Each will have an influence on the successful outcome of the research study although not all will contribute to the research study personally. The role of certain individuals (e.g. children, gatekeepers) will have a considerable impact on what happens during the research and examples of how this happens and how as a researcher you can manage and minimise the impact follows.

Listening to what Children Say

It is not unusual for novice researchers to say 'I couldn't get the children to say anything'. There may be a number of reasons for this, not least that as a (novice) researcher discussing ideas or concepts with children can be daunting (Hill, 1997). Researchers may feel the need to talk so that there are no silences but unless the children have an opportunity to speak they will feel less inclined to say anything. If, you are nervous, you may also think that the child or adolescent does not understand what you have asked and as such you ask the question in a variety of different ways in an effort to make them understand. However, this can be confusing for the child/ren you are researching with because they may not appreciate that they are being asked the same question in a different way but may simply perceive they are being asked a lot of different questions (and are not quite sure which one to answer first!). Whilst silences can become uncomfortable there is a balance between talking and allowing the time and space for answers.

There are a number of strategies to overcome the need to talk and these include making sure you have an 'ice-breaker' question (see ideas in Box 6.1). This is something the child or adolescent will find easy to answer and may be interested in. This will build their confidence and will help them become familiar with the way in which the researcher talks and asks questions. If the child appears nervous, have additional ice-breaker questions to hand or tell them something about yourself that they might find entertaining so that the pressure is not on them to speak before they feel comfortable to do so (see Box 6.2). If the child has been asked a question and they do not say anything, simply enquire if they can understand what has been asked of them. However, if they say they do understand but still do not say anything ask them to tell you what they think the question means. If the child then agrees that they do not understand what is being asked of them, then break the question into a number of parts. If the child is still unable to understand you may want to re-cap what it is that you are trying to find out. It may be that if they understand what you are trying to research they can contribute without having to go through the set of structured questions you have prepared. Be flexible and adaptable in your approach. Ensure that you have used at least one technique to engage the child (see Chapter 4) as, if they have already thought about the research (e.g. they have drawn a picture or taken a photograph, written a narrative or helped to make a collage), they are more likely to talk to a researcher about the topic.

> **Box 6.1:** Examples of ice breaker questions
>
> 1. What is your name and your favourite pizza?
> 2. If you were an animal what would you be and why?
> 3. Tell me your name and something about the shoes you are wearing.
> 4. Who is your favourite superhero?
> 5. What is your favourite kind of ice-cream?
> 6. What is your favourite TV programme or film and why?
> 7. How old are you?
> 8. Do you like playing sport? What kind?
> 9. If you could visit any place in the world where would you go?

Do not assume that if a child does not talk extensively that they have not thought about what you have asked them. The child may not have an opinion on what they are being asked or may not feel strongly about the topic area. The researcher needs to maintain a balance between asking too many and too few questions (Mauthner, 1997). Be sensitive to their level of interest and understand that an insight, however small, into the social world of a child can contribute to a more holistic understanding of the topic being researched.

Box 6.2: What children might want to know about the researcher

1.   What your favourite topic was at school and why

2.   If you have any pets and what they are called

3.   Interesting places you have visited

4.   Your favourite superhero

5.   Your favourite kind of chocolate bar

6.   How many brothers and sisters you have and how old they are

7.   Who your favourite teachers were at school and why

Children who like to talk (and know all the answers)

Although some children can be quiet and difficult to engage with, other children can be quite talkative (particularly when the topic is of particular interest to them) and the views of some young people are much more likely to be heard than those of others (McLeod, 2007). For example, teenagers will be consulted more often than younger children (Winter, 2006) whilst 'engaged' teenagers are more likely to represent the group than those who are disaffected (Cairns and Brannen, 2005). To ensure all children are able to contribute it may be useful for the children to take turns answering questions (Mauthner, 1997) although this may work better with younger children as older children may be able to sustain a discussion with little input from a researcher (Curtis *et al.*, 2004). Whilst talkative children can enhance the volume of data, as a researcher you will want a holistic view and as such it is important that all children have the opportunity to contribute. Where one or two children in particular dominate the conversation or 'answer' any questions you pose, you may want to consider if there is a special role that this child/ren can be allocated. Can they perhaps scribe what the other children say? Could they be the one that writes ideas or concepts on a piece of flip chart paper? Perhaps they can make notes about what you are asking or can write down their own ideas whilst others contribute theirs?

Children who do not want to engage

Whilst some children want to talk, others will refuse to engage. Collee (1992) indicates that it is important to let children set the agenda in conversation by avoiding questions and as such it is essential that children do not have to answer questions if they do not want to. Check carefully with these children who seem unwilling to engage if they want to take part in the study and reassure them that they can withdraw at any time. If they still want to continue make sure that they fully understand what is being asked of them. Occasionally children will be intrigued by a research topic but will not necessarily want to contribute verbally. They may just want to listen to what is being said. Research should not be considered as exclusionary and if those few children who want to listen to what is going on are not being disruptive or causing concern to the others, the researcher should not worry about what they are 'not' saying. The children may not want to talk because of the 'platform' they have been given (e.g. they are working in a creative group but would prefer a one-to-one interview). It may be that if the researcher talks to this child on a one-to-one basis that the child will offer up ideas or opinions on the task or topic being discussed. There are a number of reasons that children may not 'speak out' and these are detailed in Box 6.3.

Box 6.3: Reasons why children may not want to speak out

1. The child/ren may feel intimidated by other children in the group
2. The child/ren may not understand what is being asked of them
3. The child/ren may be interested in the topic but may not have an opinion on what is being discussed
4. The child/ren might not believe that what they say will be confidential
5. The child/ren is not feeling well/has had a poor night's sleep
6. The child/ren is shy (particularly with people unfamiliar to them)
7. The child/ren is bored
8. The child is easily distracted

Box 6.3 serves to illustrate that whilst planning and organisation are central to successful research studies with children, no one piece of research conducted with children will be without its surprises or challenges. Hopefully the children you research with will engage with the research topic you propose and, by using innovative techniques, the child/ren will both understand and be enthusiastic about the nature of the research. However, expecting the unexpected is a useful attitude to have and remaining calm and flexible in your approach to researching with children will be a great asset.

Children who want to become gatekeepers

If the gatekeeper is in view but is not engaging with the research process, it is not uncommon for a (self-appointed) child/ren to 'help' the researcher by providing information about their peers or by asking the other children to behave/keep quiet/speak out. Whilst a novice researcher may initially find this both endearing and helpful, it is confusing for the other children (in a creative research group, for example) who are unsure (and perhaps a little confused) about the ownership of the research and what their role ought to be. In the event of this becoming problematic first, thank the child/ren and tell them that they have been extremely helpful. Second, make eye contact and say to them that you are now going to ask all the children to help with the research study and ask them to sit down. If this is unsuccessful, if you are sitting down, simply stand up. This will automatically give you an 'adult role'. Speak clearly and calmly to all the children and reinforce your role and what you are proposing to explore.

Gatekeepers who want to become researchers

The degree to which a child engages with a researcher or a research topic may be influenced by the role of the gatekeeper (e.g. social worker, teacher or parent). Whilst it is essential that the research is conducted using an ethical approach and that the input of the gatekeeper in relation to a number of issues can be sought (e.g. level of literacy) the role of the researcher should be different to that of the gatekeeper. Whilst it would normally be considered bad practice for a project worker (gatekeeper) to be present during an interview, in some instances (e.g. when children are unfamiliar with group work) it can be considered as helpful (Curtis et al., 2004). The gatekeeper however should allow the researcher to conduct creative groups or scene interviews, for example, without interjecting or offering answers to the children involved. In some cases it is important to have the gatekeeper in view (e.g. if the children are known to have unpredictable behaviour, medical conditions or if the children are young and the researcher is inexperienced) but they should not contribute to the research by either asking their own questions or by indicating to the children that their responses are 'incorrect'.

The extent to which the children think the gatekeeper is listening or watching may also influence the type of data that is collated (see, for example, Irwin and Johnson, 2005). Depending on the extent of the data collection (e.g. if the research is being conducted in a variety of locations) differences in the 'findings' could be attributable to the role of gatekeeper as opposed to other moderating effects (e.g. socio-economic group, gender, etc.). As such, a consistent approach in relation to the role of the gatekeeper is necessary.

To manage the research process effectively in relation to the role of the gatekeeper it is important to identify any priorities or issues the gatekeeper has that need to be addressed before the research with children takes place (see, for example, Barker and Weller, 2003). It is useful to arrange with the gatekeeper that you will arrive at least ten minutes before researching with the children and ask the gatekeeper if you can run through with them what you propose to do. (NB the gatekeeper of the children you are researching with may not be the *same* gatekeeper who allowed you access – e.g. the head teacher may have given permission for you to have access to the children but the class teacher may not have met you before. If this is the case, the class teacher should still have been provided with information about the research topic and proposed research approach.) Provide the gatekeeper(s) with a short summary of the research proposal and the key areas you wish to address to refresh memories. Indicate the research approach you wish to take (e.g. friendship pairs, paired friends). If you have not already agreed a location for the research, ask the gatekeeper where the research should take place. If you feel the location will adversely impact on your research make an alternative suggestion. Respectfully explain that the children are not expected to provide 'correct answers' and that it is important that the children do not feel restricted in their responses in relation to the research. Additionally, respectfully ask the gatekeeper if he/she wishes to add their own thoughts or comments about the research topic or process that it is done outside the time you are able to spend researching with the children (unless the gatekeeper(s) considers the research to be causing embarrassment or discomfort to the child/ren).

Generally, if the gatekeeper(s) considers the researcher's approach to be professional and believes the research study to be well conceived and thought through then they are more likely to trust the researcher with the children. Where the gatekeepers believe the approach of the researcher is a haphazard one then they are more likely to involve themselves in the research study to ensure the safety of the children. Remember that the gatekeeper's responsibility is *not* to the researcher but to the children.

It may be in an educational setting that the gatekeeper is also the researcher (as in Appendix 3 on the 'Impact of creating dyslexia friendly classrooms on children's learning'). Homan (2001) discusses the problems that can arise as a consequence of this (e.g. lack of consent). However, as can been seen from the excerpt from Appendix 3 below, in the case of researching the creation of dyslexia-friendly classrooms the study has been rigorously planned with clear aims and objectives and measurable outcomes.

> To launch the research and provide the professional development necessary for it to proceed the Adviser led a joint INSET day involving the head teachers, teachers, teaching assistants and SENCos from each of the participating schools. This provided a forum to disseminate information, time for discussion and allowed for the training to be adapted to specific needs. During the final session participants worked in their school teams to discuss the issues relevant to them and to agree future actions based on the information provided. Using outcomes from the INSET day, each SENCo then wrote an action plan outlining how the project would be developed in school. This was linked to the SDP (School Development Plan) and indicated clear timescales and success criteria in order for these to be evaluated at the end of the project.

Gatekeepers and Power

There are instances where the gatekeeper(s) will be reluctant to be 'in view' or 'out of sight' of the children they have been charged with looking after (and whose ultimate safety is their responsibility). Where gatekeepers are aware of behavioural issues in relation to the children or are concerned about the nature of the research topic they may prefer to be 'in view' or 'in hearing distance' of what is being discussed. There are a variety of reasons for this which may include the gatekeeper not having been fully informed of the research study or approach (as access has been permitted by someone else in authority) and is unsure, suspicious or sceptical about it. Alternatively, the researcher may inadvertently get involved in internal politics. The researcher can be made to feel uncomfortable because whilst access may have been granted by a higher authority, the secondary gate-keeper may feel that this research study has been foisted upon them and may insist on being either (a) more involved in the research or (b) dismissive of it. To avoid this it is always better to try and develop a relationship with all relevant gatekeepers *before* going to the school/hospital/community centre where the re-search will be conducted as gatekeepers can have a positive effect on the research (Cree *et al.*, 2002). Where this is not possible, try to be flexible in your approach and be sensitive to the roles of all gatekeepers. It may be that gatekeepers are aware of power plays within groups (particularly amongst adolescents) and they may feel it is important to remain 'in contact' during the research. Knowledge is power and with specific reference to researching with children, the researcher (and where appropriate the gatekeeper) should consider not only what the children are being asked to contribute in relation to the topic being researched but the way in which that information is being 'shared' within or across groups.

It is important for the researcher (and where appropriate the gatekeeper) to consider how the information given by the children may be used or recounted by other children once the research is complete and the researcher is no longer present. For example, the smaller the number of children interviewed by a re-searcher at any one time may facilitate anonymity or confidentiality whereas conducting research with children in creative or focus groups may raise issues of 'in-group' confidentiality. Children have to understand that what they say in front of one another in the context of the research project should not be repeated (or 'used') elsewhere unless with the permission of the child that made the con-tribution. This is a considerable responsibility for children and it may be easier to convey this responsibility to adolescents (as opposed to younger children). Gatekeepers may be best placed to advise researchers on power plays within and across groups.

Gatekeepers and Conflicting Advice

Although policies and practices differ across disciplines when accessing and re-searching with children (see Chapter 2), gatekeepers will always make their deci-sions about involvement with research projects by taking into account the best interests of the children for whom they are responsible. However, not all gate-keepers will offer the same guidance when researchers seek advice on the best research approach to take (e.g. using friendship pairs, creative groups, etc.) as all gatekeepers have different levels of experience with a variety of young children and adolescent groups. This can be confusing for the researcher but taking into account the views of the gatekeeper is likely to enhance the data. When gate-keepers have differing views in the same locale or the advice given by different gatekeepers influences the data collection process (e.g. one gatekeeper advises friendship pairs and another advises creative groups) problems can arise. It is important that the research is conducted in a consistent manner to ensure that comparability between groups is credible. Gatekeepers may also have different views on incentives. Curtis *et al.* (2004: 169) note that the behaviour of children and teenagers may be used by gatekeepers as an inclusion criterion for access to the research process with participation viewed as a 'reward' and exclusion seen as a 'punishment'. This clearly would have an impact on the sampling frame and should be avoided. Try to ensure any incentive is equitable across groups.

Setting Parameters and Boundaries

If the gatekeeper is 'in view' or nearby but not necessarily 'in charge', the researcher may find it useful to establish a few 'ground rules' for the duration of the research. These ground rules are likely to be different depending on the type of research method employed and the age of the children involved. If the research method involves smaller groups of children (e.g. interviews or friendship pairs) it is likely that the researcher will be able to be reasonably flexible in their approach. However, when conducting research with larger groups of children or a group that may be predisposed to push boundaries (and the gatekeeper(s) may be able to advise you here) then the ground rules suggested in Box 6.4 may be a useful starting point.

Box 6.4: Suggested ground rules to be employed when researching with children

1. If one person is speaking, no one else is to speak
2. Everyone is to respect what others have to say even if they do not agree with what they think
3. Avoid the use of inappropriate language
4. Wait until a person has finished speaking before you give your thoughts or opinions
5. Mobile phones should be switched off
6. Headphones (from iPods, for example) should be removed
7. It is important to listen to everyone's contribution to prevent repetition

---

Important to note here also is the type of approach adopted by the researcher in relation to the behaviour of the children. Gersh and Nolan (1994), for example, suggest that researchers adopt a 'non-judgemental' view in the context of the research. However, as Curtis *et al.* (2004: 172) ask, just how non-judgemental should researchers be when dealing with racist or homophobic behaviour? It is useful in these cases as a researcher to make your views clear and to challenge the young people to think about their opinions and the way in which they are expressed. Nuttall and Tinson (2005) illustrate that younger children are as likely to use homophobic language as older children (although they are probably less likely to realise the significance or consequences of their choice of language). There is a fine line between being judgemental and expressing your own views but it is important to consider what young people might say during the research so that as a researcher you can prepare for, and when necessary, employ a strategy for dealing with, for example, racist or homophobic behaviour should it occur.

Other suggestions for conducting successful research with younger children (in school) are provided in Box 6.5.

Box 6.5: An expert view for research success with younger children

1. Use sticky white labels to identify the researcher's name and those of the children
2. Have toilet breaks otherwise the research will be disrupted regularly
3. Let the children go at their own pace
4. Acknowledge any response the children give
5. Make sure you have eye contact
6. The classroom assistant may be a good ally
7. Show by example (e.g. manners, behaviour etc.)
8. Make sure the children understand the role of gatekeeper (teacher) in the context of the research
9. If there is a fire alarm stay calm
10. Keep smiling!

Finally, if the gatekeeper is not 'in view' make sure you have the school's office telephone number in your mobile phone in cases of emergency

S.B. Nimmo, primary school head teacher, 33 years

Technology and Equipment

Appendix 2 considers the cumulative impact of alcohol marketing on youth drinking and illustrates that even with careful planning and organisation, recording equipment can fail. Whilst it is possible to ensure during the planning stage that equipment is in full working order and replacements are at hand (where possible) there are instances when the technology simply will not meet the needs and expectations of the researcher. This can have a significant impact on data collection particularly when the research is technology based, for example, the researcher is using a computer simulation or an online questionnaire. It may also be that you have a film clip or an advert to stimulate discussion but that the TV or DVD equipment is not as up-to-date as you had anticipated and you are unable to conduct that particular task. If any of the above scenarios happen, it is important to consider the extent to which this will have an impact on the data collection and if the research should be rescheduled (see 'Best laid plans' below). If you are planning to use technology and/or equipment it is always useful to have a contingency plan (see Chapter 5).

In some respects, finding out that the technology or equipment does not work *before* the research takes place, is the best case scenario. Sometimes when re-cording equipment fails it does so in the middle of an interview and because as a researcher you will be concentrating on the interview and not on the recording equipment it is possible that only after the interview is complete will you realise that only half of the interview has been recorded. As such it is best practice that before the research takes place ensure when you set up the equipment that it is in full working order. Whilst conducting the research, check at least once that the equipment is still running. Once the data collection is complete listen to the recording as soon after the interview as possible because if the recording is poor or non-existent you will have to write down as much as you can remember from the interview as soon as possible.

Miscellaneous

Aside from any issues that might arise from the research method, research topic or the engagement of the children with the research, there are other issues that might impact on the data collection. The safety of the children you are research-ing with is paramount and as such taking the following into account is best practice.

Fire Alarms

It may be that when you are conducting research with children that a fire alarm will go off. This could be a 'real' fire alarm or a 'test' but either way you should be aware of the nearest fire exit and where you should assemble if you have to leave the building. It is best practice to ask before you start researching with children (in school, in hospital, in a community centre) if there is a planned fire alarm test. If there is a planned fire alarm test, the gatekeeper will be able to tell you what time the alarm will be sounded and how long to expect the alarm to be sounded for. If no fire alarm test is planned and if an alarm is sounded at anytime during the research, assume it is an actual fire alarm (unless you know it is a bell to alert pupils to change class, for example). Leave all research materials and equipment, collect the children together and leave the building by the designated exit. Do not take any risks and follow procedure at all times.

First Aid/Health Related Issues

Similarly, if the child/ren you are researching with begin to feel unwell during the research or for whatever reason may need first aid (e.g. they accidentally cut themselves with scissors) it is useful to know the procedure for dealing with situations that may require minor medical treatment. If the children have medical conditions (e.g. epilepsy or a severe allergic reaction to bee stings or nuts) it is also useful to know this information so that in the event of a medical emergency you are in control of the situation. If you are researching in the area of health, it is of course more likely that medical conditions will be a more regular occurrence (see, for example, Broome *et al.*, 2001). However, this does not mean that minor or major health issues might also arise in a school or community centre setting.

Best Laid Plans

It would be unusual, but if a myriad of these issues outlined above happened in quick succession or one pertinent issue (e.g. a fire alarm) meant that the research could no longer be conducted, the researcher should not feel disheartened but simply admit that it would be better to reschedule the research. It is important to be both flexible and adaptable but there are times when it is easier to admit that the opportunity to collect reliable data has passed and that another day and time would be more suitable to conduct research with children. If this does happen, reschedule the research as soon as possible and have a positive attitude when you return. The children may remember that you tried to research with them before but they will be guided by you as to how to treat the 'false start'. Go to the venue thinking that you will enjoy the experience and try not to worry about or focus on what happened before.

Summary

This chapter was designed to illustrate the different ways in which conducting research with children can have an element of surprise. It is not written in order to make the (novice) researcher think that researching with children is difficult or, in some cases impossible, but simply to show what can happen. It may be that when you conduct your research with children, none of the above happens and your planning and organisation pay dividends. It may also be the case, however, that regardless of how well you have conceived and thought through your research approach, the mitigating factors outlined here impact on the quality and quantity of your data. This chapter is certainly not to dissuade researchers from considering researching with children but is to reinforce that doing so can be challenging at times. If the researcher is aware of what might happen then forewarned is forearmed and what may have been surprising becomes more routine and easier to manage.

Reflective Questions

1   Describe the issues associated with listening to children effectively and how these might be addressed.

2   Why is it that some children are more likely to be heard than others?

3   How would you deal with a child who dominates a discussion?

4   What should you do if a child does not engage with the research?

5   How should you manage the role of the gatekeeper during the research?

6   What should you do if you receive conflicting advice from different gate-keepers?

7   If you are planning to use equipment/technology what should you do to minimise any problems that might arise?

8   If there are a number of problems that arise in quick succession during the research and your work with the children is disrupted, what should you do?

Checklist

☐   Do you understand how important it is to maintain a positive attitude whilst researching with children?

☐   Will you remember to ask the child/ren in a variety of ways what they think and regularly summarise what they have said to you so that you can clarify what has been said and how you have interpreted it?

☐   Have you considered which appropriate ice-breaker questions you will use?

☐   Will you consider what boundaries or parameters you might set during the research to help collect the best quality data?

☐   Have you considered how to deal with both talkative and quiet children?

☐   Do you know what information the gatekeeper may require to facilitate the research process?

☐   Will you remember to ask about fire alarm tests and any medical conditions you need to be aware of?

☐   Will you remember to ask for a (class) list of those taking part so that you can be specific when referring to the children you are researching with?

References

Balen, R., Blyth, E., Calabretto, H., Fraser, C., Horrocks, C. and Manby, M. (2006) 'Involving children in health and social research: "human becomings" or "active beings"?', *Childhood*, 13, 29-48.

Barker, J. and Weller, S. (2003) 'Geography of methodological issues in research with children', *Qualitative Research*, **3** (2), 207-227.

Broome, M.E., Richards, D.J. and Hall, J.M. (2001) 'Children in research: the experience of ill children and adolescents', *Journal of Family Nursing*, **7** (1), 32-49.

Cairns, L. and Brannen, M. (2005) 'Promoting the human rights of children and young people – the "investing in children" experience', *Adoption and Fostering*, **29**, 78-87.

Collee, J.C. (1992) 'From the mouths of babes', *The Observer*, 20 December.

Cree, V.E., Kay, H. and Tisdall, K. (2002) 'Research with children: sharing the dilemmas', *Child and Family Social Work*, **7** (1), 47-56.

Curtis, K., Roberts, H., Copperman, J., Downie, A. and Liabo, K. (2004), '"How come I don't get asked no questions?" – researching "hard to reach" children and teenagers', *Child and Family Social Work*, **9**, 167-175.

Darbyshire, P., MacDougall, C. and Schiller, W. (2005) 'Multiple methods in qualitative research with children: more insight or just more?', *Qualitative Research*, **5** (4), pp.417-436

Gersh, I.S. and Nolan, A. (1994) 'Exclusions: what the children think', *Educational Psychology in Practice*, **10**, 35-39.

Gibson, F. (2007) 'Conducting focus groups with children and young people: strategies for success', *Journal of Research in Nursing*, **12**, 473 - 483.

Hill, M. (1997) 'Participatory research with children', *Child and Family Social Work*, **2** (3), 171-183.

Homan, R. (2001) 'The principle of assumed consent: the ethics of gatekeeping', *Journal of Philosophy of Education*, **35** (3), 329-343.

Irwin, L.G. and Johnson, J. (2005) 'Interviewing young children: explicating our practices and dilemmas', *Qualitative Health Research*, **15** (6), 821-831.

Mauthner, M. (1997) 'Methodological aspects of collecting data from children: lessons from three research projects', *Children and Society*, **11**, 16-28.

McLeod, A. (2007) 'Whose agenda? Issues of power and relationship when listening to looked-after young people', *Child and Family Social Work*, **12**, 278-286.

Nuttall, P. and Tinson, J. (2005) 'Exploring peer group influence by considering the use and consumption of popular music among early adolescents', *Marketing Review*, **5** (4), 357-370.

Wanat, C.L. (2008) 'Getting past the gatekeepers: differences between access and cooperation in public school research', *Field Methods*, **20**, 191-208.

Wilson, C. and Powell, M. (2001) *A Guide to Interviewing Children: Essential Skills for Counsellors, Police, Lawyers and Social Workers*, London: Routledge

Winter, K. (2006) 'Widening our knowledge concerning young looked after children: the case for research using sociological models of childhood', *Child and Family Social Work*, **11**, 55-64.

7 Analysing and Interpreting the Data

- To identify a variety of approaches that can be employed to analyse qualitative research

- To explore the ways in which analysis and interpretation overlap

- To establish the importance of 'shared meaning' and how this can be achieved through back translation, dual moderation and multiple researchers

- To consider types of quantitative data and how to code, examine and analyse numerically

- To summarise the issues associated with mixed methods analysis.

Introduction

Having successfully completed an ethical, engaging piece of research with children, the challenge that must now be met is that of analysing and interpreting the data. It is important, in order to ensure your study continues to be cohesive and focused, to review the initial aim(s) and objectives of the research before embarking on any analysis or interpretation. What did you hope to achieve overall? What 'themes' or concepts were you exploring? Did you pose questions and have these been addressed? Did the research raise issues or ideas that had not previously been considered? Once you have refamiliarised yourself with the context of your research study, you can begin to analyse and interpret the data. This chapter is designed to facilitate this process and is in three parts. In the first part, tried and tested methods which describe how to systematically analyse qualitative research will be discussed. This will be followed by an examination of qualitative analysis and interpretation by considering the possible outcomes from research approaches discussed in Chapter 3. In the second part, analysing quantitative research will be explored with some practical advice on how to interpret the findings of the research study. Third, mixed methods analysis will also be addressed.

It is important to note that whilst analytical methods for qualitative research are being described in the following section to demonstrate ways in which 'sense can be made' of the data, it is difficult to clearly separate analysis and interpretation as the two partly overlap (Gummesson, 2005). Analysis and interpretation are not necessarily discrete activities nor do they occur in ordered sequential fashion (Spiggle, 1994). Although analysis in the following section is primarily associated with techniques (to ensure studies can be replicated and/or are rigorous in their research design) and is therefore more readily associated with quantitative approaches, it is recognised that qualitative 'analysis and interpretations are part and parcel of the same issue' (Gummesson, 2005: 311).

Qualitative Research Approaches to Analysing Qualitative Data

Across disciplines (see for example: Spiggle, 1994; Jones, 2000; Mulhall, 2003; Gummesson, 2005) it is recognised that analysing qualitative research can be problematic. These concerns normally involve issues of reliability and imprecise modes of data analysis. Providing a structure for the data may ensure that the analysis is more comprehensive and often researchers will categorise and analyse thematically the data they have collected in order to provide a structure to their findings (see, for example, Coffey and Atkinson, 1996; Woods *et al.*, 2005; Sanders and Munford, 2005; Dagkas and Stathi, 2007; Horstman *et al.*, 2008). Although the issues with qualitative analysis (e.g. interpretation, the role of the researcher in the data collection, shared meaning, etc.) are not confined to researching with children, (novice) researchers are often unsure how to collect their thoughts about what they have uncovered. The following approaches may assist in structuring and interpreting the data.

The Ritchie and Spencer (1994) Framework analysis method is one which is widely used in social science and has been used to analyse data generated by health, education and social research (see, for example, Jones, 2000; Russell *et al.*, 2004). It is a method for analysing qualitative research data and it was developed in the 1980s by the Qualitative Research Unit at the National Centre for Qualitative Research in the UK. This method depends on the manual coding, charting and mapping of data and can principally be used for analysing interviews, creative (focus) groups and diaries (unstructured).

'Framework' comprises of five stages:

- *Familiarisation*: At this stage the researcher should have an overview of the range and diversity of material which has been gathered. Essentially, familiarisation allows the researcher to become immersed in the data, while listing key themes and recurrent ideas.

- *Identifying a Thematic Framework*: During this stage, the key issues, concepts and themes are further explored and a framework model can be developed by drawing upon a priori issues and emergent issues as highlighted by the interviewees, the researcher and analytical themes emerging from recurrence of particular experiences (see, for example, Table 8.1).

- *Indexing*: Having developed the thematic framework, the data collated from the interviews is systematically indexed.

- *Charting*: This stage involves compiling charts for each subject area with headings and subheadings drawn from the index. This allows comparison between the themes and issues as dictated by the respondents. The transcripts should also be referenced to allow each source to be identified.

- *Mapping and Interpretation*: At this stage, the key characteristics are drawn together to interpret the overall data. The information is used to find associations between the salient issues and should be governed by the original research questions. The associations should be mapped in the confines of the data and alternative explanations should be sought and uniformly appraised against the actual data.

If the field of qualitative research badly needs explicit, systematic methods for drawing conclusions (Miles and Huberman, 1984), then the strength of Framework is that it gives this process clarity. It provides a trace to the original data which other forms of qualitative analysis do not readily allow (see, for example, Patton, 2002). As this approach allows both the charting and mapping of the analysis, there is confidence in this method because of the visible nature of the thoughts and ideas which have been generated. As the procedures for this particular analysis are repetitive, the reliability of the interpretation is enhanced because of its rigour and systematic nature. It also prevents the researcher being caught between succumbing to confusion and choosing some simple and plausible but false explanation. Framework is also driven by the original data. A full review, as opposed to a selective reflection, of the material is possible.

Framework, of course, is not the only way to analyse qualitative data. Alternative analytic approaches are detailed in Table 7.1 and illustrate common methods employed to sort, organise, conceptualise, refine and interpret data.

Box 7.1 is an example of where the constant comparative method has been used to explore the concepts of 'borrowing' and 'sharing' between adolescent sisters. This illustrates the way in which social processes can explain something of human behaviour and experiences.

Type of approach	Key characteristics	Relevant analysis of children's research
Constant comparative analysis	As social phenomena are recorded and classified, they are also compared across categories. This involves taking one interview, one statement or one theme and comparing it with all others that may be similar/different to develop ideas about the possible relations between pieces of data Well suited to grounded theory Simultaneous comparison of all social incidents to help explain something of human behaviour and experiences	Fredricks et al., 2002 Rollins, 2005 Tinson and Nuttall, 2007 Pickler, 2007 Marshman and Hall, 2008
Phenomeno-logical	Seeks to discover the underlying structure of experience through intensive study of individual cases and more importantly how individuals make sense of their own experiences Is the philosophical science of consciousness Explicitly avoids cross comparison Set aside preconceptions and focuses not on objects but on perceptions of objects	Miller, 2003 Roose and John, 2003 Grover, 2004 De Mol and Buysse, 2008
Ethnographic	Immersion and engagement in fieldwork or participant observation Analysis uses an iterative process in which cultural ideas that arise during active involvement during the 'research' are transformed, translated or represented in a written document This analysis involves sifting and sorting through pieces of data to detect and interpret thematic categorisations, search for inconsistencies and contradictions Generate conclusions about what is happening and why	Harness Goodwin, 2002 Mulhall, 2003 Maybin, 2006
Narrative and discourse analysis	Narrative analysis recognises the extent to which the stories we tell provide insights about our lived experiences Relationship between language and the contexts in which it is used Key elements such as lexicon, phonology and grammar, for example help linguists identify and interpret samples of spoken text Discourse analysis principally tries to understand what is represented by the various ways in which people communicate ideas	Mills, 2001 Driessnack, 2006 Nicolopoulou and Richner, 2007

Table 7.1: Approaches to Analysing Data

Box 7.1: Exploring Familial Intra-generational Borrowing and Sharing

Adapted from Tinson and Nuttall, 2007

Siblings

Little research currently exists that has examined sibling influence and extended family systems beyond the parent–child relationships (Lawson and Brossart, 2004). Yet siblings can and do act as a relevant peer group for each other and may socialise each other to similar attitudes and behaviours.

Method

Teenage participants were sought to take part in this study as they were considered to be most likely to be frequently engaged in borrowing and sharing during adolescence and would be relatively close in age. Female siblings were the focus of this study. A local secondary school was most helpful in providing a purposive sample (Mills, 2001), a room and a timetable for the researcher to interview the respondents. The school duly produced a cross-sample of sisters varying in age, family type and socio-economic group. This research then involved 15 in-depth 'paired' interviews with 30 adolescent sisters. The school also carried the responsibility of writing to the parents and obtaining consent for the research to be conducted and during school time. It is important to note that the interviews were conducted just prior to the school holidays so that the chances of the girls missing salient information during class was minimised.

Data Analysis

The analysis of the data explored themes in the responses of siblings using the constant comparative method (Alvesson and Deetz 2000; Silverman, 2004) and analytic induction (Bryman and Burgess, 1994). Once the data was collected it was sorted before it was analysed. Interviews were taped and transcribed, field notes collated and observations written up.

The raw data was then written up as a mini case and were informed by the case study approach (Gummesson, 2003). The mini cases were then compared and analysed to determine categories and general patterns of borrowing and sharing activity.

Each incident was continually compared with others within the emergent categories to refine both description and explanation. Themes were identified and the data was examined and explored for detail relating to these themes.

Summary of Findings

The overall findings from the interviews conducted with pairs of sisters illustrated that borrowing and sharing are commonplace amongst sisters but that whilst sharing is frequent between sisters it is quite a different concept to borrowing. Sharing tends to be imposed (usually by the mother and/or other family members) whilst borrowing is an 'exchange' only between the siblings (where family members are only drawn in when conflict arises).

Analysis and Interpretation

Not all researchers agree on how to analyse and interpret qualitative data and there are researchers who suggest that it is difficult to disentangle analysis and interpretation (Luckman, 1999; Punch, 2002; Gummeson, 2005). Gummesson provides his own strategies for analysis and interpretation which may be useful to researchers analysing and interpreting the data they collected when researching with children. The most pertinent of these strategies are summarised as follows.

It is difficult to isolate the data into 'parts' so look for synergies (the working together of two or more people or things, especially when the result provides greater depth than the sum of their individual effects or capabilities). Look for causality and understanding. Gummeson advocates the constant comparative method (see Table 7.1) and suggests that data should be compared with data, existing theory and with results from previous research. Continuous comparison is part of the sense-making process. Further to this, he suggests recognising the role of the researcher in the data collection. He also proposes to reduce data to make it more manageable but stresses the importance of not losing its richness or depth. Given that richness, it may not always be possible to be transparent. Indeed trying to fulfil requirements for reliability and replication is difficult. However it is important to be rigorous and systematic with data and sources. For example, interviewing adolescents about their attitudes towards contraception may elicit socially desirable responses depending on the context of the interview and the 'self' the adolescent may want to convey. Finally to increase credibility, the researcher should offer possible alternative interpretations and argue both for and against them. When causal explanations are straightforward, however, they should be dealt with accordingly.

Shared Meaning

One way to ensure a reliable interpretation of the qualitative data you have collated whilst researching with children is to ask them if you have correctly interpreted what they said and did. As Chapter 3 suggested the 'philosophical stance' of the researcher is less important than having a *shared meaning* or understanding between the adult researcher and the young people or persons with whom the research is being conducted. The data analysis should also be conducted with this in mind. That is, interpretation of what has been said or done in a given context should be understood by the researcher and those being researched – and the understanding should be the *same*. This is also known as 'respondent validation' (Dagkas and Stathi, 2007).

There are a number of ways to ensure the quality of the qualitative data and the resulting analysis and interpretation. One way to find out if you have correctly interpreted the data is simply to ask the children you were researching with what they 'meant' by the data that has been produced (e.g. photograph, drawing or dialogue). Bolton *et al.* (2001) discuss 'meaning' and interpretation in the context of photographs and illustrate that it is easy to misconstrue visual data. A boy, aged 12, kept a diary for these researchers and used photographs to help construct his biography. He had a picture taken of himself on a quad bike and the researchers could have interpreted this as a child showing off his treasured possession. However, he took the photo to show that he uses the quad bike to help his father on their farm check on the animals. As such, the 'meaning' of the photograph changes considerably. Backett-Milburn and McKie (1999) also support a qualitative as opposed to a quantitative approach to analysing both drawings and the associated written material.

It is likely that 'explaining' what is meant by photos, drawings or dialogue will be easier for the children the older they are although younger children too can 'create and insist' on meaning (Rasmussen, 1999). It is best practice when researching with children to ask them about what you have 'found out' as a matter of course. Older children can be asked to read transcripts of their interviews or can be invited to review visual recordings of the research in which they were actively engaged. Additional ideas for engaging older children in the analysis and interpretation can be found in Chapter 9. This approach, known as back translation, is not always possible. This may be because of limited access to the children, a limited amount of time for the project or children's lack of engagement with the research. In these circumstances and/or when the researcher deems it necessary, the research design (see Chapter 3) can employ dual moderation or observation. That is, an additional researcher(s) can be actively engaged or can simply observe the research process. When the analysis and interpretation is conducted the additional researcher(s) can give their input and/or provide their own analysis of the data. Inconsistencies between the researchers' analyses can be discussed until an agreed 'interpretation' is arrived at (see, for example, Broome *et al.*, 2001; Fredricks *et al.*, 2002; Sanders and Munford, 2005; Horstman *et al.*, 2008).

Occasionally, researchers who have not been engaged in the fieldwork but who have been either part of the overall project or are familiar with the practices of researching with children will follow these same principles to ensure reliability of interpretation. This too is good practice although it may not be as effective as observing or engaging in the fieldwork in person.

The following section details specific guidance for interpreting and analysing data. These suggestions for data analysis complement the methods suggested in Chapter 3 for engaging the children you are researching with.

Participant Observer

As identified in Chapter 3, participant observation is an aspect of ethnographic research and ethnographers interpret the processes and products of cultural behaviour. If, as a researcher, you have chosen to employ an ethnographic approach it is likely that ideas about 'culture' will have been raised during the time you have spent being actively involved with the children. As a participant observer, you will have made field notes about your observations of this (perceived) 'culture'. Van Maanen (1988), Sanjek (1990) and Emerson *et al.* (1995) address the issue of field notes, their form, meaning, use and construction (Mulhall, 2003). Specific ideas on what field notes should refer to (and which are detailed in Chapter 3) include the suggestions of Silverman (1993) and Kelly *et al.*, (2000) who hold that details about the environment in which the study was being conducted are vital in providing a context to any dialogue. Other information that could be noted in the context of researching with children may encompass information about the gatekeepers as well as the children (how they behave and interact), rituals performed (daily activities), special events (e.g. birthdays) and reflective pieces about how the study is forming and your role in the study. This can then be interpreted to provide an account of the culture and associated practices which have been observed.

Regardless of how these notes have been structured, it is now necessary to transform these ideas into a written report or document and this will involve looking for themes, categories, similarities and contradictions. This will ensure that you are able to generate 'conclusions' from what you have observed over time. There are a number of ways of conveying these conclusions (Van Maanen, 1988). A realist approach suggests that the researcher is an impersonal channel through which information simply flows to the reader and has only been interpreted by the ethnographer. By contrast a confessional approach ensures that the reader is aware of the researcher's personal experiences but that these remain independent from the account of what happened 'in the field'. Impressionists provide accounts of different situations and allow the reader to draw their own conclusions. Regardless of how these conclusions are conveyed, additional reading on interpreting this fieldwork is recommended (see 'Reading list – ethnographic interpretation').

In Appendix 3 the data collection was twofold – observation of and questionnaires administered to the children. In analysing the observed behaviour an ethnographic approach was taken (see Table 7.1). Throughout the course of the project outlined in Appendix 3 the interim meetings were used to share observations, reflect upon the issues arising and consider reasons for these. At the end of the project, the varied collection of data was sifted to identify common themes and contradictions. This proved to be of particular significance as several anomalies were detected in some children's use of the questionnaire which, when taken into consideration with the data as a whole, indicated a possible misunderstanding of certain questions. Conclusions were then formed on the basis of this interrogation and discussion.

Paired Friends or Friendship Pairs

It is likely that either of these approaches to researching with children (paired friends or friendship pairs) will have been conducted using an interview method. As such, the interview may have been either audio and/or visually recorded (see Chapters 2 and 3 for guidance on ethics and method). You will either transcribe the interview and/or review a visual recording of the interview to facilitate your data analysis. The data analysis techniques outlined in Table 7.1 and described earlier in this chapter will ensure that you are able to effectively structure and interpret the data that has been collated. Whilst researchers may be more familiar with written text, the following will help when considering what to explore when analysing visually recorded images.

♦ What are the dynamics between the children?

♦ How often do they look at one another?

♦ Why do you think they are looking at one another? (e.g. seeking support or illustrating confusion, etc.).

♦ What do the facial expressions tell you about the topic under discussion? (e.g. happiness, discomfort, confusion, contentment etc.).

♦ Are there gestures made between the children? If so, what are they and do they impact on speech or movement?

♦ Does one look at the other before speaking (e.g. for reassurance or permission to speak)? How closely or how far apart are they sitting?

♦ Does this seating arrangement remain constant throughout the interview (e.g. are there periods of association or disassociation)?

♦ Is this a reflection on the research topic under discussion?

♦ How do they manage any tasks that they are given?

♦ Is one non-verbally 'in charge' of the task(s) (e.g. distributing the material or pointing at what needs to be done)?

♦ Do they equally share the writing or drawing or does one scribe and one watch and/or give advice/an opinion?

♦ Do they whisper to one another to exclude the researcher and, if so, why might that be?

♦ Do they play up to the camera? If so, what do you think they are trying communicate (e.g. what is it saying about them and how they are positioning themselves in this situation)?

These probes are certainly not exhaustive and it can be difficult to take a structured approach to visually recorded data.

> Highly systematic transcription schemes developed for linguistic analysis do not necessarily accommodate the complexity of dynamic visual data [and whilst the researcher] cannot reproduce all the observed interaction...all

data [has to be analysed] so that the passages selected for presentation are informed by analysis and interpretation of the complete data set.

(Flewitt, 2006: 45)

That is, the visually recorded data ought to support and reflect the verbal communication. Matching verbal and visual data can be problematic – particularly for the untrained or inexperienced researcher. When considering whether to use visually recorded data, it is also useful to consider what this will add to your research and how you will analyse all of the data you have collated.

When researching with children you may also have actively engaged them in a task and analysing what has been produced can be facilitated by reading the next section.

Creative (Focus) Groups

As suggested in Chapter 4, employing techniques to enhance children's enjoyment and engagement with research can produce better quality data. For example, using the draw and write technique with children can encourage the active participation of children (Banister and Booth, 2005) and can also be less intimidating than one-to-one interviews (Hood *et al.*, 1996). Rose (2001), however, illustrates the complexities of interpreting the images produced by the children. She indicates that there are three aspects to a drawing created by a young person and these are: the production of image, the image itself and the audience for whom the image is intended.

To this end, there will be three levels of interpretation. First, the technological aspect of creation should be considered (e.g. what materials were used and why). The researcher should explore why particular colours of pen, pencils or crayons were chosen and why a particular size or colour of paper was decided upon and the relevance of this. Second, the compositional aspect of the drawing should be considered. The researcher should be concerned with what the children has drawn (is it a picture or a series or pictures or is it merely a symbol or shape?). Has the child used letters or words in the picture? Can the child describe what they have drawn and provide a context to the image? Finally the researcher should be aware that the child has created the image because they have been requested to do so and as such the image will be one which they believe the 'audience' will want. This can be considered the social aspect. As a consequence, when discussing and interpreting the image with the child/ren it is important to remember that whilst this technique is 'projective' and as such more reflective of inner feelings, the creation of the image will be influenced by the 'audience' for whom the picture is being produced.

Scene Interviews

It may be that you have provided an image or scene for the children or adolescents that you are researching with and that this has prompted a discussion or provided a foundation on which to build a series of questions (see Chapter 4 for the implications of choosing an image for discussion). To this end, it may be less important to analyse the image or scene and more important to structure your analysis based on the discussion. As before, using one of the methods outlined earlier in this section will facilitate analysis of transcriptions of the data. If there is visually recorded data to analyse, considering the movements, gaze and non-verbal communication (as outlined in the section on 'Paired friends or friendship pairs' above) should be a useful aid to analysis. Of course scene interviews are likely to involve a greater number of young people so the dynamics under consideration will also include, for example, peer friendships, status within the cohort, responses to communication strategies by different players in the group, activity type and control of activity. The person conducting the analysis will also have to bear in mind the context of the scene or image used in the interview or group situation. That is, if the scene or image was given to the children prior to or during interview. Either way, the introduction of the scene or image chosen may have an effect on the ensuing discussion.

Diary Studies

Diary studies can be analysed using either qualitative analysis techniques as outlined above or quantitative analysis (see 'Quantitative analysis' below). The type of analysis employed will be directly related to the aim(s) and objectives of your research and this may be coupled with your research philosophy. Jones (2000) discusses the analysis of an unstructured diary and employs the Framework method (Ritchie and Spencer, 1994). He finds that there are drawbacks to employing this approach to analysing data particularly as the concepts are heavily rooted in a priori issues (i.e. Framework is based on generating ideas from a literature review before conducting fieldwork). To that end, he suggests that it may be easier to use a qualitative software analysis tool such as NUD*IST to facilitate analysis and interpretation for unstructured diaries. Software packages can be useful to help researchers analyse qualitative data generally but it is important to remember that regardless of the software package used, the 'thinking' still has to done by the researcher. That is, NUD*IST or Nvivo will help you organise your thoughts but these thoughts will still be yours. This is true of software employed for both qualitative and quantitative research.

Quantitative Analysis

Quantitative data is typically gathered via questionnaire instruments giving a numerical output that can be transformed into 'meaningful' results. The questionnaire however, is not the only form of quantitative data, and it is useful to think of quantitative data as any form of research that offers some form of numerical output. This can range from a content analysis of 10 semi-structured diaries, through to a large-scale survey involving thousands of responses. Regardless of the amount of data produced, analysis is required to generate meaning. In order to achieve this, some form of quantitative analysis must be performed. The techniques involved in quantitative analysis range from generating simple pie charts and graphs representing the data to establishing and verifying complex statistical relationships.

The purpose of this section is to provide a starting point in designing a framework for quantitative analysis. This section will offer guidance on: preparing data for analysis, types of data to be aware of and an outline of some common statistical tests. The level of expertise of the researcher will dictate the technical nature of the analysis. This is something to be mindful of when designing research objectives. If the research requires a complex level of analysis it is always recommended that researchers seek advice (Robson, 1993; Saunders *et al.*, 2002). A range of texts are available offering detailed guidance on performing statistical calculations (see 'Reading list – Quantitative analysis').

Data Preparation

Prior to conducting any tests or creating any charts it is essential to consider the quality and nature of the data to hand. The researcher should take time to examine, for example, a questionnaire to look for poor quality responses and mal response. These can take various forms including: selecting the same response continually throughout the whole questionnaire or perhaps the respondent has missed a page or certain questions and therefore the questionnaire is incomplete. This process of 'cleaning' the data is essential to ensure that the results produced are valid and reliable.

Types of Data

Kinnear and Gray (2007) state that there are three commonly-used terms which describe the different types of data that numeric responses can generate. These terms are nominal, ordinal and scale. The purpose of recognising the type of data collated is to allow the researcher to (a) understand the nature of the information contained in a variable (or question) and (b) to help determine the type of statistical test which is appropriate for the data. Nominal data refers to variables that seek to measure a category or affiliation. This could be attributes such as gender or age. These types of questions require only an indication (a tick) or a 'yes/no' response, thus the value itself does not contain any level of measurement. It is only an expression of membership or otherwise of a group. Ordinal data refers to ranks or sequences. This type of data is often designed through the use of a Likert scale indicating: 1= strongly agree through to 7 = strongly disagree. Scale data is identified as an actual numerical value that has meaning. Examples of scale data include heights and weights, level of IQ, the number of times a child recognises an advert. Scale data contains meaning and each individual response is independent of the other. Once the data has been 'cleaned' and the types of data have been identified the coding of the data can begin.

Coding Data

There are a variety of software packages that can be utilised for data analysis. SPSS, Minitab and Excel all provide the function to perform statistical calculations. Specialist survey design software, including Survey Monkey and SNAP, also has dedicated analysis packages. To allow data input to be performed quickly and accurately it is necessary to devise a range of codes which represent the responses on the questionnaire. Recalling the types of data discussed above; nominal, ordinal and scale data are required to be coded in slightly different ways. Boxes 7.2, 7.3 and 7.4 demonstrate these differences.

Box 7.2: Nominal Data

Example question:
Please indicate your gender:　　Male　　☐
　　　　　　　　　　　　　　　　Female　☐
Male could be assigned 1 and female 2. This means when entering the data into a spreadsheet the number '1' is entered, ensuring quick and accurate input.

Box7.3: Ordinal Data

Example question:
I desire to give up smoking in the next 12 weeks:

False						True
1	2	3	4	5	6	7

This example of an ordinal Likert scale, if the respondent selected 4 in response to the question the number '4' would be entered into the spreadsheet.

Box7.4: Scale Data

Example question:
How many hours do you play on the computer when you come home from school?
Answer: 3 hours.

When categorising scale data it is common to use the actual number indicated by the respondent. In this example you would input '3'.

Data Examination

It is a good idea to begin the data analysis by performing some form of descriptive statistics. This performs two functions. First, it will allow any errors in data entry to become apparent, for example if a Likert scale has values from 1 to 7 and there is the number 77 appearing in the frequency output then this can easily be rectified. Second, frequency outputs allow the researcher to become familiar with the data and in a sense get a 'feel' for it. This stage of exploring the data can generate ideas and perhaps inspire other areas of enquiry; although this does not discount the importance of keeping focused on the initial research aim(s) and objectives. Frequency outputs can be represented in various forms depending on the software of choice. Tables, bar charts, pie charts and histograms are common frequency outputs.

Data Analysis

A number of statistical textbooks will offer guidance on the type of statistical test required for a given scenario or desired outcome. However, Kinnear and Gray (2007) consider it unrealistic to pose a definitive 'decision tree' suggesting that the correct test that should be performed is not always immediately obvious. Instead it is recommended that (novice) researchers first become familiar with their data and then reflect on the research questions posed. The design of the research and the nature of the data will all impact on the style of analysis performed and statistical analysis often falls into one of two types of research: experimental research and correlational research. Experimental researchers often seek to make comparisons between variables. Common tests applied to this research style are t-tests and ANOVA (analysis of variance). Conversely performing correlational research focuses on the statistical associations that can be made. This often involves the use of correlation tables and regression calculations.

Box 7.5 ('Gender role orientation and involvement in family decision making') illustrates a variety of different approaches to analysing data (e.g. frequencies, cross-tabulations, correlations) whilst maintaining a focus on the aims and objectives of the research. As there is a wealth of statistical tests that can be performed on data, it is highly recommended that dedicated textbooks (see 'Reading list – Quantitative analysis') are consulted before embarking on statistical analysis on the data you have collected with children.

Box 7.5: Gender role orientation and involvement in family decision making
Adapted from Tinson and Nancarrow, 2007

Introduction

Role expectations and preferences within families are reportedly changing (Engel et al., 1990) and supporting this assertion are the increasing number of women holding full-time, career-type jobs and their amount of influence in the decision making process that is said to be significant relative to non-working mothers (Lee and Beatty, 2002). It is possible that families are becoming more liberal or egalitarian in their approach to decision-making not (just) because of time pressures but as a result of a more 'modern' or 'enlightened' outlook.

Studies that consider this phenomenon (increasing democratisation within the family) often focus on sex role orientation preference (SRO) or 'gender role orientation' (GRO). That is, both parents and children can be categorised along a 'traditional' to more 'modern' (egalitarian) continuum depending on their preferences towards traditional household tasks such as childcare (Tinson and Nancarrow 2005). Lee and Beatty (2002) describe egalitarian parent(s) as being more 'liberal' in their attitude towards family decision-making. The more egalitarian tend to share responsibilities and decisions in the household. This being the case it is suggested that where egalitarian parents are present, it is more likely the egalitarian disposition might extend to children and purchase decisions. If there is a shift in GRO preference towards a liberal approach to decision making amongst parents then children's involvement in purchase decision-making will increase. As such, there is a need to research the assumption underpinning this hypothesis, namely that GRO is related to involvement in decision-making.

Method

We decided to concentrate on 10-12-year-olds to represent tweenagers at this stage of research because of their probable greater influence on purchasing than 8-9-year-olds and on the basis of consultations with teachers, the proposed method using self-completion questionnaires. This decision is supported by the meta-analysis on research methods for children (Melzer-Lena and Middelmann-Motz, 1998).

Research Approaches

This research involved not just a quantitative study but also follow-up qualitative research. The former was to determine how many children were involved in decision-making across various categories, the associated level of disagreement within the family unit relative to purchase decisions and who these children were in terms of GRO. The qualitative research was designed to explore the perceptions of modern versus traditional roles, family strategies, purchase role preferences and ways in which conflict was dealt with, and so build on the quantitative findings.

For the quantitative research we used a self-completion questionnaire. A UK nationally representative sample of mothers with children aged 10-12 was recruited by a major marketing research agency. A total of 350 mothers agreed to participate in a university survey on family purchase decision-making which involved the husband/partner, the children and themselves self-completing questionnaires independently (to be returned in separate envelopes to try and encourage confidentiality within the family and so maximise honest assessment and disclosure). 106 families responded with 101 family units being usable – a total of 264 respondents (children, mothers and partners). The response rate, including sending out a reminder pack 4 weeks after the first batch was sent, was around 30%.

Analysis

Adults and children were scored in terms of their GRO preference or orientation and then, each within each group (children, mothers and their partners), respondents were divided into high and low scorers based on the median score within each respective group. This permits examination of those who are more liberal in outlook and those less so or more traditional. As it seems likely that gender role orientation might be correlated with gender, we examined the gender composition of the GRO preference groups. For both children and adults the GRO preference groups exhibited no statistically significant difference between the sexes. So we can examine the effect of GRO preference on involvement in the decision-making process and eliminate gender as a moderator variable. MAS analysis was also used to determine the extent of agreement with each family unit of perceptions of relative influence.

Findings

In the case of casual clothes and 'looking around' at potential purchases the more egalitarian/liberal mother, as one might anticipate, sees her child as more involved than the traditional mother sees her offspring (egalitarian: 52% versus traditional: 38%). As regards packed lunches for school the above finding was mirrored. Further to this compared to the more traditional children, the more egalitarian children see themselves and their mothers being more often involved in talking about purchases. Finally perceptions of who had most say frequently conformed to the expectation that the more liberal children see themselves as having more say than is the case for more traditional children. Traditional mothers see themselves as having more say than egalitarian mothers. Compared to traditional children, the more egalitarian children regarded themselves more often as having the most say in the final purchase decision on casual clothes.

In parallel, the more traditional children often see their mother as having most say compared to the perception by the more egalitarian children. For packed lunches for school there is no difference between egalitarian and more traditional children. Traditional mothers see themselves as having most/some say more often than do modern mothers.

To conclude there seems to be evidence that the more liberal outlook correlates with greater decision-making involvement but this relationship is far from perfect. Clearly there are different family compositions in terms of GRO preferences and this might also explain the complicated nature of family decision-making and one potential cause of friction in it.

Mixed Methods

Mixed methods approaches can take two main forms: a 'mixed model' (which involves mixing qualitative and quantitative approaches within or across the stages of the research process) or a 'mixed method' (which includes a quantitative phase and a qualitative phase in an overall research study). If, as a researcher, you employ the mixed method approach the analysis may be more complex. Exploring and explaining the similarities and inconsistencies between the research findings from a qualitative and quantitative piece of research can make the analysis complicated and cumbersome.

Where a mixed method approach is employed, it may be to explore the key concepts or themes in-depth (qualitatively) before developing a quantitative phase (see, for example, Appendix 2). In this scenario, the qualitative research would be analysed (using one of the methods outlined in 'Qualitative research approaches to analysing qualitative data' above) before the quantitative research was conducted. Buchanan (1992: 118) suggests that qualitative research used in this way relegates it to an epistemologically subordinate role and that it implies 'results from qualitative studies must await the true test of valid and reliable knowledge that is gained only through quantitative, hypothesis-testing, experimental designs'. It has, however, been known for a qualitative method to follow after a quantitative one to 'flesh out' the findings (Clarke, 2003). For example, when researching adolescent romantic relationships, Giordano *et al.* (2006: 271) used qualitative research after the quantitative phase 'to validate the quantitative findings, give depth to conceptual arguments and provide a starting point for reconciling results with themes about gender and relationships that have predominated prior research'. Box 7.5, 'Gender role orientation and involvement in family decision-making' (Tinson and Nancarrow, 2007) also illustrates this approach. Either way, the integration of the qualitative and quantitative data at the analysis stage has been cause for concern (see, for example, Buchanan, 1992; Moran-Ellis *et al.*, 2006). These anxieties include trying to reduce the qualitative data to a quantitative form, what to do with singular responses in qualitative research and how to employ logical inference between the qualitative and quantitative findings.

Pawson (1995) and Coxon (2005) both argue for research where methods have been integrated and Pawson (1995) particularly is critical of multiple data approaches that primarily generate more data about a phenomenon without addressing how the plurality of data will be combined analytically. Moran-Ellis *et al.* (2006) illustrate how their data analysis is integrated and explore in depth the concepts of analysis and integration with specific reference to mixed methods. When analysing mixed methods data, it would appear to be important to focus on what needs to be 'found out' as opposed to the type of method which provided the 'answer'. It may also be that the quantitative results collected from research with young people may illustrate a difference to those collated qualitatively. In some cases it could be simply truer in reality to acknowledge that children do not necessarily believe one way or the other and that conflicting results reflect the true diverse nature of their behaviour, attitudes and motivations (Buchanan, 1992).

Whilst there are many benefits to conducting a mixed methods study with children these benefits have to be set in context by taking into account the timeframe of the project (e.g. projects with a short time frame do not lend themselves to mixed method approaches), the aim(s) and objectives of the project (e.g. why the research is being conducted) and the experience (and perhaps the research philosophy) of the researcher.

Summary

This chapter sought to explore different ways in which the data collated whilst researching with children can be analysed. Although the chapter cannot replace more specialised texts in this area, qualitative research approaches to analysing qualitative data and quantitative approaches to data analysis have both been examined. A Framework method commonly employed to analyse qualitative data has been detailed in addition to describing the constant comparative method, phenomenological and ethnographic approaches to data analysis and narrative and discourse analysis. This chapter was designed to facilitate analysis of the methods for researching with children proposed in Chapter 3. This chapter included suggestions about analysing data collected from observation and/or from interviews conducted with children in groups or pairs. Back translation and dual observation were also considered to ensure reliability and the quality of the data and subsequent interpretation. As such, this chapter reflected a more child-centric approach to analysing research. Employing a mixed methods approach and the complexities that may result as a consequence have also been summarised. The following chapter will discuss 'good practice' in relation to presentation of the data that has been analysed and interpreted as well as offering a variety of options in terms of presenting qualitative and quantitative data.

Reflective Questions

1   What are the five stages of the Framework analysis and what are the benefits of employing this approach?

2   What are the key characteristics of constant comparative analysis?

3   Why is a shared meaning important and how might this be achieved?

4   When analysing field notes, what might a researcher specifically look for?

5   How might the analysis of visual data differ from that of the written or numerical form?

6   Diary studies can be analysed quantitatively or qualitatively. Outline the advantages of both.

7   How might you prepare quantitative data before analysing it?

8   What three different types of quantitative data are there and why, as a researcher, is this important to know this?

9   Suggest three difficulties that may arise when conducting mixed methods analysis and detail how these issues could be overcome.

Checklist

☐   Have you refamiliarised yourself with the original research aim(s) and objectives and have you a clear understanding of what you are looking for in the data you have collated?

☐   Are you aware of the differences and commonalties between qualitative approaches to analysis?

☐   Are you able to identify the best method of analysis for your own research project taking into account the method, techniques and any other circumstances particular to the children you researched with?

☐   Do you understand the difference between analysis and interpretation and how the two overlap?

☐   Do you know how to clean the quantitative data you may have collected when researching with young people?

☐   Have you considered how you will ensure a shared meaning when analysing your data?

☐   Have you considered how you will interpret visual data where appropriate?

☐   Do you understand the importance of integration when analysing a mixed methods approach?

Reading List – Ethnographic Interpretation

Denzin N.K. and Lincoln, Y. (2003) *Landscape of Qualitative Research*, Sage.

Gobo, G. (2008) *Doing Ethnography*, Sage.

Madison, D.S. (2005) *Critical Ethnography: Method, Ethics, Performance*, London: Sage.

O'Reilly, K. (2008) *Key Concepts in Ethnography*, Sage.

Pink, S. (2006) *Doing Visual Ethnography*, 2nd edn, London: Sage.

Reading List – Quantitative Analysis

Creswell J.W. and Plano Clark, V.L. (2006) *Designing and Conducting Mixed Methods Research*, Sage.

Faherty, V.E. (2007) *Compassionate Statistics: Applied Quantitative Analysis for Social Services*, Sage: CA

Kinnear, P. and Gray, C.D. (2007) *SPSS Made Simple*, Psychology Press: East Sussex

Rowntree, D. (2003) *Statistics without Tears: A Primer for Non-Mathematicians*, Allyn and Bacon, Pearson Education

References

Alvesson, M. and Deetz, S. (2000) *Doing Critical Management Research*, London: Sage.

Backett-Milburn, K. and McKie, L. (1999) 'A critical appraisal of the draw and write technique', *Health Education Research: Theory and Practice*, **14**, 387-389.

Banister, E. and Booth, G. (2005) 'Exploring innovative methodologies for child-centric consumer research', *Qualitative Market Research*, **8** (2), 157-175.

Bolton, A., Pole, C. and Mizen, P. (2001) 'Picture this: researching child workers', *Sociology*, **35** (2), 501-518.

Broome, M.E., Richards, D.J. and Hall J.M. (2001) 'Children in research: the experience of ill children and adolescents', *Journal of Family Nursing*, **7** (1), 32-49.

Bryman, A. and Burgess, R.G. (1994) *Analysing Qualitative Data*, London: Routledge.

Buchanan, D.R. (1992) 'An uneasy alliance: combining qualitative and quantitative research methods', *Health Education Behaviour*, **19** (1), 117-135.

Clarke, P. (2003) 'Towards a greater understanding of the experience of stroke: integrating qualitative and quantitative methods', *Journal of Aging Studies*, **17** (2), 171-187.

Coffey, A. and Atkinson, P. (1996) *Making Sense of Qualitative Data*, London: Sage.

Coxon, T. (2005) 'Integrating qualitative and quantitative data: what does the user need?', FQS (Forum: *Qualitative Social Research*) **6** (2) http://www.qualitative-research.net/fqs/fqs-eng.htm (accessed Feb 2009)

Dagkas, S. and Stathi, A. (2007) 'Exploring social and environmental factors affecting adolescents' participation in physical activity', *European Physical Education Review*, **13** (3), 369-384.

De Mol, J. and Buysse, A. (2008) 'The phenomenology of children's influence on parents', *Journal of Family Therapy*, **30** (2), 163-193.

Driessnack, M. (2006) 'Draw and tell conversations with children about fear', *Qualitative Health Research*, **16**, 1414-1435.

Dunn, J. (1983) 'Sibling relationships in early childhood', *Child Development*, 54, 787-811.

Emerson, R.M., Fretz, R.I. and Shaw, L.L (1995) *Writing Ethnographic Fieldnotes*. Chicago: University of Chicago Press.

Engel, J.F., Blackwell, R.D. and Miniard, P.W. (1990) *Consumer Behaviour*, London: Dryden Press.

Flewitt, R. (2006) 'Using video to investigate preschool classroom interaction: education research assumptions and methodological practices', *Visual Communication*, 5 (1), 25-50.

Fredricks, J.A, Alfeld-Liro, C.J., Hruda, L.Z., Eccles, J.S., Patrick, H. and Ryan, A.M. (2002) 'A qualitative exploration of adolescents' commitment to athletics and the arts', *Journal of Adolescent Research*, 17 (1), 68-97.

Giordano, P.C., Longmore, M.A. and Manning, W.D. (2006) 'Gender and the meanings of adolescent romantic relationships: a focus on boys', *American Sociological Review*, 71, 260-287.

Grover, S. (2004) 'Why won't they listen to us? On giving power and voice to children participating in social research', *Childhood*, 11 (1), 81-93.

Gummesson, E. (2003) 'All research is interpretive', *Journal of Business and Industrial Marketing*, 4, 482-492.

Gummesson, E. (2005) 'Qualitative research in marketing: road-map for a wilderness of complexity and unpredictability', *European Journal of Marketing*, 39 (3/4), 309-327.

Harness Goodwin, M. (2002) 'Exclusion in girls' peer groups: ethnographic analysis of language: practices on the playground', *Human Development*, 45 (6), 392-415.

Hood, S., Kelley, P. and Mayall, B. (1996) 'Children as research subjects: a risky enterprise', *Children and Society*, 10 (2), 117-128.

Horstman, M., Aldiss, S. and Gibson, F. (2008) 'Methodological issues when using the draw and write technique with children aged 6 to 12 years', *Qualitative Health Research*, 18 (7), 1001-1011.

Jones, R.K. (2000) 'The unsolicited diary as a qualitative research tool for advanced research capacity in the field of health and illness', *Qualitative Health Research*, 10 (4), 555-567.

Kelly, D, Mulhall, A. and Pearce, S. (2000) 'A good place to be if you are having a bad time: an ethnographic evaluation of a teenage cancer unit', report to the Teenage Cancer Trust, London.

Kinnear, P.R. and Gray, C.D. (2007) *SPSS 14 Made Simple*. Psychology Press: London.

Lawson, D.M. and Brossart, D.F. (2004) 'The association between current intergenerational family relationships and sibling structure', *Journal of Counseling and Development*, 82, 472-482.

Lee, K.C.C. and Beatty, S.E. (2002) 'Family structure and influence in family decision making', *Journal of Consumer Marketing*, 19 (1), 24-41.

Luckmann, T. (1999) 'Remarks on the description and interpretation of dialogue', *International Sociology*, **14**, 387-402.

Marshman, Z. And Hall, M.J. (2008) 'Oral realth research with children', *International Journal of Paediatric Dentistry*, **18** (4), 235-242.

Maybin, J. (2006) *Children's Voices: Talk, Knowledge and Identity*, Basingstoke: Palgrave Macmillan.

Melzer-Lena, B. and Middelmann-Motz, A.V. (1998) 'Research among children', in C. McDonald and P.Vangelder (eds), *ESOMAR Handbook of Market and Opinion Research*, European Society for Opinion and Marketing Research

Miles, M.B. and Huberman, A.M. (1984) *Qualitative Data Analysis: A New Sourcebook of Methods*, Beverly Hills, CA: Sage.

Miller, S. (2003) 'Analysis of phenomenological data generated with children as research participants', *Issues in Research, Nurse Researcher*, 1 June.

Mills, J. (2001) 'Self construction through conversation and narrative in interviews', *Educational Review,* **53** (3), 285-301.

Moran-Ellis, J., Alexander, V.D., Cronin, A., Dickson, M., Fielding, J., Sleney, J. and Thomas, H. (2006) 'Triangulation and integration: processes, claims and implications', *Qualitative Research*, **6** (1), 45-59.

Mulhall, A. (2003) 'In the field: notes on observation in qualitative research', *Journal of Advanced Nursing*, **41** (3), 306-313.

Nicolopoulou, A. and Richner, E.S. (2007) 'From actors to agents to persons: the development of character representation in young children's narratives', *Child Development*, **78** (2), 412-429.

Patton, M.Q. (2002) *Qualitative Research and Evaluation Methods*, 3rd edn, Thousand Oaks, CA: Sage.

Pawson, R. (1995) 'Quality and quantity, agency and structure, mechanism and context, dons and cons', *BMS, Bulletin de Méthodologie Sociologique*, **47**, 5-48

Pickler, R. 'Evaluating qualitative research studies', *Journal of Pediatric Health Care*, **21** (3), 195-197.

Punch, S. (2002) 'Research with children: the same or different from research with adults?', Childhood, 9, 321-341.

Rasmussen, K. (1999) 'Om fotografering on fotofgrafi som forskningsstrategi I barndomsforskining', *Dansk Sociologi*, **2** (10), 63-78.

Ritchie, J. and Spencer, L. (1994) 'Qualitative analysis for applied social policy', in A. Bryman and R.Burgess (eds), *Analysing Qualitative Data*, London: Routledge, pp. 173-193.

Robins, L.N. (1966) *Deviant Children Grown Up*, Baltimore, MD: Williams and Wilkins.

Robson, C. (1993) *Real World Research: a Resource for Social Scientists and Practitioners-Research*, Oxford: Blackwell.

Rollins, J.A. (2005) 'Tell me about it: drawing as a communication tool for children with cancer', *Journal of Pediatric Oncology Nursing*, **22** (4), 203-221.

Roose, G.A. and John, A.M. (2003) 'A focus group investigation into young children's understanding of mental health and their views on appropriate services for their age group', *Child: Care, Health and Development*, **29** (6), 545-550.

Rose, G. (2001) *Visual Methodologies*, London: Sage.

Russell, B., Richards, H., Jones, A. and Hoddinott, P. (2004) 'Breakfast, lunch and dinner': attitudes to infant feeding amongst children in a Scottish primary school. A qualitative focus group study', *Health Education Journal*, 63 (1), 70-80.

Sanders, J. and Munford, R. (2005) 'Activity and reflection', *Qualitative Social Work*, **4** (2), 197-209.

Sanjek, J. (1990) *Fieldnotes: The Makings of Anthropology*, Ithaca, NY: Cornell University Press.

Saunders, M., Lewis, P. and Thornhill, A. (2002) *Research Methods for Business Students*, Harlow: Pearson Education.

Silverman, D. (1993) *Interpreting Qualitative Data*, London: Sage.

Silverman, D. (2004) *Qualitative Research: Theory, Method and Practice*, 2nd edn, London: Sage.

Spiggle, S. (1994) 'Analysis and interpretation of qualitative data in consumer research', *Journal of Consumer Research*, **21**, 491-503.

Tinson J. and Nancarrow C. (2005) 'The influence of children on purchases: the development of measures for gender role orientation and shopping savvy', *International Journal of Market Research*, **47** (1), 5-27.

Tinson J. and Nancarrow C. (2007) 'Growing up: tweenagers' involvement in family decision making', *Journal of Consumer Marketing*, **24** (3), 160-170.

Tinson, J. and Nuttall, P. (2007) 'Insider trading? Exploring familial intra-generational borrowing and sharing', *Marketing Review*, 7 (2), 185-200.

Van Maanen, J. (1988) *Tales of the Field: On Writing Ethnography*, Chicago: University of Chicago Press.

Waddell, J., Pepler, D. and Moore, T. (2001) 'Observations of sibling interactions in violent families', *Journal of Community Psychology*, **29**, 241-258.

Woods, S.E., Springett, J., Porcellato, L and Dugdill, L. (2005) '"Stop it, it's bad for you and me": experiences of and views on passive smoking among primary-school children in Liverpool', *Heath Education Research*, **20** (6), 645-655.

8 Presenting and Disseminating the Data

Objectives

- To explore the ways in which data can be presented for different types of audiences

- To establish why it is important to maintain the interest of the gatekeeper(s)

- To consider how best to acknowledge the children you have researched with in your published work

- To identify best practice for the completion of your project

- To summarise how to prepare your work for publication.

Introduction

Previous chapters have explored and explained an ethical approach to researching and engaging with children and latterly data analysis has also been examined. This penultimate chapter is designed to demonstrate different ways in which the data you have analysed, coupled with initial theoretical concepts that have underpinned your study, can be presented. The ways in which this presentation will differ by audience type (e.g. academics, children and gatekeepers) will also be explored. Maintaining ethical practice when researching with children will be addressed here too with specific reference to acknowledging respondents whilst retaining their anonymity and the storing and destroying of information (see Chapter 2 for additional information on the ethical aspects of this and the Data Protection Act).

Presenting Qualitative Data

(Novice) researchers are often unsure how to structure the findings of the research they have conducted with children as the information they have collated and analysed may be complex, vast or simply overwhelming. Before attempting to structure and present any piece of work, it is important to return to the initial aim(s) and objectives of the research study. This will help to establish the key areas or themes initially under examination and may also facilitate the development of headings or subheadings for the presentation of the data. Table 8.1 illustrates the way in which themes and sub-themes can be identified from data. This particular study considered adolescent identity expression and music consumption.

Table 8.1: Overview of Consistent Key Themes

Agency themes	Identity themes	Agent themes
Socialisation	**Self**	**Families**
• Artificial agency	• Selfhood	• Family studies
• Consumption skills	• Social construction	• Parent-peer influence
• Consumer socialisation	• Multiple selves	• Situational influence
• Social meaning	• Normative behaviour	• Family type
• Social consumption	• Signature	• Private consumption
	• Social self	
Product conspicuousness	**Semiotics**	**Peers**
• Materialism	• Symbols	• Peer influence
• Values	• Sign system	• Friendship groups
• Self esteem	• Symbolic context	• Type of peer influence
	• Cultural text	• Inter-relationships
		• Peer orientation
		• Public consumption
	Music consumption as a semiotic in identity formation	**Media**
	• Conveying meaning	• Expectations
	• Escaping boundaries	• Expression
	• Interpreting meaning	• Conforming
	• Personal meaning	• Type of influence
	• Type of music	
	• Social significance/ judgement	**School**
	• Cultural capital	• Type of music
	• Convergence	• Public consumption
	• Divergence	• Private consumption
		• Social capital
		• Escape
		• Boundaries
		• Access

Having identified the recurrent themes and having utilised a method of analysis and interpretation it is important to consider how this information will be presented. In the example of the study on adolescent identity and expression of self, the analysis can be presented using the three categories – agency, identity and agent themes but can be further subdivided by the areas recurrent in the data, for example, sign systems or social capital.

Woods *et al.* (2005) employed a mixed methods approach to explore the experiences of and views on passive smoking among primary school children in Liverpool. They chose an integrated approach to present their data. That is, drawings, quotations and statistics were presented, where relevant, under headings so that rather than simply reporting what was 'found' from employing the draw and write technique or the questionnaire or the focus groups, the presentation of the research told a cohesive story. As such, what children understood by 'passive smoking', how children felt about being in a smoky place and the health concerns children had in relation to smoking were discussed and explored comprehensively under 'themes' as opposed to method.

Presenting Quantitative Data

It is important when presenting quantitative data that graphs, pie charts, diagrams or tables help to summarise the data in a way that can be understood. Using diagrams or tables that simply confuse the reader will not help the researcher explain their findings. It is important to be as explicit as possible when presenting quantitative data so that it is clear how you arrived at your findings. Table 8.2 illustrates the presentation of factor analysis that was conducted on data collated from adolescents attending their senior prom (high school leaving dance). The table clearly shows which statements refer to the relevant statistics. The type of prom attendee has been 'interpreted' by the researcher.

Where the analysis has been conducted with reference to hypotheses, it is still useful to group the results together so that the information can be summarised succinctly. Table 8.3 shows the difference between socio-economic group and use of information from different sources during teenage pregnancy.

Of course the presentation of quantitative data will largely depend on the type of analysis used. The presentation of structural equation modelling (SEM), for example, will by its very nature be more complex. The converse of this is that sometimes there will be no need for tables or pie charts if you are presenting simple information. For example, if your data has been collated from 54% of boys and 46% of girls, this simple frequency can be expressed in words and a pie chart is not necessary to facilitate the readers' understanding of this 'finding'.

Whilst the presentation of research here principally refers to journal articles and dissertations, the notion of qualitative data presentation may not be as relevant for a report and this may be because of the audience for whom the report is being written. The presentation of data is now discussed in the context of the 'audience'.

Table 8.2: Types of adolescents attending the senior prom

Type of prom attendee	Corresponding statements	Cronbach alpha	Cumu-lative loading (%)
Anxious	I am apprehensive about not finding someone to go with	.701	74.5
	I am anxious about not looking as good as others		
	I will be nervous about making sure I get to sit with friends		
	I am anxious about not being left out of my group		
Celebratory	I am very excited and full of anticipation	.656	78.8
	I am looking forward to really dressing up		
	I am expecting one of the best nights out so far		
	I am really looking forward to sharing the experience with all my friends		
Image conscious	I am anxious about how my partner will feel if I dance with someone else	.706	64.3
	I am worried about dancing with people who can't dance		
	I am concerned about how much it will all cost me		
	I'll probably get anxious about taking enough good photos		
Needing to belong	I'll probably get upset if I don't get invited into a limo	*	*
	I am worried someone else will be wearing the same outfit		

Table 8.3: Category respondents' use of referent groups and literature

Usefulness of information	Z	2 tailed p	Result
From mother	-2.5385	.0111	Significant
From sister	-.6706	.5025	No significance
From community midwife	-1.9045	.0568*	Significant*
From antenatal classes	-5.4852	.0000	Significant
From GP	-1.4228	.1548	No significance
From friends with children	-1.0588	.2897	No significance
From literature	-1.9964	.0459	Significant

Writing for your Audience

When structuring and writing up your research findings, it is important to re-member who will be reading the work you submit and what their expectations will be. If you are submitting work in the form of a dissertation or thesis, it is likely that you will need to consider how your findings reflect previous studies or build on theoretical models (see 'Academic work', below). Alternatively, if you just want to let the children share in your analysis and interpretation of the data then a simpler and perhaps illustrative approach should be taken to display what you have 'found out' (see 'Ensuring the children know how the data has been used' below). The gatekeepers may be satisfied with what is provided for the children but they may also want additional information (which may be a shortened form of the academic submission). This additional information may have been asked for during the research design phase as part of negotiating access to the children.

Academic Work

There is a particular way in which academic work or reports should be struc-tured and this may be particular to your university or organisation. It is always useful to consult your own university handbooks or organisation guidelines be-fore designing a structure for your work. There are a plethora of texts that can be accessed to help in the structuring of dissertations (see, for example, Murray, 2005; Oliver, 2008). However, to summarise it is likely that if you are submitting a thesis that you will have:

- *An introductory chapter* outlining the basis for the research study which will also include the aims and objectives of your project. It will be forward looking (i.e. it will tell the reader what you are proposing to do).

- *A literature review* should also be included and will highlight the salient issues of previous research in the area you are researching. Whilst it is im-portant for your research to be innovative, it is very unlikely that you are the only person who has researched the topic under consideration. Even if no-one has written on exactly the same topic, there will be associated research that has been published which will be of use to you. Perhaps your research builds on theoretical models or frameworks and these should be critically evaluated here. It should be self-evident to the reader why the research needs to be conducted having read the literature review you have produced. It is always useful to identify where you can add to existing knowledge in the area particularly in the concluding section.

- *Your methodology chapter* should explore your research design, planning issues and sampling frame. It is likely to contain research objectives and may contain a section on your research philosophy. Ethical issues in relation to your project should be addressed here with details on how any barriers to researching with children were overcome. Limitations of the research approach can also be discussed here. Details of disclosure or negotiation over access should also be included here.

♦ *The analysis chapter* will follow your methodology and your findings will be presented in this chapter. *Qualitative research* is typically presented by using illustrative quotes within themes to support the analysis. If you have employed a *Framework* approach (see Chapter 7), it is usual to include a table that expresses the way in which the thematic framework has been developed. The indexes used to facilitate analysis of the data (see 'Presenting qualitative data' above) should also be presented. For *quantitative findings* it is commonplace to use graphs or tables to express and explain what you have discovered. The use of hypotheses may help you to explore the data but it is best practice not to simply type the hypotheses on the page and give the 'answers'. Rather, think about categorising your hypotheses in groups or themes so that the reader can get a 'feel' for what the data is actually 'telling' us (see 'Presenting quantitative data' above).

♦ The chapter that follows the one on analysis should be '*Conclusions and Recommendations*'. If your analysis chapter has focused on simply illustrating the findings, this chapter too may include some discussion on the previous chapter. Usually this chapter summates what has been 'found out' and reflects on how these findings contribute to knowledge in this area using academic underpinning (the salient issues from the literature review) to support the work. Overall limitations of the work as well as suggestions for future research should be identified here.

♦ The thesis will conclude with a robust bibliography and appendices that may contain examples of creative work produced by the children and/or, for example, creative group moderator guidelines.

The above outlines a 'typical' academic dissertation. This is not to say that all dissertations are written in this way. If, for example, a student has used a *grounded* approach to research, it may be the case that the research will be conducted before the literature review has taken place. In this scenario, the methodology chapter should come before the literature review.

It may be that you are a researcher who is not writing a dissertation or thesis but a report for an organisation. A report is quite different to a thesis or dissertation and it is likely that there will be an expected format for your report depending on who the report is for (e.g. funding body, etc.). Again specific texts can be accessed to facilitate report writing (see, for example, Forsyth, 2006; Bowden, 2008). As a general guide a report should have the following headings and should be succinct in comparison to a dissertation (although will be no less important with regard to the information that it is conveying):

♦ An executive summary

♦ An introduction

♦ The main body or core

♦ Conclusions.

The report will also contain fewer references than a thesis although it is common practice to use footnotes to provide sources for statistical output or theoretical background. When compared with a dissertation or thesis you will have less opportunity to include illustrative rich qualitative data as the structure for a report is less flexible than that of a more academic piece of work. Always have the qualitative data and analysis to hand if presenting a report to an organisation, however, as those who read the report may need additional information or may wish to check interpretation of important points or may simply want to enhance their understanding of the topic under discussion.

Ensuring the children know how the data has been used

Younger children especially will be less concerned about how your work has built on or developed a theoretical model but will be interested in how what they have said and/ or the way in which they have behaved has contributed to the research study overall. They may even want to reflect on their participation (see Goodenough *et al.*, 2003). Sometimes for younger children, where the research has been visually recorded, it will be enough to show the children themselves on video or DVD. Younger children tend to respond better to visual images and negotiating a space on the wall of a classroom or hospital ward where you can display some of the creative work or photographs that have been taken whilst researching with children may be rewarding. Younger children too like to be able to show their parent(s) or guardian what they have been doing at school. A 'take away' in the form of a letter, postcard or certificate to say the child has been involved with the research (and to thank them for their input) is also something that could enhance the research experience for younger children. Coad (2007) suggests that if the young person wishes to keep the work produced, one commonly used approach is to photograph the work and for the facilitator/ researcher to use the photographs to facilitate the analysis (leaving the artwork with the child).

Older children will be less impressed by a letter, postcard or certificate and are likely to have greater literacy skills. As such a 'take away' in the form of an A4 sheet summary (use bullet points where possible) to indicate the key or significant issues of the research findings and how this might impact on (a) current understanding or thinking in the area (b) improving services where relevant and/ or (c) policy development where relevant may be well received. This will not be immediately available, of course, so it may be that other incentives (see Chapter 5) are more appropriate at this juncture. Whilst older children may appear less impressed with being able to see themselves visually (e.g. on video or in photographs) they too will be interested in how the research is presented and how what they have said has been interpreted. A short presentation by the researcher to the adolescents may be an interesting mechanism for 'feeding back'. Equally an A4 folder with clear plastic inserts which will simply holds and records the 'findings' of the research which is easily accessible to the children you have researched with might also be appreciated. Coad and Lewis (2004) employed an IT web-based facility to enhance the feedback regarding the research project for the children they researched with.

The older the child the more likely they are to be able to engage fully with the research analysis (e.g. become involved in back translation, see Chapter 7) and the subsequent presentation of those findings. Dockett and Perry (2007) refer to this as 'co-construction of the research interaction' or where 'each participant in the dialogue strives to grasp the subjective perspective of the other' (Berk, 2001: 42). That is, when data and interpretation are discussed with research participants to develop a shared or agreed meaning (see also Thomas and O'Kane, 2000). However, just because the adolescent can engage further with your research does not mean they will either be interested enough or have enough time to involve themselves further in the project. Be sensitive to the adolescents' other interests and do not expect them to be as interested in your research as you are likely to be. Remember that however your relationship has developed with these children over time, it is important to maintain ongoing consent and not simply assume that because these children know you that they will want to continue being involved in the research project.

Maintaining Gatekeepers' Interest

The gatekeeper(s) may be very interested in your research depending on the aim(s), objectives and possible implications for policy, service provision or curriculum development. It is unlikely, however, that the gatekeeper(s) will have time to read a thesis or dissertation. They probably will be interested in a shorter executive report. It is important to maintain the gatekeepers' interest for a number of reasons and these will be considered in turn.

The gatekeeper(s) will initially have been the one who either gave permission for access to the children and/or will have negotiated access with regard to the research data you have been able to collate (with appropriate ethical considerations having been addressed). You will be fulfilling your obligation to 'give something in return'. It may also be that the gatekeeper(s) assisted in the development or design of the research approach and they will probably be interested to know if and how their suggestions were useful. Depending on the type of research method you employed, you may have made a number of return visits, particularly if, for example, you used a back translation approach. As such you may have built up your relationship with the gatekeeper(s) over time. They will have invested their time and effort as well as the children. This will need to be considered and, where possible, rewarded. Furthermore, where gatekeeper(s) have had a positive experience of dealing with researchers (e.g. the researcher has turned up on time, they have not been disruptive, they have been respectful of the children and the gatekeeper, they have informed the gatekeeper of their key findings) then the gatekeeper(s) will be more inclined to work with other researchers in the future (and that might include you as a researcher if you want to conduct studies with children in the future). You have a responsibility as a researcher to maintain a positive relationship with the gatekeepers you come into contact with even if you have no intention of researching with children in that particular environment again.

It is imperative to remember, however, in the case of qualitative research that the findings or information given to the gatekeeper(s) will *not* allow them to identify any individual child who you researched with. This is important for two reasons: first, you will have promised confidentiality and anonymity to the children you were researching with and this means that they think you will not tell their gatekeeper (e.g. social worker, teacher, ward sister) what they have said. Their responses may have been different if they thought you were going to report to the gatekeeper(s) what they said. Second, and equally important, is that the gatekeeper(s) will continue to have a working relationship with these children in their capacity as caregiver, for example, after your research has been completed. It is self-evident that your research findings should not impact on or seek to undermine this working relationship. Also, if the gatekeeper(s) is given access to specific quotes then it may be that this discourse would have been taken out of context and the meaning of what was being discussed could be misinterpreted by the gatekeeper. It is important then to provide general or 'overall' findings to the gatekeeper(s) whilst ensuring that your promise of confidentiality and anonymity is met.

Acknowledging your Respondents

When you obtained initial and ongoing consent to research with children you will probably have promised that the respondents and their comments would remain anonymous. As such when presenting your findings it is important to use pseudonyms for the child whose discourse you are using as part of your work. This ensures that individual contributions cannot be attributed to specific respondents when others (e.g. gatekeepers) access the findings. It is also common practice to ascribe the gender and age of the child to the discourse used as part of the presentation of findings as this is normally relevant to ideas or concepts being conveyed. However, there are exceptions to this. For example, when a child can be identified be a gatekeeper(s) simply by their gender and age (e.g. if there was only one 8-year-old boy in the sample). In this scenario you must ensure that the child is not identifiable and the age and gender should not be included. It is also important that the discourse does not contain any other information that will make the respondent identifiable outside of the research context (e.g. will not be able to be identified other than by his 'friendship pair' or members of his creative group).

Where appropriate you can thank the school and the children for taking part in your study. This too has exceptions as it is normally more appropriate to thank the school and the children where the research has been *quantitative* in nature. This is because it is difficult, if not impossible, to identify individual respondents. If in doubt, ask the gatekeeper(s) what their preference would be. If the research has been small scale and has explored a sensitive topic it is wise to thank the participants individually and, if the report is published to simply thank the participants without specifically naming them or the school, hospital, community centre involved.

Do provide a summary of your 'findings' for the children you researched with (See Writing for your Audience, above) and enclose a formal thank you letter to the department, class, school, youth group or community centre that took part in your study. This will show your appreciation without having to formally recognise their involvement where this may be deemed inappropriate (see above).

Storing and Destroying Information

If you have conducted your research using an ethical approach you will have ensured that during the data collection phase that you stored the data in a safe place where it is inaccessible to anyone other than yourself or recognised members of the research team. It is extremely important that if you share computer facilities that the data you have collated is not available on a shared drive. It is best practice to have your own printing equipment. However, if you share other equipment with other students or colleagues (e.g. a printer) it is essential that you do not sent data to print without making sure you immediately retrieve your data from the printer. This can become problematic which is why it is best to have your own printer. Where possible have the data in the same place all the time so that you are secure in the knowledge that the data is 'safe'. If you have to take data with you (e.g. outside the confines of your office to read on an airplane or train) make sure that you have thought about the possible consequences and implications of doing so and *do not* leave that data on the plane or train.

Once the project has been completed, you will need to destroy all related data produced as part of the study (unless you have specifically sought permission to re-use the data or use the data elsewhere). The data should be erased from any computer(s) and/or memory stick(s). Any data in paper format should be shredded. It is particularly important that any data that identifies the children you have been working with (e.g. name, age, address, class/year group, school, hospital attended, social worker) is destroyed first and is *completely* irretrievable.

Publishing your Work

There are a number of texts that can be read to facilitate publication of your work. For academic researchers, Epstein *et al.* (2007) provide a number of generic issues around academic writing (including intellectual property rights) as well as writing for refereed journal articles, books and book chapters. Other less common forms of publication for academics are also considered. As such, this text does not seek to replicate what can be found elsewhere. However, there are some simple suggestions that may be useful in helping the (non-academic) researcher to consider when preparing material for publication.

As a researcher you will have read a wide number of texts, articles and reports. It is likely that you will have used a number of journals to support your own work and/or you may have identified some key developments in the popular or trade press. This should be your starting point for considering publishing your own work. These different types of publications have different audiences and, consequently, different types of writing style. Is there an audience you particularly want to communicate with? Or is there a writing style you prefer? Once you have decided on the publication you want to write for, look for the most recent articles and study the structure of what has already been published. Is there an in-depth literature review? How much detail is needed for the methodology section? Does the publication lend itself to qualitative or quantitative data?

It may be that the publication you choose will have a 'guidelines for authors' section which will indicate the length of the articles that are normally published, what the editorial position is (e.g. who the editor thinks the audience is and what s/he is hoping to achieve) and the types of articles s/he is looking for authors to submit. If you are a novice researcher it is common to write articles or conference papers with your supervisor although this will largely depend on the relationship you have with them and the resources available to you both. There is a significant difference between writing articles and writing dissertations and these require different skill sets. It is not unusual for a researcher to be able to write a thesis well but struggle to write smaller more succinct pieces of work. It is best to write a small piece initially and then develop your writing over time. It is important to keep writing (and practice writing for different audiences) to develop your skills in this area.

Summary

This chapter was designed to help researchers organise and present their findings, having analysed and interpreted the data they collated while researching with children. Both qualitative and quantitative (and mixed methods) presentation was explored and the complexity of these presentation approaches acknowledged. Writing for a particular audience was discussed with specific reference to dissertations and reports, and suggestions for the researcher with regard to their potential for publishing has also been addressed. Importantly, the children you have researched with and the gatekeeper(s) you have developed relationships with and what they should expect at the end of the project have been considered. Acknowledging the respondents and gatekeeper(s) as well as providing them with the findings has been explored, and destroying the information from the project once it has been completed has also been addressed.

This concludes the main body of the text. The previous chapters have detailed how to employ an ethical approach when researching with children and have described a number of methods that can be used to engage the children you are researching with. Specific techniques to enhance the enjoyment of the children during the research process have also been discussed. The importance of planning has been considered and the timing of research addressed. The element of surprise, that is what might happen during the research project with children, has been discussed. Analysing and presenting data has also been considered.

The following chapter is designed not only to illustrate an innovative approach to researching with children but to highlight the implications and consequences of employing such a method. Those seeking to employ an innovative approach and those researchers who perhaps are more experienced researching with children may find the following chapter illuminating. Novice researchers may find the approach appealing but the caveats (e.g. ethics, engagement and researcher role) are all still relevant regardless of the method employed.

Reflective Questions

1   What do you need to consider when writing for a particular audience?

2   What are the three key differences between writing a dissertation and writing a report?

3   What might younger children like the researcher to provide on completion of the project?

4   Why should you be sensitive regarding adolescents and 'back translation' or 'respondent validation'?

5   Give three reasons why you want to maintain the gatekeepers' interest.

6   What should you be careful of when acknowledging your respondents?

7   What should you be aware of when presenting quantitative data?

8   In what circumstances should you not destroy the data from the study?

Checklist

☐   Do you understand why data should be presented in different ways for a variety of audiences?

☐   Do you know why it is important to maintain the gatekeepers' interest?

☐   Do you understand the differences between acknowledging the children you have researched with and respecting their anonymity?

☐   Do you understand why you should destroy all materials (e.g. transcripts) on completion of your project?

☐   Have you considered the age of the young people you have been researching with and what adolescents may expect the researcher to provide on completion of the project?

☐   Do you know how to consider if your work is suitable for publication?

References

Berk, L. (2001) *Awakening Children's Minds*, Oxford: Oxford University Press.

Bowden, J. (2008) *How to Prepare, Write and Present Really Effective Reports*, Oxford: How to Books.

Coad, J. (2007) 'Using art-based techniques in engaging children and young people in health care consultations and/or research', *Journal of Research in Nursing*, 12 (5), 487-497.

Coad, J. and Lewis, A. (2004) 'Engaging children and young people in research: a systematic literature review for the national evaluation of the children's fund', www.ne-cf.org (accessed Feb 2009)

Dockett, S. and Perry, B. (2007) 'Trusting children's accounts in research', *Journal of Early Childhood Research*, 5 (1), 47-63.

Epstein, D., Kenway, J. and Boden, R. (2007) *Writing for Publication, The Academic's Support Kit*, London: Sage.

Forsyth, P. (2006) *How to Write Reports and Proposals*, Oxford: How to Books.

Goodenough, T., Williamson, E., Kent, J. and Ashcroft, R. (2003) '"What did you think about that?" Research children's perceptions of participation in a longitudinal genetic epidemiological study', *Children and Society*, 17, 113-125.

Murray, R. (2005) *How to Write a Thesis*, Maidenhead: Open University Press.

Oliver, P. (2008) *Writing Your Thesis*, London: Sage.

Thomas, N. and O'Kane, C. (2000) 'Discovering what children think: connections between research and practice', *British Journal of Social Work* 30, 817-33.

Woods, S.E., Springett, J., Porcellato, L. and Dughill, L. (2005) '"Stop it, it's bad for you and me": experiences of and views on passive smoking among primary school children in Liverpool', *Health Education Research*, 20 (6) 645-655.

9 Young People as Researchers

by Dr Pete Nuttall

Objectives

- To explore the concept of young people as researchers and to critique the scope and limitations of current research practice in this area

- To identify methods for advancing the notion of young people as researchers and to establish the ethno-participatory model as a methodological innovation

- To consider the practical organisation, design parameters, training and research roles implicated in a youth-focused approach

- To explore the possible contrasts between researcher and adolescent interpretation of findings

- To summarise the limitations and scope of the ethno-participatory approach.

Introduction

The vast choice of qualitative and quantitative methods and approaches that are commonly found to resource the capture of data surrounding the actions, behaviour, attitudes and perceptions of children and adolescents have been already explored. Throughout the text, but particularly in Chapter 3, reference has been made to the qualitative research field of ethnography (and more specifically 'Participant observation'). Ethnography, in the context of children's research is a largely underused research approach and this may be because this style of study is located in the child's naturally occurring setting. This data collection is conducted by methods which capture the child's social meanings and ordinary, everyday activities. This requires the participant researcher to be directly involved in the setting and, in some cases, the activities themselves. There are a number of issues that arise as a consequence of employing this approach most notably an ethical approach to researching with children and the philosophy of the researcher.

The role of the researcher in ethnography facilitates a systematic collection of data that remains free from predetermined (or positivistic) order (see Chapter 3 for a discussion on methodology). Whilst the range of methods used in ethnography can be employed in a variety of research approaches, for example, in-depth interviews and diaries, ethnography is distinguishable by its proximity to the research field and desire to explore and uncover the 'lived order' of the respondents. The notion of proximity to the research setting, in this case the child's everyday life, is the salient issue posed by this particular field of research, and one that is addressed specifically in this chapter.

Ethnographic studies that require the researcher to immerse her/himself in the community under investigation as an active participant remains impossible for the adult researcher wishing to gain the benefits of this style of research when the study is with young people. Employing adolescents or children as researchers may overcome this barrier, however, and the first part of this chapter explores this concept further. A teen–centred model for organising this type of research is proposed and the practical considerations for employing such a design are considered. The chapter concludes by identifying the interpretive attributes, research roles and ethical issues associated with a youth-focused study.

Young People as Researchers

The range of limitations and caveats attached to the research methods and techniques explored throughout this book are largely as a result of the physical and psychological distance between the researcher and those with whom they are researching. Morrow and Richards contend that 'the biggest ethical challenge for researchers working with children is the disparity in power and status between adults and children' (1996: 98). For example: 'when kids talk to researchers, they assume the adult is a kind of teacher and that the questions are, again, about getting it right or being wrong. Overcoming that mindset is crucial (Roper, 1989: 17).

Ethnographic research, through various forms of participant observation, aims to research the lived order of the respondents without the influence, shaping or reconstruction produced by introducing extraneous and traditional research tools. Techniques that employ participant observation through long-term immersion are considered to be important and are increasingly popular methods for social scientists aiming to unearth a complete picture of the topic under consideration and to develop 'thick descriptions' of social behaviour (Elliot and Jankel-Elliot, 2003). Observational data is attractive as it affords the researcher the opportunity to gather 'live' data from 'live' situations and allows for an understanding of the context of the research and the discovery of ideas or issues the respondents might not talk about freely in interviews (Cohen *et al.*, 2000). Ethnographic research could involve the participation of parents or gatekeepers to help record events over a period of time. This might be particularly valuable when attempting to observe critical moments during the period of socialisation (see, for example, Nutbrown, 1999) although the power imbalance inherent in this approach and parents being considered in some cases as 'agents of survellience' (Danby and Farrell, 2002) may influence the data collected.

A point to note is that, depending on the aims and purpose of the research study (and in some cases the reason for conducting the research) it may be important to be able to generalise the findings of the study and thereby utilise a set of methods that remain objective and external to the respondent's immediate context.

From a qualitative perspective, the aim of any credible piece of exploratory research is to unmask the genuine motivations, reasons, interactions and influences that help to explain and assist in our understanding of the behaviour and actions of the respondents whether the focus is on educational development, health awareness or social behaviour. Children and adolescents are increasingly aware of research and its purpose and, if you have followed the ethical path to completing your fieldwork as outlined in Chapter 2, young people will also recognise and comprehend your role as a researcher. Inevitably this 'research awareness' increases as a result of the perceived demographic and psychographic distance felt by the child or adolescent towards the (adult) researcher. Indeed, in an effort to circumvent this research awareness (and the influence it may have on the data collection) some researchers may be tempted to try and 'become' an adolescent (see for example Llewellyn's 1980 unfinished study on teenage girls). However the prospect of this approach succeeding is remote and may as a consequence create a greater perceived distance than would have been achieved by simply behaving as normal adult researcher.

It has been argued that the inseparability of research and researcher is an essential and desirable characteristic of social science studies and that the methodology which underpins the research design is as much to do with personal values as it is to do with rigour and 'hygiene' in the research process (Clough and Nutbrown, 2002). However, researchers have also sought to limit the extent to which this inseparability pervades the whole research process and indeed promote the notion of natural separation (Pole *et al.* 1999). Natural, in this sense, means that there are normal and desirable differences between an adult world from which the research aim ordinarily originates from and the child's world we are seeking to understand in more depth. Child or youth-centred research promotes the concept of children as active generators of data and encourages a more reflexive research process on behalf of both the adult researcher and the child respondent (see Jenks, 2000). Researchers from a range of disciplines including sociology, management and marketing, health research and cultural studies have embraced this stream of methodological development and have employed qualitative methods that involve children's active participation. The methods range from interview and discussions with children, observations, projective techniques, through to full involvement in the research process and young people as co-researchers (see Bannister and Booth, 2005). This reflects a shift that involves repositioning children as collaborators with rather than objects of research and is an emerging paradigm that places the child at the centre of the research and accords value to a child's point of view as a competent individual and social actor.

The idea of employing adults as co-researchers, involved in the production and analysis of data is already widely acknowledged (Alderson, 2000) and the benefits of involving children as active participants or collaborators and partners in the research process are equally apparent. In the first instance, developing a rapport and cooperative relationship and being viewed by the child respondent as 'interested parties who could be trusted and to whom the children would enjoy talking and communicating' (Pole *et al.*, 1999) is likely to improve the quality, authenticity and analysis of the data. In addition, to enhance the level of understanding between researcher and respondent, other benefits of children collaborating with the research include the likelihood of the respondent feeling more comfortable and at ease with the researcher, the research environment and the focus and aims of the research (Peracchio and Mita, 1991).

Research projects that have employed a more child-focused approach (see for example, O'Kane, 2000) also display limitations that typically reflect a desire to control the research and operate in a governing role to ensure the validity of the work (as determined by the methodological frameworks endorsed by their respective research communities). There is a tendency to group children into samples defined by age both for access and ethical reasons rather than by considering their social environment which cuts across institutionally constructed age groups. Power relations are still present irrespective of the notion of a joint and collaborative process. Interview arrangements are potentially problematic given the importance of privacy and confidentiality, especially in relation to the power imbalance between children and adults. There is also the emphasis on the adult researcher and their communication skills to create the rapport needed to build and sustain trust, confidence and commitment on behalf of the child respondent. Of course when employing this approach, negotiating access and consent is of primary concern and the ethical considerations in developing a more collaborative approach are exacerbated. A youth-focused piece of research requires a more reflexive approach on behalf of the researcher and whilst it is useful to acknowledge the implications and influence of autobiography in the research process (James, 1993) it nevertheless remains a significant constraint when attempting to derive the respondent's view of the topic that is as faithful as possible.

Advancing the Notion of Young People as Researchers

Is it possible then to maintain the benefits of employing an ethnographic approach whilst minimising our 'governing role' as researchers? Closing the perceived gap between the adult researcher and the child respondent presents a challenge for the child-centred research process and developing a rapport with young people in their space and on their terms becomes an integral aspect of this process (Bannister and Booth, 2005). Several authors have argued for a reduced or 'least-adult' role in the field (see for example Mandell, 1991) which requires suspending all adult-like traits and adopting as much of a child-like persona as is possible. This reflects an ethnographic approach and has clear limitations in the context of researching young people as cited above. Others recommend a more participatory approach that centres on the development of methods or media that facilitate both a greater engagement on behalf of the child respondent but which also allows the children to relate their experiences through an active role in the data collection, providing them with the voice, tools and shared understanding of the research process with which to relate their experiences (see Christensen and James, 2000). This can be particularly relevant when researchers are engaged in participatory action research (Dick, 2004).[1]

In essence, participatory research techniques give children control over the methods by which data is derived and allows the young people to give meaning to the research whilst the process itself remains under the governance of the researcher. Morrow and Richards (1996: 100) suggest that:

[U]sing methods which are non-invasive, non-confrontational and participatory, and which encourage children to interpret their own data, might be one step forward in diminishing the ethical problems of imbalanced power relationships between researcher and researched at the point of data collection and interpretation.

Thomas and O'Kane (2000: 820) support the notion of 'an open minded commitment to hearing what children have to say about the subjects they want to talk about, and in ways they want to talk about them'. They provide examples of the way in which opportunities are created for children to participate in the interpretation and analysis of research data. These can be summarised a follows:

---

1   Participatory Action Research (PAR) involves all relevant parties in actively examining a practice they are all engaged with (which typically is problematic) in order to change and improve it.

first, children are given a choice of subjects for discussion and can decide what to say about them by selecting from a range of research instruments. Second, children are given the chance to review and refine what they said in the original interview via a second interview. Third, via small groups, children are able to collectively reinterpret the research questions and the material from the individual interviews. Finally, volunteers from the original sample compile an audiotape of children's comments from the research by selecting and editing comments which best reflected the messages that ought to be taken from the research (Thomas and O'Kane, 1998).

This participatory approach offers a degree of agency to the child within the process managed by the researcher. For example, interviews with the children may be based around discussions using activities chosen by the children from those designed and prepared by the researcher. An ethno-participatory approach takes this a stage further and applies what Kroll (1995: 98) refers to as the art of '*being*' rather than '*doing*'. This corresponds closely with ethnographic research situated in the research site with the added emphasis on children's agency that spans the entire research process. What further differentiates participatory research from ethnographic studies is the less invasive and more transparent nature of the methods used which are chosen and actioned by the children rather than the participant observer (O'Kane, 2000). These differences in agency afforded to young people through each stage in the various types of research are illustrated in Table 9.1.

Table 9.1: Research stage management by research approach

	Research Approach			
Research Stages	Traditional	Ethnographic	Participatory	Ethno-participatory
Choice of research topic	Theoretical/ pre-determined	Theory guided/ grounded	Theory guided/ consultative	Theory guided/ potential to modify/ agreed
Research design	Removed from research site	Situated in research site	Contextualised by research site	Developed within the research site
Research methods	Actioned by methodology	Actioned by researcher	Actioned by respondents	Produced by respondents
Fieldwork	Controlled by researcher	Controlled by research site	Controlled as a partnership	Controlled by respondents
Analysis and interpretation	Analytical modelling	Conceptual framework	Reflective framework	Co-produced framework
Dissemination	Institution directed	Researcher directed	Ethically directed	Respondent directed

There are a number of examples of research projects that have been initiated and directed by children and adolescents (see, for example, Alderson, 2000). These are typically characterised by the young person taking ownership for the design, production, analysis and dissemination of the research. It is noted how effective these approaches are in discovering the child's eye view of the issues under investigation which inevitably lead to a more appropriate and child-focused set of conclusions and recommendations. Hart (1992) compares different ways of sharing control with young people by illustrating children's participation in the context of rungs on a ladder. The lowest rung represents the 'pretence' of shared work – a superficial gesture to make the project appear more attractive. The next level is more authentic and involves direct participation by the child in activities shared between children but initiated by adults. The top rung represents projects more fully initiated and controlled by children.

Conceding control to the young people you are researching with may appear a daunting prospect and is certainly one that is likely to challenge both novice and experienced researchers. The balance achieved between retaining a level of control over the research process and ascribing autonomy to the children or adolescents will be guided by a combination of the research objectives, your ontological position, your own limitations and the perceived limitations of the capabilities of the children with whom you are researching.

Your decision to extend the autonomy of your respondents will most likely be influenced by the level of engagement the young people in your study are likely to display when taking part in an ethno-participatory research process. Okely (1992) points out that social research is always about social relationships and argues that in studies with young people an essential ingredient is the relationship that is created between the researcher and the child. It is a bond that secures a continuous dialogue over which researcher and child feel they have control and encourages a willingness to participate throughout the research process.

The young person's motivation to be more engaged in an ethno-participatory research process is derived from the characteristics inherent within the process of research itself and these attributes can be illustrated using a personal account from a young researcher involved with several ethno-participatory projects (see Box 9.1).

This young female researcher identifies several aspects of the research study that inspired her to take the initial step of getting involved with research projects and also to seek out and volunteer for additional projects utilising a similar ethno-participatory approach. Most notable is the acknowledgment of her role as an 'insider' able to gather information about her peers. Also significant is the recognition of the skills and experience that were developed as she became more involved with research studies and how these skills informed her understanding of research methods. Prominent is the reflexivity she demonstrates in accounting for the differences in the methods used and the variety of responses they produced, some of which surprised and led her to question her own beliefs about the behaviour of her peers.

Box 9.1 Adolescent Researcher's Account of Ethno-Participation

I first took an active and key role in the research projects being carried out by the lecturers (I was asked to by a friend) when I was 13. I have always had a great curiosity about research and I enjoyed the interviewing process and the wide variety of responses and then the conclusions that are clear at the end. It is all greatly interesting and good fun too. I have since been involved in numerous projects such as finding out the influences behind different music tastes and also the drivers behind the significance of the 'senior dance' or 'high school prom' held at schools. As adolescents and their thoughts and opinions are central to research, what better way to gain this information than through another adolescent acting as an adolescent researcher? I was trained and given the opportunity to write my own questions for the research topics. I then had to think about who to research with. Initially, it proved difficult to find and recruit people to interview as although there were many friends available, factors such as an individual's reliability and willingness to participate had to be considered.

It was always really interesting when people were asked to specify what they liked and why as it opened people's minds and created insightful discussions. The different ways in which the volunteers were interviewed also provoked different responses. For example, discussions in small groups highlighted points that others didn't think of but did agree or disagree with and questionnaires allowed people to keep their thoughts to themselves. Conducted in whichever way, the responses were always varied and sometimes very surprising and unexpected (even with people I thought I knew quite well!). Frequently, problems did arise in connection with the questions as many people found they were unsure or did not know the reasons why they behaved a certain way. One of the main reasons for this, I learned, was that they hadn't really thought about their behaviour before, that is, it was subconscious or the reason was not at the forefront of their mind. Yet, as more questions were asked and the greater the discussion, it was great to see that the interviewees got more involved and interested in the research and its purpose. When questions were broken down to help prompt answers the interviewees seemed more aware of how they could answer and then they felt more comfortable.

Helping out with the research not only gave me and all of us involved the experience of communication, responsibility and at times teamwork, it was also good fun. I would definitely encourage other people to get involved for experience and to benefit from the discussions.

Youth-Focused Research Designs and Practical Implications

Setting the Scene: Realistic Aims and Objectives

Developing and testing theory are not easily separated. Theory can emerge from data, although any interpretation of emergent themes is subject to mediation by the author's own assumptions and perspectives. At the same time, an ethno-participatory approach demonstrates a commitment to gaining a more in-depth understanding of the thoughts, motives, perceptions and cultural contexts which structure the lives of young people and as such falls within the interpretive tradition of research. Employing this approach requires an acknowledgement of the issues of power and authority in the research process and a balance that confers much of the control to the child (see 'Advancing the notion of young people as researchers' above). Setting and developing aims, objectives and the research topic can be seen in Chapter 1.

Research Design

An ethno-participatory technique is fundamentally guided by the researcher's agenda and does not fall into the category of grounded research in its purest sense. It remains a versatile method that, when combined with other methods can harness the benefits accrued from a participatory research approach and can alleviate many of the drawbacks (see 'The concept of young people as researchers' above). Ethno-participatory research equates with the top rung of Hart's (1992) ladder analogy discussed earlier and advocates the initiation and direction of the study by the young people who are the focus of the study. The range of activities and methods employed by the adolescent researchers (or 'experts') can vary greatly and involve research in groups or individually. Adolescent experts can select research topics, themes, specific research questions or interview topics and select the sample and research site(s). They may run a pilot and/or a review and modify the original research design, then collect and collate the data, analyse it and produce and disseminate the report using a range of creative and often highly effective methods (see, for example, Alderson, 2000). One aspect of the design is the choice of a qualitative and/or quantitative approach and an important component of the training the 'experts' (adolescents) ought to receive is a discussion of the merits of each type of research and the associated methods (see 'Training and research methods' below).

Sampling, Recruitment and Adolescent Roles

Key to the success of an ethno-participatory approach is to work with a group of children or adolescents who reflect the population you are studying and who actively want to participate in the research. As a consequence of the resources required by both the researcher (organiser) and the adolescent (researcher), the sample of young researchers you choose is likely to be fairly small and grouped geographically and based on convenience sampling or purposive sampling as discussed by Cohen *et al.* (2000) for practical reasons. This clearly has consequences for the nature of the sample in terms of a potential lack of diversity in socio-economic status and ethnic background, common behavioural norms associated with urban/rural dwelling and the predominant influence of local social institutions (schools, youth clubs, local newspapers, magazines, etc). The opportunity for increasing the diversity of the sample comes from the choice of peer respondents chosen by the young researchers. A youth peer group is not necessarily bound by the social norms cast by the traditional adult segments and as such affords an opportunity to cross many of the artificial boundaries ascribed by society. Friendship and peer groups can include a great variety of young people brought together by alternative strands of shared values and culture often displayed through musical taste, lifestyle and recreational activity. Encouraging the child to focus on their peer and friendship groups to find recruits for their interviews and focus groups has a motivational benefit and provides an element of familiarity for the child researcher. Indeed, to enhance the ethnographic element of the study, it would be important not to restrict or limit the sample chosen by the experts as the data collection would be more effective and the data itself more illuminating. The process and the ethical issues surrounding the recruitment of young respondents by the adolescent experts are discussed below (see 'Fieldwork and data collection').

In seeking active agreement (consent) on behalf of the children (supported with the passive consent of the gatekeepers) you should aim to provide an information pack about your research project without biasing the outcome of the project, for example, disclosing what it is you hope or expect to find as a result of doing the research. There are a number of innovative ways this can be achieved and consideration for the type of media young people find interesting may be a greater success than standard letters or A4 sheets explaining the project. You could consider creatively designed leaflets, audio recordings about the research on CDs or as an MP3 file, excitingly displayed activity sheets and flowcharts to show what is going to happen with the project, dynamic mini-presentations at schools or at youth clubs, an interactive project website with an email contact address or a research activity afternoon designed to pique their interest in research and provide the opportunity to enrol on the project.

Whichever method is chosen to reach and influence your potential adolescent experts the focus of the communication must be on the collaborative nature of the study and the autonomous role and control the young person will have to shape the design and destiny of the research. Any young person given the responsibility to research is likely to respond more positively on the basis that they are aware of (and can sometimes resent) the limitations of their 'pre-adult' status. This corresponds with the notion of children as 'competent witnesses' and promotes children's agency.

Recruiting adolescent researchers could be facilitated by conducting initial interviews with the young people identified in a sample designed and executed in a traditional manner to explore the themes of a research topic in greater depth. The appealing feature of interviews as a research tool is the opportunity for the interviewee to respond in their own words to express their own personal perspectives. At this stage the respondent has already expressed an interest by agreeing to take part and once rapport and a level of trust has been established it would be possible to seek volunteers from this group to become your adolescent researchers or *'experts'*.

Training and Research Methods

Alderson (2000) argues that working with child researchers will not necessarily resolve the problems of power and may indeed amplify them unless working methods are planned, tested, evaluated and developed with the young researchers. A critical component of this methodical approach is the quality of the training provided for the sample of adolescent experts volunteering to design and conduct research.

If the young researcher is already familiar with the research project (for example they volunteered after being interviewed during an initial research phase) their training has effectively begun. As these adolescents are aware of the research project already you can assume that their initial interest in being 'involved' will carry over into the next phase and provide you with an engaged individual when it comes to more formal training. Training for research is essential in building the confidence of the adolescent expert. A training programme that focuses on developing the essential skills required to conduct the research as professionally as possible also conveys to the adolescent experts a sense of faith in their abilities as competent young people and reinforces their responsibilities and role as researchers. How to train young people as researchers is covered in detail elsewhere (see Clark *et al.*, 2001) but in developing a training programme you would need to address at least the following: the importance of securing consent before starting, designing interview questions, recruiting friends and organising interviews, choosing appropriate locations for the interviews to take place, operating recording equipment, using observational techniques and compiling and storing data and anonymity and confidentiality. It is equally important to reflect on the following aspects before, during and after the training session: understanding what was required, time constraints, the learning environment and confidence.

The methods for the study should be chosen and selected by the adolescent experts. After the training session they should be more aware of the nuances and attributes of the available research methods and will be able to make a more informed choice. They should have an understanding of the implications for the fieldwork in terms of their personal resources and how acceptable the methods are for researching with their peers.

Based on the research themes modified and agreed with the researcher, specific interview questions should be designed by the experts themselves. An example of the type of questions that can emerge can be seen in Table 9.2 which compares the questions developed by two groups of experts (12-14-year-olds and

Table 9.2: Interview questions designed by groups of experts

Interview themes	Early (younger) adolescent sample	Later (older) adolescent sample
1. Things which are really important	**Questions E1** • What is important to you in life generally? • Give examples of brothers and sisters, other family, friends, fashion, money, health, lyrics, advice on life, looks and appearance, clothing, etc. • Do you have a role model? If so, does it affect you in the way you dress, talk and behave?	**Questions L1** • Would you listen to music just because it made you laugh? • Do you listen to music just because other people do? • If you could only take one thing with you to a desert island would it be music related? • What is really important to you and why?
2. Places they would listen to music on their own	**Questions E2** • Do you listen to music on your own? • If so, where do you listen to music on your own? • Would you rather listen to music through headphones or in a room on your own with the door closed and blast it out?	**Questions L2** • Where do you listen to music? • If you listen to music alone will it be of a more subdued genre than that which you would listen to amongst companions? • Do you need to listen to music to help you concentrate? • Do you feel less on your own when you listen music on the bus?
3. Music they would listen to with their friends	**Questions E3** • Would you be influenced by your friends? • What types of music would you listen to with your friends? • (If female/male) Is it just male/female artists you listen to? And why?	**Questions L3** • Do you dance when you listen to music with your friends? • Do you feel that you have to listen to certain types of music to get new friends? Or more better friends? • Do you feel more free when you listen to music with friends? • Would you sing along to music with friends in public?

15-18-year-olds) who were invited to participate in a study of adolescent music consumption (See Nuttall, 2006). The table illustrates that the interview questions designed by the older adolescent group differ in various ways from the questions created by the younger group. The older group, perhaps not surprisingly, produced on average a greater number of questions under each theme. They tended to be more sophisticated and enquiring in nature. The older group also demonstrated a better understanding of the research and its objectives by positing questions that were designed to explore in more depth, aspects related to the research project (e.g. identity, social contexts and behaviour relating to music consumption and use).

In this particular case the questions culminated from discussions that centred on collages the recruited experts made together during one of the training sessions. The adolescent researchers were given a variety of music/adolescent interest magazines and asked to generate collages using clippings from the magazines under a number of relevant headings. The adolescents then made up their own questions which were discussed and agreed within the group. They were then supplied with the materials to conduct the interviews, instructions on ethical issues and means of contacting the researchers in cases of difficulty and/or need for more general support.

There are various ways to facilitate the design of questions by adolescent researchers. Box 9.2 presents an alternative approach that demonstrates how a small group of adolescents, if asked, would design and implement a research approach with a particular focus on the methods and fieldwork.

Box 9.2: How Would Adolescents Research if Asked?

Three 17-year-old females were recruited via the researcher's social network to come to the university to discuss how they, as adolescents, would design and conduct a research project with their friends and peers. This was to be a youth-focused piece of research. The contribution made by the adolescents would, therefore, not only ensure the discussion was grounded in the context of what the adolescents considered to be important about the forthcoming event but would also give an indication of the best approach to adopt when the research was conducted. The topic for the research was their forthcoming 'senior dance' or end-of-year celebration. The researcher provided the girls with a few general areas of interest in relation to the senior dance which would facilitate the beginning of the discussion. The areas of interest included: deciding on an outfit, shopping (and who funds the shopping), transport to the event, additional celebrations, friendship groups, people who do not attend the dance and how the dance would be recorded (e.g. photographs). The researcher provided the females with a room, flipchart paper, A4 paper, pens, pencils and soft drinks. They were left to discuss the research on their own and took approximately two hours to arrive at their conclusions. The discussion was audio-recorded for the benefit of the researcher with relevant consent given by the adolescents.

Initially the discussion focused on the event itself. The girls discussed the emotions and anxieties associated with the dance including whether a boy had asked them to the dance, their outfits (e.g. how they would feel if someone was going to be wearing the same outfit as them), the cost of the event, feeling excluded if they had not been asked by a friendship group to share a limo to the event and who they would sit beside for the meal at the senior dance. They also considered what would happen 'after' the senior dance had taken place, where the 'after party' was (who would be invited) and how the event would be recorded. One girl commented that everyone would 'take lots of photos to put on Bebo etc. as if to prove how much of a good time they had'.

Having explored all the aspects of the forthcoming event they were interested in, the adolescents began to form a plan to research with their friends and peers about the senior dance. Before the research could take place, the girls recognised that not everyone would want to participate. Those, for example, who were studying hard for exams would be too busy, there were those known to be 'unreliable' or 'not entirely honest' and those who 'may not take it seriously'. Sampling clearly would be an issue. Research methods were then explored.

The use of diaries, photographs, questionnaires and the setting up of a Bebo senior dance page were considered. The adolescents then discussed the management of a project this size. They decided that they would need someone to be in charge of each research method, for example, someone who would manage the questionnaire distribution or the Bebo site and an additional number of researchers (six) to assist if all the methods were to be employed. Meetings for those managing each of the methods were to be set up to maintain open lines of communication and to benchmark the progression of the study.

However, given the length of time the adolescents had before the research took place and taking into account their own personal commitments (and how difficult they thought it may be to recruit other researchers), the girls decided on a questionnaire approach. This they could manage between themselves and thought their friends and peers would prefer this approach to research as it would be less time-consuming and would require less of a time commitment than other forms of research (e.g. in-depth interviews).

With thanks to Rebecca Tinson, Emma Watson and Justine Hughes

Fieldwork and Data Collection

Organising the fieldwork is a critical aspect of the training of young researchers. Their understanding of the ethical implications of the study they are about to conduct will encourage them to ensure that the friends they want to interview and their parents have completed consent forms and are fully aware of the origins of the project and the dissemination of the findings (see Chapter 2). For example, you could co-produce with your experts a 'consent pack' to give to their peer interviewees which would contain letters to the parent and adolescent explaining the research, consent forms and a return-paid envelope to have the completed forms sent back to the adult researcher (who can manage the administrative aspects of the project). You should insist that peer interviews are only allowed to take place once the consent forms have been received. Parent signatures should be checked and follow-up calls made to a sample of parents to ensure the consent forms had been legitimately completed. Once the consent forms have been received, and you are happy with the legitimacy of the forms, a simple phone call can be made to the experts to give them the go-ahead to conduct the interview(s).

Before the fieldwork begins it is important that channels of communication between yourself and the young researchers are open and fully understood. Each expert should have the telephone number of the researcher and should be encouraged to maintain regular contact during the period of interviewing. Follow-up calls could be made during and after the data collation, although care needs to be taken that this is not perceived as 'monitoring' or that the adult researcher becomes overbearing.

The training session will have provided instructions on how to use the recording devices chosen for the study and tuition on interview techniques. It is worth supporting this with a 'research pack' that might contain written instructions for the recording device(s), hints and tips for the interview, collating and storing data and a reminder about issues regarding confidentiality and the respect they need show their respondents during the interviews (e.g. informed dissent). One technique for preparing the adolescent researchers for their peer interviews is ask them to first interview one of their parents or a guardian as this will allow the adolescent to practise their research skills, familiarise themselves with the recording equipment and give them an opportunity to immerse themselves in the research topic.

In accordance with the principles underpinning the ethno-participatory approach the research is conducted *in situ* and some consideration of the recording devices made available to the young researchers is important. Traditional recording devices such as tape recorders can be bulky, intrusive and ineffective particularly given that the data collection is likely to take place in a variety of non-formal locations and possibly noisy environments for example, on the bus on the way to school, in school playgrounds or at a youth centre. Where resources allow, capturing data by using smaller (and clearer) digital recording devices or capitalising on the recording functions offered by lifestyle products familiar to young people such mobile phones or MP3 players would potentially address some of these issues effectively.

Depending on the nature of the study it is advisable to encourage the experts to complete their interviews within a specific time frame, for example, within a fortnight of the training session. Clearly, given the ethnographic foundations of this approach, it is necessary that the interviews are conducted at the convenience of the interviewer and interviewee. At the same time, consideration must be given to the length of time a young researcher will be able to sustain the necessary level of motivation and interest in the project required to complete every stage including analysis and interpretation.

Self-Interpretation and Analysis

According to James *et al.* (1998) we need to address the perception that children are less active social beings or less competent than adults and remove the tendency to adopt a *top-down* perspective when analysing and interpreting data produced by, in this case, adolescent interviewers, and read adult meanings into what is recorded (for a consumer research perspective see Hyatt, 1991). Bartholomew and O'Donohoe (2003: 434) also support 'look(ing) through the eyes of a child rather than the lens of adult researchers'. By adopting an ethno-participatory approach, you have already accepted the notion supported by Holstein and Gubrium (1997) that it is essential to view children as *constructors of knowledge* in their own right and in collaboration with the researcher as opposed to being the simply the subject of the research process.

In establishing a dialogue with young people about the themes and issues raised by the research that includes their own interpretations as a researcher you have reduced some of the methodological problems around the interpretation of children's responses and activities by adults (Solberg, 1996). See also Chapter 7. Thomas and O'Kane (1998) also argue that the use of participatory methods can enhance validity and reliability of your findings.

As can be seen in the following example, the research approach taken by Nuttall (2006) afforded the adolescent experts the chance to analyse their own interviews which explored identity formation and music consumption. That is, having conducted the interviews with their friends, all of the experts provided an interpretation of their peer interviews. To facilitate this interpretation, the experts were provided with the transcripts of the interviews they conducted with their friends and audio recordings of the same interviews. The experts were then asked to go through the transcripts and listen to the tapes after which they were asked to interpret the findings. A tape-recording was made of the experts' interpretations as they discussed their own interviews. The interpretation of each interview transcript was divided into the 10 themes related to the meaning of music, identity and self expression through music and music listening and consumption identified by the adult researcher during the initial phase of research. At each stage, very brief prompts were provided by the researcher and are summarised below:

♦ In your own words, what did you understand about what your friend was telling you here?

♦   How easy was it for your friend to answer these particular questions?

♦   Do you think your friend was hiding anything or did s/he surprise you with anything they said?

♦   How honest do you think your friend was being?

An extract from one of these interpretative interviews is presented in Box 9.3.

Box 9.3: Expert Adolescent's Interpretation of Interview Data

Transcript from adolescent researcher (AR) interviewing their friend (F)

AR What is important to you in life generally?

F   My family and friends.

AR Anything else, like looks, appearance, clothing, money?

F   I like what I wear.

AR Do you have a role model?

F   Yeah my mum.

AR And does it affect the way you dress, talk and behave?

F   It effects the way I behave because I don't act silly and immature, like when I'm around my mum and stuff, so I guess it does.

AR Do you have like a role model that's like a celebrity or not really?

F   No.

AR No pop stars or anything like Christina Aguilera or.....?

F   Celine Dion.

Adolescent researcher and principal investigator (PI) reflecting on the interview

PI   Tell me about this friend's response to question one.

AR   I thought she was being very honest, I don't think she hesitated a lot, I think she was just thinking of how to say it. I think she was.....well not quite embarrassed but quite shy of saying that she didn't have a role model, I think because when I said it she was a bit, no I don't have one.

PI   Why do you think she responded like that?

AR   She probably just thinks that because I asked her that, that most people have one maybe and she thought, oh I don't have one and she was trying to think whether she should say yes and just think of one, or say no. I think she was being very honest when I said, if looks or appearance were important, she just said no because I like what I wear. I think that was quite an honest one, I think that was a good one.

Limitations and Scope of the Ethnoparticipatory Approach

Whilst this chapter and indeed this text advocates engaging children with the research process, not all children can or will be involved in participatory or ethno-participatory research. As levels of children's participation and control are affected by their capacity to understand the relevant issues and apply critical analysis and evaluation (Alderson, 2000), the social and cognitive development stage of the child/ren may limit the role of the young persons and in some cases become counterproductive. That is, the child/ren may not want the responsibility and/or may simply not understand what is required of them and may become uncomfortable and unsure how to continue in their role. The role of the adult researcher in this context is extremely important and if you have adopted the persona of the *interested adult friend* as suggested by Fine and Sandstrom (1988) and James *et al.* (1998) it is essential that you look for signs of discomfort and are sensitive to the implications of delegating responsibility for your research study to young people. In this chapter ethno-participatory research has been illustrated by employing adolescent experts to minimise difficulties of comprehension.

Individual agency promoted through this type of research is constrained by the social pressures as adult researchers we may not be aware of as they are forged and sustained within the social context. As such, it may only be when the adolescent researchers go out into the field that design issues (e.g. types of questions agreed amongst the adolescent researchers) or the new role of the adolescent in their social or peer group becomes problematic. The adolescent researcher may not have anticipated that their friends or peers would behave differently towards them and that their new role may change their social position within the group (if only temporarily).

Sustaining the adolescents' level of interest in the research can also limit the scope of ethno-participatory research. Although the interest in the research tends to be a factor in recruitment, using this approach means that those with good communication skills are more likely to volunteer to become adolescent researchers and it may be that their sample of friends chosen for interview may reflect this. As such, adolescents with poorer communication skills and their input would not be included in the research. There are of course ways of overcoming this as ethno-participatory research can be both exploratory and experimental and can be used with more traditional forms of research to ensure a more representative sample.

Ensuring confidentiality and anonymity for the research participants is essential (see Chapter 2) and it is important that the young people researching with other young people can be trusted and are aware of the importance and significance of employing an ethical approach whilst researching. Depending on the social network and the experience of the adult researcher, again these considerations may limit the sample. The topic and the aims and objectives of the research may also influence the decision to attempt an ethno-participatory approach. If, for example, the topic is of a sensitive nature, children may not want to discuss their concerns with another child. It is important then to always reflect on the reason for researching with children and take a balanced approach to the design and data collection of any research project that includes the world view of young people.

Children are the primary source of information about their own social world and this chapter has illustrated how it is possible to move from a child being asked by an adult researcher to 'do' research to 'being' a researcher. Whilst there are a wide-ranging number of caveats to employing ethno-participatory research, adolescents appear to be motivated by this approach perhaps driven by responsibility and the notion of managing their own projects and having control over the output which may, for example, determine changes in social policy that affects them directly. As employing a traditional ethnographic approach has a number of limitations (e.g. the researcher will never be a child) using participatory approaches can be a means of access to other children (albeit that additional and possibly unique ethical issues such as ensuring anonymity and confidentiality amongst the children may have to be taken into consideration). It has been shown here that the novelty and immediacy of using participatory methods for a research project can help produce greater interest and may enhance the speed and efficacy of dissemination. It can also add to the range of skills and to the confidence of young people.

Summary

This chapter has considered the concept of young people as researchers and has attempted to advance this notion further. Differences in agency afforded to young people through different levels of participatory research have been explored and examples of how adolescents would conduct research if asked have been considered. An adolescent researcher who has taken part in a variety of research projects also contributed their own view on participatory research. Although this chapter discusses the significance of youth-focused research design, the practical implications of managing such a project have also been addressed. There are a number of requirements to employing a participatory approach (such as level of training) and these too have been identified and explored.

Reflective Questions

1   List three methods used in ethnography.

2   What is the biggest challenge for researchers working with children?

3   Why should children become collaborators in research?

4   How can researchers minimise their 'governing role' when researching with children?

5   What is an ethno-participatory research approach?

6   How might a researcher recruit adolescent researchers?

7   What might be the limitations of employing adolescent researchers to research their friends and peers?

8   What ought to be taken into consideration when training adolescent 'experts'?

9   How might a researcher facilitate interpretation of adolescent researchers' research data?

10 How and why would adolescent researchers have to understand anonymity and confidentiality?

Checklist

☐   Have you considered the ethical implications and consequences of employing a participatory approach?

☐   Are you aware of the benefits of employing an ethnographic approach?

☐   Do you understand how employing an ethnographic approach may affect sampling and validity?

☐   Do you know what to take into account when training adolescent researchers?

☐   Do you know what may affect your decision to extend the autonomy of adolescents when researching with young people?

☐   Have you thought how to motivate adolescents to become researchers?

☐   Do you understand why the adult researcher/adolescent researcher power imbalance may not be resolved by employing a collaborative approach?

☐   Have you considered how to facilitate interpretation of the research data?

References

Alderson, P. (2000) 'The effects of participation rights on research methodology', in P. Christensen and A. James (eds), *Research with Children: Perspectives and Practices*, London: Falmer Press.

Bannister, E. and Booth, G. (2005) 'Exploring innovative methodologies for child-centric consumer research', *Qualitative Market Research: An International Journal*, 8 (2), 157-175.

Bartholomew, A. and O'Donohoe, S. (2003) 'Everything under control: a child's eye view of advertising', *Journal of Marketing Management*, 19, 433-457.

Christensen, P. and James, A. (eds) (2000) *Research with Children: Perspectives and Practices*, London: Falmer Press.

Clark, J., Dyson, A., Meagher, N., Robson, E., and Wooten, M. (2001) 'Involving young people in research: the issues', in Clarke *et al.* (eds), *Young People as Researchers: Possibilities, Problems and Politics*, Leicester: Youth Work Press (National Youth Agency).

Clough, P. and Nutbrown, C. (2002) *A Students Guide to Methodology*, London: Sage.

Cohen, L., Manion, L. and Morrison, K. (2000) *Research Methods in Education*, 5th edn, London: Routledge Falmer.

Danby, S. and Farrell, A. (2002) 'Accounting for young children's competence in educational research: new perspectives on research ethics', *Australian Educational Researcher*, 31 (3), 35-50.

Dick, B. (2002). 'Action research: Action and research', http://www.scu.edu.au/schools/gcm/ar/arp/aandr.html (accessed Feb 2009)

Elliott, R. and Jankel-Elliott, N. (2003) 'Using ethnography is strategic consumer research', *Qualitative Market Research: An International Journal*, 6 (4), 215-35.

Fine, G. and Sandstrom, K. (1988) *Knowing Children: Participant Observation with Minors*, London: Sage.

Hart, R. (1992) *Children's Participation: From Tokenism to Citizenship*, London: Earthscan/Unicef .

Holstein, J.A. and Gubrium, J.F. (1997) *Active Interviewing*, London: Sage.

Hyatt, C. (1991) 'Qualitative and quantitative approaches to child research', *Advances in Consumer Research*, 18, 117-28.

James, A. (1993) *Childhood Identities: Self and Social Relationships in the Experience of the Child*, Edinburgh: Edinburgh University Press.

James, A. and Prout, A. (eds) (1990) *Constructing and Reconstructing Childhood*. Basingstoke: Falmer Press.

James, A., Jenks, C. and Prout A. (1998) *Theorizing Childhoodi,* Cambridge: Polity Press.

Jenks, C. (2000) 'Zeitgeist research on childhood', in P. Christensen and A. James (eds), *Research with Children: Perspectives and Practices*, London: Falmer Press, pp.62-76.

Kroll, B. (1995) 'Working with children', in F. Kaganas, M. King and C. Piper (eds), *Legislating for Harmony: Partnership under the Children Act 1989*, London: Jessica Kingsley.

Llewellyn, M. (1980) 'Studying girls at school: the implications of confusion', in R. Deem (ed.), *Schooling for Women's Work*, London: Routledge, pp. 42-51.

Mandell, N. (1991) 'The least-adult role in studying children', in F. Waksler (ed.), *Studying the Social Worlds of Children*, Basingstoke: Falmer Press.

Morrow, V. and Richards, M. (1996) 'The ethics of social research with children: an overview', *Children and Society*, 10 (2), 90-105.

Nutbrown, C. (1999) 'Literacy in the earliest years: Alex's story', in E. Millard (ed.), *Enquiring into Literacy*, Sheffield: Sheffield University, Sheffield Papers in Education, pp 37-52.

Nuttall, P. (2006) 'Exploring the consumption and use of popular music as a means of expressing an adolescent's identity during the socialisation process', unpublished PhD thesis, University of the West of England, Bristol.

O'Kane, C. (2000) 'The development of participatory techniques: Facilitating children's views about decisions which affect them', in P. Christensen and A. James (eds), *Research with Children: Perspectives and Practices*, London: Falmer Press, pp 136-159.

Okely, J. (1992) 'Anthropology and autobiography: participatory experience and embodied knowledge', in J. Okely and H. Callaway (eds), *Anthropology and Autobiography*, London: Routledge.

Peracchio, L. and Mita, C. (1991) 'Designing research to assess children's comprehension of marketing messages', *Advances in Consumer Research*, 18, 23-34.

Pole, C., Mizen, P. and Bolton, A. (1999) 'Realising children's agency in research: partners and participants?', *International Journal of Social Research Methodology, Theory and Practice*, 2 (1), 39-54.

Roper, G. (1989) 'Research with marketing's paradoxical subjects: children'. *Marketing Research*, June, 16-23.

Solberg, A. (1996) 'The challenge in child research: from "being" to "doing"', in J. Brannen and M. O'Brien (eds), *Children in Families: Research and Policy*, London: Falmer, pp 53-65.

Thomas, N. and O'Kane, C. (1998) 'The ethics of participatory research with children', *Children and Society*, 12, 336-348.

Thomas, N. and O'Kane, C. (2000) 'Discovering what children think: connections between research and practice', *British Journal of Social Work*, 30, 819-835.

Glossary

Assent (informed)
This means the child is told about what will happen during the research process and agrees to the plan. Informed assent is normally used with younger children, who will not be required to sign a consent form but their parent/guardian will.

Back Translation
Children can be asked to read transcripts of their interviews or can be invited to review visual recordings of the research in which they were actively engaged to help the researcher in their interpretation of the data.

Collages
Made by assembling and or sticking a variety of materials onto a piece of paper or canvas. The materials can be, for example, newspaper clippings, pictures or words from magazines, photographs and/or pieces of coloured ribbon.

Consent (informed)
A person's independent agreement to participate in research. This can be provided by a parent/guardian but older children too could sign a consent form.

Contingency
A contingency or a contingency plan involves having a flexible approach to researching with children and can be employed when there are factors outside of the researcher's control that impact on their research plan.

Covert Research
This uses informed consent to bypass research responsibilities. That is, once a researcher has a signature on paper to agree to the child being involved in the research process the researcher (and not the participant) is protected from any risks or outcomes as a result of the study.

Creative Groups
Creative groups can involve the children with whom you are researching in role play, drawing, collages or inventing stories and are akin to focus groups.

Credence
This is when the participant and their parents/guardians cannot fully comprehend what is being tested or the way in which it is being researched, but are comfortable to delegate the responsibility to those with the credibility or authority.

Data Protection Act (DPA)
The Act which details the way in which sensitive information is collected and stored during the research process.

Disclosure
Disclosure (or Disclosure Scotland) is where an individual (or organisation) can apply for police checks through the Criminal Records Bureau (CRB) in accordance with the Police Act 1997. The applicant can be checked against police records for convictions, cautions, reprimands and warnings and enhanced disclosure will provide detail on any records that are held about an individual by the Department for Education and Skills, the Department of Health and any other relevant bodies.

Dissent
This means the child withdrawing their consent for their involvement during research at any time.

Draw and Write Technique
Drawing is often referred to as the universal language of childhood as it reflects the feelings and information concerning psychological status and interpersonal style of the child. Allowing the child to draw and write can elicit more information from the child/ren being researched with.

Friendship Pairs
These are usually 'best friends' or children who know one another very well.

Gatekeepers
Parents, head teachers, teachers, social workers, members of ethics committees, ward sisters, managers of after-school clubs and others who are charge of children in a social or community context (scout leaders, guiders, youth club organisers etc.). In the context of researching with children, the *gatekeepers* are the persons, who control access to young people and who, in some cases, are present when the research is being conducted.

Incentives
A motivation or reward given to the child as a thank you for taking part in the research.

Interlocutors
See *Gatekeepers*

Learning Styles
These are the preferences individuals have for visual, auditory or kinaesthetic learning also known as VAK.

Mixed Methods
This is when qualitative and quantitative methods are used together.

Ontology
The researcher's theory of existence, that is, his/her view on what really exists outside that which simply appears to exist. In sum, it is how a researcher defines the form and nature of reality and what may be known about it.

Paired Friends
These will typically be children known to one another but will be part of a wider circle of friends (e.g. members of a friendship group).

Participant Observation
A research approach which allows the researcher to understand the attitudes, behaviours and/or motivations of individuals (or groups of individuals) simply by watching and noting the way in which he/she/they interact and behave.

Participatory Action Research (PAR)
This involves all relevant parties in actively examining a practice they are all engaged with (which typically is problematic) in order to change and improve it.

Projective Techniques
These involve the use of vague, ambiguous, unstructured stimulus objects or situations in which the children can project his/her personality, attitudes, opinions and self-concept to give the situation some structure.

Research Ethics Committee (REC)
A committee designed to both protect the general public from unethical research and to improve research practice. These committees will advise researchers on their research proposals before any research takes place.

Research Philosophy
This is an explanation of the researcher's assumptions about the nature of knowledge and the methods through which that knowledge can be attained.

Respondent Validation
This is when the interpretation of what has been said or done in a given context should be understood by the researcher and those being researched and the understanding should be the *same*.

Risk Assessment
This involves taking all reasonable steps to ensure that hazards to children, both indoors and outdoors, are kept to a minimum.

Scene Interviews
Scenarios or 'scenes' used during interviews are also known as vignettes and may involve role play.

SEAL (The Social and Emotional Aspects of Learning)
A system used by both primary and secondary schools, which offers a framework for promoting the social and emotional aspects of learning: self-awareness, managing feelings, motivation and social skills.

Social Constructivism

This is who we are and how we come to see ourselves. It is the ongoing and changing story we tell about our lives which is actively constructed from our roles at home, school, and the community.

Visual Data

This type of research material could include photographs, video recording and recordings taken on mobile phones.

Appendices

1 Evaluation of the Youth Counselling Service, Airdrie Local Health Care Co-Operative

by L. Bondi, L. Forbat, M. Gallagher, V. Plows and S. Prior, University of Edinburgh, 2006

Introduction

In July 2004, Airdrie Local Health Care Co-operative set up the Youth Counselling Service (YCS) as a two-year pilot project. A project was conducted by researchers at the University of Edinburgh to evaluate the success of the YCS in providing an independent counselling service for young people of secondary school age in school and in the community.

The YCS responds to Scottish Executive and North Lanarkshire policies for providing multi-agency, community-based, early intervention mental health support for children and young people. The Service has its origins in the identification of a gap in the availability of therapeutic support for young people in the area. The YCS was set up with counselling delivered in one secondary school and a local community centre. It accepts self-referrals as well as referrals facilitated by parents, pupil support staff, health professionals and a wide range of other organisations.

The aim of the evaluation was to identify how successful the Service (including confidential counselling and the 'drop in') has been in providing an independent and confidential counselling service for young people in school and in the community. The evaluation focused on supporting young people experiencing behavioural, social or emotional problems in their personal development and in fulfilling their potential.

Mixed methods were used by the research team. They included:

♦ Interviews with service-users (including school pupils and young people in the community)

♦ Interviews with pupil support staff

♦ Interviews with staff in partner agencies and other referrers

♦ Interviews with members of the YCS advisory group

♦ Questionnaires completed by young people in the school

♦ Service-provided data about referrals and service-users.

Guided by the project's advisory group, the research team identified a range of informants and stakeholders who would be consulted as part of the evaluation of the YCS:

♦ Young people who have used the service. Data from this group provide the most immediate measure of how successful the counselling provided by the YCS has been to date.

♦ Young people who have not used the service. It was essential to gather the views of potential users of the service, particularly the reasons why they might be disinclined to seek counselling, and what could be done to make the YCS more accessible and appealing to them.

♦ Community partners, both actual and potential. To evaluate how the YCS fits in with other services, it was important to gather the views of those who have referred young people to the YCS, or who might do so in future.

♦ Referrers, who include representatives of school-based staff, parents and community-based agencies.

A range of qualitative and quantitative methods were used to gather data from each of these groups.

Ethical Issues

The evaluation study was submitted to Lanarkshire Local Research Ethics Committee, and was approved to proceed on 1st March 2005. Following approval, information was supplied to parents of all pupils at Airdrie Academy, with an invitation to opt their child out of the research if they wished. The parents of 19 pupils took up this offer. Logistical difficulties made it impossible to reach the parents of all young people who might use the community centre. The research team therefore determined to limit the recruitment of young people to those aged 16 or over. Information about, and invitations to participate in, the project were then circulated in the school and at the community centre. In all the ensuing contacts between researchers and participants, the voluntary nature of participation has been stressed, and informed consent has been negotiated orally.

The Evaluation Methods

Interviews with Service-Users

To obtain an in-depth understanding of the effectiveness and experience of using the youth counselling service, service-users who had completed counselling contracts were invited to participate in confidential semi-structured research interviews. This invitation was extended to 19 service-users who finished counselling sessions after ethical approval was granted at the beginning of March 2005 and the end of November 2005. Of these, ten agreed to participate in interviews, of whom one did not attend the interview offered because of another commitment, so that a total of nine interviews were conducted. This response rate (47%) is very high for opt-in recruitment, and substantially higher than rates typically achieved in self-completion questionnaires.

The interviews were conducted between August and December 2005 at a location suitable for the service-user. For those who had used the Service at the school (eight), the counselling room was used. For those who had attended the Service at the community centre (one), alternative accommodation was found. Seven of those interviewed were female and two were male. They were aged between 13 and 17. All had seen the counsellor for at least seven sessions.

Service-users invited to participate in interviews were explicitly informed that they would not be asked about their reasons for attending counselling or the content of the counselling sessions; however, if they wished to talk about these subjects, they could do so. The schedule for the interviews covered experiences of accessing counselling (the referral process); expectations of counselling; experiences of therapeutic change inside themselves and in their ways of engaging with their external environments and satisfaction with the Service. Eight of the interviews lasted for between 25 and 40 minutes, with one being shorter (13 minutes) because the young person forgot to attend and was contacted confidentially via pupil support staff, as a result of which the start time was delayed. Eight of the nine interviews were digitally recorded. One interviewee did not wish to be recorded, but gave permission for written notes to be made. In this case, the interviewer wrote detailed notes of the interview immediately afterwards from memory.

The researcher who conducted these interviews is a counsellor with extensive clinical experience of working with children and young people, including referrals via statutory services. He was selected to conduct this component of the study because of this background, which ensured that he would be able to address the research questions at the same time as being mindful of the potential for these conversations to stir up difficult feelings or memories for the young people concerned.

Young people self-selected to be interviewed and may therefore include those who felt especially satisfied with their experience of counselling. Compared to all service users who had completed their counselling sessions by the end of January 2006, the interview sample was representative in terms of presenting issues, waiting time, referral route and age. It was not representative in terms of:

♦ The balance of service-users seen at Airdrie Academy and the community centre, with the latter under-represented

♦ Gender, with boys under-represented

♦ The number of sessions attended, with service-users attended fewer than seven sessions under-represented

♦ Experience of positive benefits, with those reporting little or no improvement under-represented.

The Questionnaire Survey at the School and the Community Centre

A questionnaire survey was designed to gather data about young people's awareness of the YCS, their thoughts on the location of counselling provision, the extent of young people's worries and the sources of support to which young people expect to turn if they experience difficulties. It was piloted with two groups of pupils in the school and revised according to their suggestions.

A total of 431 questionnaires were completed by school pupils, amounting to 39% of all pupils at the school. This return rate was lower than initially anticipated due to difficulties administering it and pupil absences, as well as pupils 'opting out' of completing the questionnaire.

Of the questionnaires completed by pupils at Airdrie Academy, 52% were completed by girls, 46% were completed by boys and 2% did not answer the question about gender. The gender mix of respondents is close to that of the school as a whole, representing a response rate of 40% of girls and 38 per cent of boys.

To reach young people in the community, questionnaire surveys were distributed at the community centre. This location presented a number of challenges. In the school, large numbers of children could be given a paper exercise as part of their classes, but many young people use the community centre in a transitory way, often for social and leisure activities at weekends or in the evenings. It was therefore difficult for the researchers to administer the survey effectively. Initially 200 questionnaires were left for young people to pick up, complete and return. This yielded no returns at all. An organisation working with young people at the centre was then approached and asked for assistance. A further 40 questionnaires were made available in this way but the return rate was still disappointing, amounting to only 13 (5% of the total number distributed and 33% of those distributed via the local organisation). Of the 13 young people at the community centre who returned completed questionnaires, three were girls and ten were boys. Ten were aged 16, two were 17 and one was 18.

Focus Group and Paired Interviews with Young People

Focus group interviews with young people were conducted with a view to complementing and extending the evidence gathered from the questionnaire survey. The groups discussed a range of issues, including awareness and perceptions of counselling, the kind of difficulties faced by young people and their relative importance, sources of help for young people with worries, and what young people would want from a counselling service, including the preferred location. Data from these discussions provided more detailed insight into the beliefs and perceptions of potential users of the YCS, complementing the data collected in the questionnaire survey.

Interviews were carried out with 11 groups of pupils at Airdrie Academy and three groups of young people at the community centre. In the school, groups of five to six pupils were selected at random from those who had opted in. As far as possible, pupils from the same classes were grouped together in order to maximise the chance of working with friendship networks. Care was taken to create some mixed sex groups and some single sex groups. Some pupils who volunteered for focus group interviews did not attend, and in practice group sizes varied from two to six.

Ten young people in the community centre were recruited into one mixed-sex group on behalf of the research team by a worker based there. The focus group interview used the same approach that had worked well with pupils of similar ages in Airdrie Academy. However, most members of the group at the community centre were very reticent to speak. The reasons for this are not known, but the larger size of the group and its mixed sex composition may have been factors. Two further paired interviews were therefore carried out in this setting, one with two young men and one with two young women, which enabled the collection of more detailed data.

Limitations of the Evaluation

As the summary of data collection methods indicates, the evaluation gathered some forms of evidence more easily than others. It proved much more difficult to recruit young people in the community than in Airdrie Academy, especially for the questionnaire survey and for interviews with service-users. Moreover, although a total of 14 young people participated in focus groups or paired interviews, it proved harder to engage them effectively in the community than in the case of pupils within Airdrie Academy. Had additional resources been available for the evaluation, a range of methods might have been used to assist recruitment among young people in the community. These include extended periods of participant observation at the community centre and intensive follow-up work to reach service-users.

Findings

Service-users who participated in in-depth interviews report high levels of distress immediately prior to seeing the counsellor and describe not knowing who to turn to for support. Some were already in contact with statutory services; others described a series of escalating problems that would have resulted in referral to statutory services had they not accessed counselling. All derived substantial benefit from counselling and expressed very high levels of satisfaction. They described improvements in relationships with others and in their capacity to regulate their emotions. They describe the YCS as highly trustworthy, and their counselling work as both challenging and effective.

The great majority of school pupils (89% of those surveyed) are not aware of the existence of the YCS. They are well aware that young people may have worries with which they need help, and have a rich understanding of the range, complexity and intensity of problems that can affect young people. Their understanding of counselling varies, with confusion and misunderstanding common among younger school pupils. School pupils express a high degree of concern about confidentiality and trustworthiness, and tend to doubt the trustworthiness of teachers. Nevertheless, the majority of school pupils consider it important to have a youth counselling service available to them (56%, with 36% not sure).

Young people who use the community centre at which the YCS is based proved difficult to reach. Of the small number who completed the questionnaire survey the majority (77%) were not aware of the existence of the YCS. When engaged in conversation they demonstrate a high level of awareness of the problems that young people face. Those surveyed were equivocal about the importance of having a youth counselling service available to them (31% considered it important, 31% considered it unimportant and 38% had no opinion or did not respond).

Pupil support staff at the school in which the YCS operates, consider it to be a much-needed, and very useful, supportive and effective innovation. They stress the prevalence of needs among school pupils to which they are not qualified or equipped to respond. They describe how the presence of the YCS supports them in their own roles as well as providing important benefits for service-users. They are very satisfied with the operation of the YCS and would like the availability of the youth counsellor in the school to be increased.

Staff in partner agencies and other potential or actual referrers varied widely in their awareness of the YCS. Despite networking activities, and the availability of information in paper form and on the Web, the existence of the YCS has not yet registered with staff in half of the partner agencies. Staff in other agencies and other referrers are strongly supportive of the YCS, considering it to be a useful addition to the range of resources available to young people in the area. They are very satisfied with the operation of the YCS, finding it accessible, effective and complementary to existing forms of provision.

Membership of the YCS advisory group reflects the partnership approach that underlies the pilot project. Members are pleased with how the pilot has progressed and support its continuation based in partnership working.

Overall, the YCS pilot project has been highly successful in addressing unmet needs of young people experiencing behavioural, social and emotional problems. It is strongly supported by actual and potential service-users and referrers. Awareness of the existence of the YCS among partner agencies and young people could be improved. However, the YCS has built up a waiting list and care is therefore required in balancing additional promotional activities with the availability of counselling sessions.

The evaluation made a number of recommendations:

- Mainstreaming the YCS within a partnership approach
- Expanding provision at the Airdrie YCS
- Retaining the systemic and flexible therapeutic approach adopted by the YCS to date
- Further awareness-raising activities for potential service-users
- Further networking activities with partner agencies
- Continuing work with referrers
- Further development of service-user monitoring and feedback forms
- Rolling out the YCS across North Lanarkshire.

2 Assessing the Cumulative Impact of Alcohol Marketing on Youth Drinking

Gordon, R. (2008) University of Stirling

Project Outline

The last decade has seen a 20% increase in alcohol consumption in the UK (ISD, 2004). There has also been a growth in binge drinking with young girls now reporting higher levels than their male counterparts (Currie *et al.*, 2002). The UK has one of the highest recorded rates of binge drinking and associated harm in the whole of Europe (Hibell *et al.*, 1999). Alcohol consumption is associated with a broad range of social and health problems in the UK, at both personal and societal level (WHO, 2002; Klingemann and Gmel, 2001).

Alcohol is currently a major topic given the considerable health and social impact generated by problem drinking (Prime Minister's Strategy Unit, 2004). This has led to significant interest in the factors which potentially influence drinking behaviour. One such factor that has been identified is alcohol marketing – but there is no consensus on its role, if any, in the problem. The alcohol industry has persistently argued that alcohol marketing has no effect on drinking behaviour but merely affects brands choice (Henry and Waterson, 1981). Meanwhile the health lobby generally take the view that alcohol marketing communications increase consumption of alcohol and are influential in the recruitment of new, often under-age, drinkers. Previous research has produced conflicting evidence with some econometric and consumer studies suggesting there may be an effect on behaviour with others suggesting little effect. Therefore doubt remains over the strength and comprehensiveness of the evidence base, certainly in the minds of policy makers:

> There is no clear case on the effect of advertising on behaviour. One recent study suggests that such an effect may exist, but is contradicted by others which find no such case. So the evidence is not sufficiently strong to suggest that measures such as a ban on advertising or tightening existing restrictions about scheduling should be imposed by regulation.

(Prime Minister's Strategy Unit, 2004: 32)

This demonstrates the necessity to construct a strong evidence base through primary research. There are undoubtedly gaps in the evidence base on the impact of alcohol marketing on drinking behaviour; there has been no longitudinal research carried out in the UK, no studies have looked at the impact of new media and viral marketing, there has been no attempt to examine the cumulative impact of marketing communications and branding and no one has checked for any differential effect in terms of gender and inequality.

This research aims to examine the marketing communication techniques used by the UK alcohol industry to assess its impact on youth drinking and risk taking during the period when most young people start experimenting with alcohol (from ages 13-15 years). The study will use a tried and tested research design adapted from the field of tobacco control research; with the inclusion of a longitudinal survey component and study cohort to provide an assessment of causal links between marketing communications and under-age drinking. The study will address the gaps in the evidence base as longitudinal research on the topic has not been carried out previously in the UK and previous studies have not assessed the cumulative impact of the whole marketing mix on youth drinking.

This case study will consider the research methodologies used to collect data with the young people who were the focus of the research.

Research Methodology

The first stage of the research involved conducting an audit of contemporary alcohol marketing communications in the UK through observation research including a press audit, website audit and interviews with selected marketing and alcohol experts.

The second stage of research involved conducting a series of focus groups (n=64) with the target audience of 13-15 year old children to explore their attitudes towards alcohol, drinking behaviours and how the young people responded to alcohol marketing communications.

This stage of the research was to be largely exploratory and would help inform the development of research hypothesis and the survey questionnaire for use in the next stage of the project. Focus groups emerged as a natural choice for exploring the attitudes and behaviour of young people with regards to alcohol and marketing allowing a wide range of information, insight and ideas. Employing a focus group methodology also allowed for the interaction between young people to be observed offering the researchers an insight into the environment and context in which the respondents socialised.

Focus Group Brief

The groups were conducted in neutral venues such as community halls with each group being facilitated by two researchers and attended by 6-8 respondents. Each group was digitally recorded with the consent of respondents and the discussions were subsequently transcribed again with full consent being sought prior to each group. Practical issues regarding holding focus groups with young people also had to be addressed such as seeking parental consent from each of the respondents, ensuring that transport was arranged for each respondent, group times fitted in around the school and family timetables of participants and booking adequate venues to hold each group. Furthermore during the process of holding the focus groups one of the major logistical issues that should be considered when carrying out qualitative research arose in terms of equipment. During one particular focus group the recording equipment failed, highlighting the requirement to ensure that any equipment is in full working order and replacements are readily at hand should equipment failure occur.

A semi-structured group discussion guide was drafted to ensure that the major topics of the research were covered and to stimulate active participation in the groups a mapping exercise task was performed with the respondents in each group.

Focus Group Findings

The transcriptions from the focus groups were then thematically analysed using QSR NVivo 7 software. The findings from the qualitative research carried out with young people for stage 2 of the project offered insights into their drinking behaviours, attitudes towards alcohol and alcohol marketing amongst this age group and their level of brand awareness.

Behaviour

It was found that all of the groups interviewed had a reasonable level of awareness of alcohol and had personal experiences with alcohol. Experimentation with alcohol was a key theme amongst the younger age groups and it was fairly common to try different drinks or even mix various drinks together during each drinking occasion.

Yeah I drink quite a bit. You want to get a wee buzz out of it. It feels good.

(Males, 13, C2DE, Drinkers)

One night my pal did it. He was just mixing it putting anything in and he just put it in his bag, so his mum wouldn't see it. Everything was in it.

(Male, 13, ABC1, Non Drinkers)

Awareness and Attitudes

Some groups displayed a sophisticated level of awareness of issues surrounding alcohol including cost, availability, % ABV, brand awareness and brand image. Most of the young people knew the cost of a wide range of alcoholic drinks and could identify several of the brands shown to them. However it was fairly common for the younger drinkers to be unable to distinguish the difference between alcohol brand and type of drink.

The two vodkas are dead strong cos they are 37%.

(Male, 13, ABC1, Non-Drinkers)

For the tonic wine it's £5.15 for a full bottle and for a half bottle, it's £2.89 in my local shop.

(Female, 14, ABC1, Drinkers)

In terms of awareness of and exposure to alcohol marketing most of the respondents could name adverts or forms of alcohol marketing they had seen. Both males and females commonly named TV adverts, football adverts or sponsorship of football teams including shirt sponsorship as channels in which they had seen alcohol marketing. A few respondents also mentioned seeing adverts on websites and pop-ups featuring alcohol brands. Print media including newspapers and magazines were also mentioned as well as price promotions in shops and supermarkets. A few respondents were able to name specific deals available in shops in their area at that time.

In the Strongbow advert they go round this bar and ask men to drink it and they all say it's great.

(Males, 13, ABC1, Non-Drinkers)

Rangers and Celtic are sponsored by Carling. It would be hard to find someone who didn't know what Carling was.

(Males, 13, ABC1, Non-Drinkers)

On the internet I get pop ups for alcohol, and if you go to the Rangers website, or Celtic then a Carling sign comes up.

(Females, 14, ABC1, Drinkers)

Branding

Brand image was an important issue with certain brands such as a brand of vodka achieving a level of kudos whilst others such as an alcopop brand were thought of as undesirable. However marketing activity was not always a strong predictor of a good brand image as several of the brands preferred by the young drinkers are not marketed strongly. A key issue when choosing a brand were image, strength and value for money with brands that had a higher % ABV and therefore were more likely to offer 'a buzz' being the preferred options. Several of the brands preferred had various urban myths or stories attached to them that seemed to be passed around by word of mouth or in Internet chat rooms.

Smirnoff vodka is cool.

(Female, 13, C2DE, Drinkers)

I prefer WKD to Bacardi Breezer. It's just because most people would probably rather drink that one and be seen with it, it's got a better image. I've seen them advertised, the WKD.

(Females, 14, ABC1, Drinkers)

You hear Buckie more than Buckfast. You see it and hear people talking about it.

(Males, 13, ABC1, Non-Drinkers)

It's just like a tradition thing where you see all these people drinking Buckfast and you think, oh, that must be nice.

(Female, 14, ABC1, Drinkers)

Quantitative Questionnaire Survey

The next stage of the research which was informed by the previous stages was the development and administration of a survey questionnaire to measure respondents' awareness of, exposure to and attitudes towards a wide range of alcohol marketing activities and also to measure their drinking behaviour and associated behaviours (such as risk taking whilst drinking).

Sampling Issues

The first challenge at this stage of the research was to obtain a sample frame that was large enough to achieve the required total sample size that would ensure any research findings would be statistically significant. This proved to be particularly problematic given the relatively large sample size required ($n=1760$) and also the fact that we were dealing with children as our respondents. There are many issues that require to be addressed when attempting to conduct questionnaire surveys with children including data protection issues, dealing with consent from parents or guardians as well as respondents, accessing a sample frame through negotiation with various gatekeepers and also the resources in terms of time and costs of materials involved in carrying out a survey. For this project our initial intention was to obtain a sample frame from the local health board; however it transpired that due to data protection issues this would not be possible.

It followed that there were months of careful and at times delicate and difficult negotiations with gatekeepers of other potential databases of children aged 13-15 years that could provide a suitable sample frame. Finally after considerable negotiations and at a not insignificant cost, the research team was able to obtain a sample frame through the local authority that enabled the team to invite participation in the research to school pupils aged 13 by direct mail. An information pack was sent out directly to the homes of each school pupil in S2 that attended a school within the particular local authority with parental and respondent consent forms being included, and an incentive of a gift token for each respondent was offered. However due to data protection issues there were strict limitations on the research team as to how the process was carried out and only once respondents agreed to take part in the research was data passed on to the researchers. Therefore it became clear during this process that the various data protection laws and issues surrounding accessing the data of children as respondents are complicated and it takes some time, effort and understanding to negotiate.

Once the invitation packs had been sent out to all S2 pupils in the local authority area the response rate was found to be considerably lower (12%) than expected (35%). It was therefore necessary to boost the sample by drawing respondents from neighbouring local authorities. This involved another round of negotiations as due to logistical issues it was not possible to invite participation in the study by direct mail, therefore invitation packs were distributed through schools.

Questionnaire Design and Administration

Once the sample was drawn, the next stage of the process was to design the questionnaire. Using previous research knowledge and experience, information gathered from other research projects on alcohol with young people and also the findings from the first two stages of the project, a draft questionnaire was designed by the research team. This was then extensively pretested with the children aged 13-15 to assess content and comprehension of the questionnaire. This process involved conducting a series of focus groups (n=20) and observed interviews (n=12). This piloting process was essential in ensuring the acceptability, appropriateness and comprehension of the questionnaire content, and to ensure respondents can accurately reflect their views and experiences without constraining responses.

Once the final questionnaire design had been reached, a team of professional market researchers was then briefed and administered the questionnaire in the home of respondents with parental or guardian consent and presence. To limit the potential for bias in answering the questionnaire due to parental or guardian presence especially given the sensitive nature of the research topics, showcards were used for much of the interviewer-administered questionnaire with alcohol consumption being measured through a self-completion questionnaire which was then placed in a sealed envelope.

Currently the data from the first wave of the questionnaire survey is being analysed with findings expected to be published during 2008 and the second wave of the survey to be started in late 2008/early 2009.

Learning Points

The two stages of research with children in this study highlighted that there are a number of issues that must be addressed when considering doing this kind of research. Consideration should be made on the logistics of the research, recruitment, equipment issues, group tasks and discussion guides, sampling issues such as data protection, issues with gatekeepers, consent, response rates and costs and resources required. Furthermore questionnaires should be extensively pre-tested for content and comprehension with children and the questionnaire design should be representative of what it is you are trying to measure. Finally the administration of the questionnaire should consider any potential for bias and aim to ensure that representative data is obtained. If these considerations are addressed when conducting research with young people the more likely it is that the study will be successful.

References

Currie, C., Fairgrieve, J., Akhtar, P. and Currie, D. (2002) *Scottish Schools Adolescent Lifestyle and Substance Misuse Survey*, National Report for the Scottish Executive, TSO.

Henry, H.W. and Waterson, M.Jj (1981) 'The case for advertising alcohol and tobacco products', in D.S.Leather, G.B. Hastings and J.K. Davis (eds), *Health Education and the Media*, Oxford: Pergamon Press, pp. 115-127.

Hibell, B., Andersson, B., Ahlström, S., Balakireva, O., Bjarnason, T., Kokkevi, A. and Morgan, M. (1999) *The 1999 European School Survey Project on Alcohol and Other Drugs* (ESPAD) *Report.*

ISD (2004) 'Alcohol briefing' (unpublished report).

Klingemann, H. and Gmel, G. (2001) *Mapping the Social Consequences of Alcohol*, Dordrecht: Kluwer.

Prime Minister's Strategy Unit (2004) *The Alcohol Harm Reduction Strategy for England*, London: The Stationery Office.

World Health Organization (2002) *The World Health Report 2002: Reducing Risks, Promoting Healthy Life*, Geneva: WHO

3   The Impact of Creating Dyslexia Friendly Classrooms on Children's Learning

Ridsdale, C., Teaching and Learning Adviser (Literacy), South Gloucestershire LA

Project Outline

Dyslexia is a specific learning difficulty which affects approximately 10% of the population to some extent (Myomancy, 2007). As a consequence of greater awareness and media coverage over recent years, accompanied by the National Strategy's promotion of personalisation within the curriculum, it is not surprising that parents are increasingly raising the dyslexia issue and becoming vociferous about the rights of their child (BDA, 2008). This move is directly impacting upon schools' accountability, with a growing number of schools being forced to explain the strategies they employ to meet pupils' individual needs and prove that these are successful.

The approach to addressing learning difficulties has changed significantly over recent years. Historically, many schools relied upon Local Authority funding and support systems to meet the needs of pupils with a range of learning difficulties, a long-drawn out process that demanded significant paperwork. With a high number of referrals and limited resources available this often resulted in children with relatively lesser needs having to wait for support, wasting valuable time. In 2002, the National Curriculum fully endorsed the shift towards a more inclusive approach, emphasising the importance of providing effective learning opportunities for all pupils and offering three key principles:

♦   Setting suitable learning challenges

♦   Responding to pupils' diverse needs

♦   Over-coming potential barriers to learning and assessment for individuals and groups of pupils.

With the current emphasis now placed firmly on inclusion, schools are encouraged and supported to consider how the organisation of resources and development of the environment can be used to support learning effectively, rather than seeking external support as a first step. The guidance 'Inclusive Schooling' clearly states:

Schools, supported by local education authorities and others, should actively seek to remove the barriers to learning and participation that can hinder or exclude pupils.

(DfES, 2001)

It is widely accepted that the key to addressing literacy difficulties in children is through early intervention and the adoption of a multisensory, structured approach. (SEN Code of Practice, 2001: 1:6, 1:11). These principles underpin the theory behind the National Strategy's Inclusion Statement and the BDA Dyslexia Quality Mark, both of which advocate quality-first, inclusive teaching for all pupils. The Primary National Strategy's publication of materials to support schools in making effective provision for dyslexic pupils in 2005 served to further endorse the benefits of this, at the same time also highlighting the dyslexia issue as a growing concern.

Following their attendance at dyslexia training in July 2006, several Special Educational Needs Coordinators (SENCos) raised concerns about the growing number of parents paying for external assessments and subsequently putting pressure upon the school to take action. This small-scale research project was established in order to address the emerging dyslexia issue. The primary aim of the research was to consider how the creation of dyslexia friendly classrooms and the development of strategies to promote quality-first teaching can be used as an effective tool to raise the attainment and self-esteem of pupils with dyslexic tendencies. In addition, the research also considered the impact of this upon other pupil groups; pupils with identified learning difficulties working below national expectations and those causing no concerns, working in line with or exceeding national expectations.

The schools involved were all within South Gloucestershire, an area north-east of Bristol which became a unitary authority in 1996, following the disbandment of Avon. South Gloucestershire's attainment is above the national average in relation to its Key Stage 1 (age 5-7) and Key Stage 2 (age 7-11) results, also performing favourably when compared to statistical neighbours.

Methodology

The project was conducted through an action-research based model in four primary schools and took place over a six-month period from January to June 2007. In order to lead the project and provide strategic direction, a steering group was identified at the outset. This comprised the SENCo from each school, the Teaching and Learning Adviser for Literacy and the Inclusion Support Coordinator, both representatives from Local Authority's Achievement and Inclusion Division. The steering group met four times during the research period and jointly determined the structure to be used. To help facilitate the project each school was also allocated £1000 from the Local Authority's Wave 3 budget.

To launch the research and provide the professional development necessary for it to proceed the Adviser led a joint INSET day involving the headteachers, teachers, teaching assistants and SENCos from each of the participating schools. This provided a forum to disseminate information, time for discussion and allowed for the training to be adapted to specific needs. During the final session, participants worked in their school teams to discuss the issues relevant to them and to agree future actions based on the information provided. Using outcomes from the INSET day, each SENCo then wrote an action plan outlining how the project would be developed in school. This was linked to the SDP (School Development Plan) and indicated clear timescales and success criteria in order for these to be evaluated at the end of the project.

The approach towards the research was twofold. Each school identified a minimum of two focus classes, where the research was concentrated. A focus group was identified in each of these, representing children with varying abilities:

♦ Children identified as having dyslexia/dyslexic tendencies

♦ Children with other identified learning difficulties

♦ 'Control' children, achieving well with no apparent difficulties.

In total the focus groups were predominately boys (70%) and from Key Stage 2 (61%). There were no girls at all in the 'other identified learning difficulties' category.

The second part of the research involved identification of strategies and approaches to be adopted within all classes to promote a whole-school approach and provide a greater evidence base upon which to inform evaluation and future planning.

In addition to this in-reach work, schools within the Local Authority with recognised strengths in the areas being developed were identified. Part of each participating school's additional funding was then allocated to provide release time for teachers to undertake visits to these schools in order to observe good practice, ask questions and deepen their understanding of the principles in action.

Data Collection

A variety of data was collected for evaluation of the project. In order to measure progress within writing, quantitative data based on National Curriculum sublevels was used. Teachers used the South Gloucestershire levelling document to inform a 'best fit' judgement based on a selection of writing completed in January, with the process being repeated in June.

It was decided that quantitative data would not be sufficient to fully measure the impact of the work and as such, qualitative approaches were also adopted. A questionnaire was devised by the steering group using and adapting some of the questions from the Primary National Strategy SEAL (Social and Emotional

Aspects of Learning) materials and the attitude surveys from the PNS/UKLA Boys' Writing Project (2004). This aimed to elicit children's emotional responses and to provide more in-depth information about the affects of the project on motivation and self-esteem, a key contributing factor to academic attainment (Goleman, 1995).

A simple scale using the common 'smiley face' system, familiar to the children and used widely in schools, was used for Key Stage 1 pupils, with a more sophisticated scale for pupils in Key Stage 2, allowing for greater choice and more specific responses. Questionnaires were completed with the focus groups in January to provide benchmark data and repeated in June. In order to promote consistency and ensure as clear an understanding as possible, teachers completed the questionnaire with the pupils, reading the questions and providing clarification where necessary.

The SENCos also collated qualitative responses from children and staff during a final review in June. In order to capture thoughts not explored through the questionnaire, the children were encouraged to record their reflections on Post-it notes. The staff completed a similar exercise, the outcomes from which were then used to inform a more in-depth discussion at a review staff meeting. After this, the steering group's final meeting was used to review and evaluate the impact of the project.

Findings

From the findings it emerged that the major impact creating dyslexia friendly classrooms had overall was in raising children's self-esteem and emotional well-being, although analysis of the three focus group categories indicated varied outcomes.

Percentage increases for the control group were relatively low. 66% of the total responses indicated no change, with the only significant differences being in children who worried less about things they didn't do well (63%) and those who believed their teachers showed greater interest in their ideas (50%). These outcomes are potentially attributed to the fact that at 88%, responses from children in this category were considerably more positive from the outset, signalling generally higher self-esteem and motivation amongst this pupil group.

Results from the group with other identified learning difficulties showed less cohesion, with fewer patterns emerging. There was a 71% decrease in the number of children who felt worried about the things they didn't do well and a 57% decrease in children who said they wandered around the classroom. Interestingly however, the highest negative response was also demonstrated by this group, 21% of the questionnaires completed in June showing a negative impact, compared to 11% for the control group and 6% for the dyslexic group. There were a number of possible reasons for this. Many of the children in this category were

	🖐	👍	🤏	👎
About me				
I like coming to school				
I like being in my classroom				
I like me				
I feel safe at school				
I am good at some things				
I often forget what I should be doing				
I worry about the things I can't do well				
I can take turns				
I get up and wander around the classroom				
I want to do well in my work				
I know what things I'm good and bad at				
I am happy being me				
I'm learning a lot at school				
About my work				
It is easy to work in my class				
I find lessons interesting and fun				
When I start my work I usually understand what I have to do				
I think my targets help my work to improve				
When I have homework I usually understand what I have to do				
My work is put on display for other people to see				
I can work without my teacher's help				
If the work is hard I still try to do it				
I get upset if I can't do my work				
I feel pleased with myself when I've done a good piece of work				
I get annoyed when I make mistakes				
I can learn from my mistakes				
I find it easy to pay attention in class				
How I work with others				
Sometimes I do class work in pairs with a friend				
I can work by myself				
I can work well with others				
About adults in school				
I can talk to my teachers about anything				
My teachers like to listen to my ideas				
My teachers like to help me with my work				
I get on well with my teachers				
Sometimes my teachers let me choose what work to do				
People in school teach me well				
My teachers try to make the work easy for me to understand				

Table A3: Sample questionaire

working significantly below national expectations and/or had a variety of specific needs, both behavioural and cognitive. Even with adult support to complete the questionnaire it is possible that they did not fully understand the questions or the scoring system. Teachers also reported that several of these children had been reprimanded on the day the questionnaire was repeated and that they were unhappy at the time, possibly influencing their responses.

Outcomes for the dyslexic group showed the most significant impact. There was a 75% increase in those that understood their tasks, a 63% increase in the number of children who were able to remember what they had to do and a 63% increase in those who felt able to work without their teacher's help, all of which indicate greater independence and confidence. Improvements in self-esteem were also noticeable with the number of children who got upset when they couldn't do their work, who worried about things they couldn't do and who got annoyed when they made mistakes decreasing by 75%, 63% and 50% respectively. There was also a 50% rise in the number of children who felt able to talk openly to their teachers.

Qualitative feedback from teachers noted many benefits, including:

♦ Increased enthusiasm for school generally and for Literacy in particular;
♦ Greater motivation, especially during the afternoons, through increased use of practical activities;
♦ Increases in the percentage of time children were on task;
♦ A rise in purposeful, work-related talk during lessons;
♦ Significant improvements in self-esteem, especially for the dyslexic group;
♦ Improved social and emotional development demonstrated through children's increased ability to deal with challenging tasks;
♦ Higher numbers of children who presented as happy and comfortable in school;
♦ Better quality and increased quantity of homework;
♦ Less low-level disruption during lessons.

Comments collated from the children's post-it notes showed positive feedback in relation to the range of strategies adopted. A large number of the dyslexic group made positive comments about the variety of new resources used to support learning:

(Coloured acetates) They help me with my reading. I used to lose where I was reading a lot but they've helped me find where I am.

(Y4 Female)

(Reading rulers) They help me when my eyes are tired.

(Y2 Female)

(Maths cards) It makes me better at adding and subtracting.

(Y4 Female)

(Using over-learning strategies) It's quick and makes you get faster. You can work things out quicker.

(Y4 Male)

A small number of responses also demonstrated an impact at home:

(Coloured acetates) I took one home and my dad's even started to use one now. They really help me with my reading.

(Y5 Male)

Providing a greater choice of homework activities with visual, auditory and kinaesthetic options was well-received by children across the age range:

I think it's better. If you get a choice and have options you can choose one. If you can't find something on it you can change your option.

(Y5 Male)

It's better. You can choose what you think you're good at and what you enjoy doing.

(Y4 Female)

It helps you try new stuff

(Y2 Female)

Children also responded favourably to the development of joined handwriting in KS1:

It was exciting, I'm learning a different way of writing

(Y2 Male)

It made my writing look neater. It has helped me.

(Y2 Female)

In relation to expectations based on their comparative abilities, increases in academic attainment were marginal and of little significance for all focus groups. Considering the improvements noticed through the qualitative data this would seem to corroborate the belief that self-esteem and motivation are linked to attainment. The 'control' group had higher self-esteem levels to begin with and therefore whilst the adoption of a dyslexia friendly approach did not hinder their learning, it did not significantly accelerate it. For the children with identified difficulties, whose self-esteem, motivation and attitude were poorer at the outset, it suggests that improvements in these areas need to take place before increased attainment can be realised.

Limitations

The research highlighted the difficulties that can arise when using questionnaires with young children. Understanding, attitude and emotional state are all contributing factors to children's interpretation of the questions, which can affect their responses and therefore influence the consistency of the data.

The timing of the research also proved to have an impact. The significant pressure placed upon schools at the time due to implementation of the Revised Primary Framework, as well as other key initiatives, meant that attention could not be focused on the project to the extent that may have otherwise been possible. Accompanying this it needs to be recognised that whole school development of an initiative takes time to embed. The six month period of the research provides useful information that can be used to inform future planning; however a more longitudinal study would provide greater insight and allow for greater consideration of the impact upon academic attainment.

Developments

As a result both of this research and a continued increase in requests from schools to support their development of dyslexia friendly classrooms, a further 30 South Gloucestershire schools are currently participating in a second research cohort. These schools have been organised into locality based networks and are being led by the same Local Authority representatives. Learning from cohort 1 is being used to inform the research which it is hoped will provide a greater evidence base to inform future recommendations and support.

References

BDA (2008) Quality Mark Position Statement.

Bearne, E., Grainger, T. and Wolstencroft, H. (1994) *Raising Boys' Achievements in Writing*, UKLA.

DfES (2001) *Special Educational Needs Code of Practice*, Ref: DfES581/2001

DfES (2001) *Inclusive Schooling: Children with Special Educational Needs*, Ref: DfES 0774 2001

DfES (2005) *Learning and Teaching for Dyslexic Children.*

Myomancy (2007) *Dyslexia Action*, http://www.myomancy.com/2007/02/who_are_dyslexi

Goleman, D. (1995) *Emotional Intelligence*, New York: Bantam Books.

QCA (2000) The National Curriculum Handbook for Primary Teachers in England Key Stages 1 and 2.

PNS/UKLA (2004) *Raising Boys' Achievements in Writing: joint research project*, UKLA and the Primary National Strategy.

4   Structured diary example

Date _____   Time_____   am/pm

People involved (please circle):

Mum   Dad   Mum's partner   Older brother

Younger brother   Older sister   Younger sister

Other (please state): _____

What was the decision about (please state):

_____

_____

_____

(Please circle):
Was the decision important to you?
    very important   1 2 3 4 5   not important

Was your opinion considered to be?
    very important   1 2 3 4 5   not important

Was there any conflict?
            a lot   1 2 3 4 5   none

Was the conflict resolved?
        entirely   1 2   3 4 5   not at all

When a decision like this normally has to be made what happens?
(Please circle)

My mum tends to side with me on my view
    Always 1 2 3 4 Never

My parents narrow down the options and then allow me to choose
    Always 1 2 3 4 Never

My parent(s) listen to my point of view but make(s) the final decision
    Always 1 2 3 4 Never

As a family we discuss all the options until we all can agree on one
    Always 1 2 3 4 Never

My dad/mum's partner tends to side with me my view
    Always 1 2 3 4 Never

My parent(s)give(s) in if I offer to do something in exchange
    Always 1 2 3 4 Never

My parent(s)give(s) in if I get very upset
    Always 1 2 3 4 Never

None of the above (please state what happens):

_____

_____

_____

This decision recorded here made me feel:

(Use drawings, words or symbols)

Index

Lightning Source UK Ltd.
Milton Keynes UK
29 June 2010

156273UK00001B/117/P

9 781906 884024